P9-DOA-876

Class Conflict,
Slavery,
and the
United States Constitution

Staughton Lynd

Class Conflict,

Slavery,

and the

United States Constitution

TEN ESSAYS

THE BOBBS-MERRILL COMPANY, INC.
A Subsidiary of Howard W. Sams & Co., Inc.
INDIANAPOLIS   NEW YORK

DEDICATED TO THE MEMORY OF

Robert K. Lamb and Franz L. Neumann

Contents

Preface, ix

Preface

Staughton Lynd is already known to many people outside the United States in his person as a responsible and alert internationalist—as a good citizen of that immanent, more rational world which must come into being if any world is to survive our time. This is to say that he is known, to those who are able to take a long and settled view, as a good American.

For some reason his kind of good American, who combines a Yankee energy and irreverence with a moral toughness which comes from older, more puritan, timber, has been seen around the campuses of the United States a good deal in the past few years.

It is only to be expected that such people will run into misrepresentation of various kinds. This generally awaits those who have the temerity to object within the heart of a swollen imperial consensus. Nor should this bother them much, since they know that it is one plain part of their business to *be* objectionable.

It is perhaps because I am also an objector (although within an imperial power now growing impotent and merely tetchy) that Staughton has done me the honour to invite me to put some words down here. At first I thought that our common objectionableness—our brotherhood in the shadowy international of revolutionary humanism—was scarcely relevant to the matter on hand. After all, Staughton appears here as Professor Lynd: not in his person as an arch-seditionist or arsonist (or whatever the mutton-fisted narks of academe suppose) but simply as a master of his chosen trade. And although we are both of the same trade, we deal in such different and highly-specialised branches that it seemed beyond my competence to offer comment on much of the detail in his intricately-wrought historical argument.

As a fellow-tradesman I can, of course, see that the workmanship in these pages is of the first order: the command of the subject assured: the argument open, sinewy, and challenging an open response: the texture scrupulous as to detail and yet impatient of marginalia, insistent upon essentials. It is the large kind of historical argument, which demands the total attention of the intellect. We are not "carried along" by Professor Lynd or snowed by the choice flowers of his rhetoric: he asks, all the time, that we stay with him and reason with him. Moreover, he does not waft around us some attenuated "climate of ideas": he immerses us within particular, and significant, historical contexts and demands that we think in actualities. And this seems to me to be the primary discipline of history (and the one which distinguishes it from sociology): the discipline of context.

I can see also that every chapter of this book is locked into the next, in such a way that the total argument presented both draws upon and feeds strength back into each part. Some parts arise from original research while others arise from thinking about and connecting in new ways long-familiar sources and the recent research of colleagues. The old kinds of argument for and against Beard, over which generations of students have grown weary (and whose echoes have become even a little tedious across the Atlantic) have now been superseded; and a new stage of argument (into which much of the heritage both of Beard and of his critics has been assimilated) has been initiated. Professor Lynd would not wish anyone to claim that he has initiated this single-handed: it has been the work of many hands. Still, with the greatest clarity, this book signs off the old and announces the definitions of the new.

Reading these pages it has occurred to me that Professor Lynd and I encounter some similar problems in our work as tradesmen, just as we share common aspirations in our more objectionable roles. In Britain also there was a radical and humanitarian ascendancy in some areas of historiography in the early twentieth century (at the time when the history of our industrial revolution and of popular movements in the nineteenth century was first being mapped out) followed, in more recent years, by a long conservative ascendency, whose products have been valuable as correctives and have been enriching in the detail of research, but whose total emphasis has been such as to fragment the full historical process—to celebrate interest and contingency, and to deny any area to rational historical agency except in its most trivialised and personalised expression.

At the same time the historian in the radical tradition has sometimes had most to fear from the friends, fighting with blunt instruments and bandaged eyes, at his own side. There have been the sentimentalists with their vapid portrait of the all-holy-common-people, touched up with real heroic instances, but with every interesting wart and wrinkle erased. And there have been the Marxists of various tendencies (to whom both Lynd and I are closely related in a continuing dialectic of argument) who have so often handled historical problems as if they were settled theorems for which proof only was required ("a truth to be established by means of accepted truths," my dictionary has it); and some of whom have handled the essential historical concepts of class in such a bald and hectoring way that they can only be rehabilitated, as they are by

Professor Lynd in this book, by the utmost precision as to context, and the utmost delicacy before the creative vitality—and the contradictoriness—of culture.

I may misunderstand the signs. But it would seem, from this side of the Atlantic, that the position of the American historian who is now seeking to recreate the radical tradition is an enviable one. For Professor Lynd is one among a large, and growing, group of younger scholars who combine the old zest with a professional excellence and human maturity which are ridding the radical tradition of the bad intellectual habits into which it fell so often in the past. Those parts of the established professional ascendancy which are somewhat comfortable, somewhat fashionable, and somewhat conservative, are coming under a criticism very much more searching than anything to which they have been accustomed.

To challenge established positions in this way requires, in the challenger, something of the awkwardness of an Objector. It would seem, then, that Staughton Lynd and Professor Lynd are in fact the same person. To write old history afresh cannot be done without un-writing other people's history; as Lynd reexamines the meaning of the 1770's and 1780's, so he must also reexamine the meaning of these decades as they appeared to minds in the 1830's, and 1890's, and at different decades in this century. And this way of seeing events, both as they occurred and as they were refracted, with changing emphases, in the historical memory, enforces the realisation that as we argue about the past so also we are arguing about—and seeking to clarify—the mind of the present which is recovering that past. Nor is this an unimportant part of the mind of the present. For some of the largest arguments, about human rationality, destiny, and agency, must always be grounded there: in the historical record.

That is why the writing of history, in this kind of way, is also an act of contemporary self-consciousness and social control. It should be unnecessary to keep on reminding oneself of ultimate purposes in the pursuit of a profession. But one does sometimes doubt the usefulness of history today, when the present appears to be so perilously near to the edge of all of it. If Professor Lynd, in his other, more objectionable, person, has his doubts, I trust that he will set them at rest. This book should provide that person with his answer.

E. P. Thompson

The University of Warwick
August 1967

Class Conflict,
Slavery,
and the
United States Constitution

1

Introduction: Beyond Beard

For more than half a century now, historians have been engaged in dubious battle with Charles Beard's *An Economic Interpretation of the Constitution of the United States* (1913) and *Economic Origins of Jeffersonian Democracy* (1915). What has been at issue in this debate is much more than an appraisal of the formation of the Constitution and the early Republic.

In *The Rise of American Civilization* (1927), Beard and his wife extended his hypothesis to include the origins of the Civil War. The "conflict between capitalistic and agrarian interests,"[1] previously presented as the basis of both the conflict of Federalists and Antifederalists in 1787-1788 and the conflict of Hamiltonians and Jeffersonians in the 1790's, was held to be also the root of the

[1] The phrase is taken from Beard's summary of the "general conclusions" of both the 1913 and 1915 books in *Economic Origins of Jeffersonian Democracy* (New York, 1915), pp. 464-467. The following pages focus on these general

3

"Second American Revolution" of 1861-1865. Hence the controversy over Beard involves our assessment of the entire period between the Revolution and the Civil War.

Moreover, Beard offers the most substantial American version to
date of an economic approach to history in general. The specter of
Marx has haunted historians' responses to Beard. Although Beard
was careful (as he observed in introducing a 1935 reprinting) to
call his 1913 work *an* economic interpretation, not " 'the' economic
interpretation, or 'the only' interpretation possible to thought,"[2]
one of Beard's prominent critics asserted in his rebuttal that "eco-

---

conclusions rather than on the detailed argument of each of Beard's two books.
"It is established upon a statistical basis," Beard concluded,

> that the Constitution of the United States was the product of a conflict be-
> tween capitalistic and agrarian interests. The support for the adoption of the
> Constitution came principally from the cities and regions where the commer-
> cial, financial, manufacturing, and speculative interests were concentrated,
> and the bulk of the opposition came from the small farming and debtor
> classes, particularly those back from the sea board. . . .

The general conclusions then asserted that the same conflict was the basis of
party strife in the 1790's:

> The men who framed the Constitution and were instrumental in securing
> its ratification constituted the dominant group in the new government formed
> under it, and their material measures were all directed to the benefit of the
> capitalistic interests—i.e., were consciously designed to augment the fluid
> capital in the hands of security holders and bank stock owners and thus to in-
> crease manufacturing, commerce, building, and land values, the last inciden-
> tally, except for speculative purposes in the West. The bulk of the party
> which supported these measures was drawn from the former advocates of the
> Constitution.
>
> The spokesmen of the Federalist and Republican parties, Hamilton and
> Jefferson, were respectively the spokesmen of capitalistic and agrarian inter-
> ests. . . .

The general conclusions characterized Jeffersonian Democracy as "the possession of the federal government by the agrarian masses led by an aristocracy of
slave-owning planters." They did not resolve Beard's lack of clarity as to whether
the slave-owning planters had supported the Constitution or, together with the
"backwoods agrarians," had opposed it.

[2] Charles A. Beard, *An Economic Interpretation of the Constitution of the
United States* (New York, 1935), p. viii.

nomic interpretation of the Constitution does not work."[3] Since those who have sought to revise Beard have not systematically explored alternative economic interpretations, the historian finds himself forced to choose between Beard's inadequate economic interpretation and a variety of eclectic treatments which agree only in filiopietistic admiration for the founding fathers.

These overtones are the more apparent when it is recalled that sustained criticism of Beard's work is largely a product of the Cold War years.[4] At a time when the politics of dead center and an end to ideology prevailed in American society at large, historians rather suddenly discovered that Americans had always shared a consensus about fundamentals that enabled them pragmatically to muddle through. Thus Richard Hofstadter, who concluded one book in 1948 with the warning that "it would be fatal to rest content" with Franklin Roosevelt's

belief in personal benevolence, personal arrangements, the sufficiency of good intentions and month-to-month improvisation, without trying to achieve a more inclusive and systematic conception of what is happening in the world,

wrote another in 1955 which praised the New Deal's "opportunism" and repudiation of "the European world of ideology."[5] Thus Daniel Boorstin, who in *The Lost World of Thomas Jefferson*

[3] Forrest McDonald, *We The People: The Economic Origins of the Constitution* (Chicago, 1958), p. vii.

[4] The two book-length critiques of Beard's *Economic Interpretation* were Robert E. Brown, *Charles Beard and the Constitution: A Critical Analysis of "An Economic Interpretation of the Constitution of the United States"* (Princeton, 1956) and McDonald's *We The People* (1958).

[5] Richard Hofstadter, *The American Political Tradition and the Men Who Made It* (New York, 1948), p. 347, and *The Age of Reform from Bryan to F.D.R.* (New York, 1955), pp. 314-326. In *The American Political Tradition*, Hofstadter referred to Beard's "great study" on the Constitution as the "high point" of "modern critical scholarship," while in "Beard and the Constitution: The History of an Idea," *American Quarterly*, II (1950), 195-213, he debunked it as an expression of Progressive debunking.

(1948) found in that ideology the germ of a dangerous pragmatism, presented in 1953 the view that the American Revolution's salutary undogmatic character anticipated "the genius of American politics."[6] Thus Louis Hartz, author in 1940 of an article on "Seth Luther: The Story of a Working Class Rebel," argued in an article of 1952 that "the central course of our political thought has betrayed an unconquerable pragmatism" and expanded this thesis in his influential *The Liberal Tradition in America* (1955).[7]

Beard's critics charge him with selecting facts favorable to his thesis and with interpreting where he claimed to narrate. They are vulnerable on the same score. Robert Brown, for example, repeatedly cites John Adams in contending that New England society was democratic even before the Revolution;[8] but Brown (as Samuel Brockunier points out) does not quote John Adams' statement that

the state of Connecticut has always been governed by an aristocracy, more decisively than the empire of Great Britain is. Half a dozen, or, at most a dozen families, have controlled that country when a colony, as well as since it has been a state.[9]

Cecilia Kenyon, who has effectively criticized Beard's assumption that Antifederalism was democratic, reveals her own assumptions in an essay called "Where Paine Went Wrong." Paine (she says)

---

[6] Daniel J. Boorstin, *The Lost World of Thomas Jefferson* (New York, 1948), pp. 237-248, and *The Genius of American Politics* (Chicago, 1953), p. 68 *et passim*.

[7] Louis Hartz, "Seth Luther: The Story of a Working Class Rebel," *New England Quarterly*, XIII (1940); "American Political Thought and the American Revolution," *American Political Science Review*, XLVI (1952), 326; *The Liberal Tradition in America: An Interpretation of American Political Thought Since the Revolution* (New York, 1955).

[8] Robert E. Brown, *Middle-Class Democracy and the Revolution in Massachusetts, 1691-1780* (Ithaca, N. Y.; 1955), and *Reinterpretation of the Formation of the American Constitution* (Boston, 1963).

[9] S. Hugh Brockunier, Foreword to Richard J. Purcell, *Connecticut in Transition: 1775-1818*, second edition (Middletown, Conn.; 1963), p. x.

was "incurably naive"; he espoused an "idealized conception" rather than observing "historical actuality"; he failed to recognize that the proper task of the Founding Fathers was to achieve "at least a moderate measure of justice in a society ruled by men who would always and unavoidably be influenced by private and sometimes selfish interests": in a word he was "essentially alien."[10] The process of reading Paine and Paine's ideas out of the American tradition culminated in Forrest McDonald's treatment of the period in *E Pluribus Unum:*

> Sometimes in the course of human events, as the Declaration of Independence had proclaimed, it becomes necessary for people to dissolve political bands. . . . The American Revolution was only a beginning in teaching men the process, but once it was done—once the vulgar overstepped the bonds of propriety and got away with it—there was no logical stopping place. *Common Sense* led unerringly to Valmy, and Valmy to Napoleon, and Napoleon to the Revolution of 1830, and that to the Revolutions of 1848, and those to the Paris Commune of 1871, and that to the Bolshevik Revolution, and that to the African and Asian Revolutions in Expectations, and those to eternity.[11]

Lucky America, McDonald concluded, had Founding Fathers who were able to check the popular revolutionary forces they had unleashed.

I.

In 1959 when I began the studies collected in these pages, my own initial attitude toward the Progressive historiography of Frederick Jackson Turner, Charles Beard, Carl Becker and Vernon Parrington, was uncritical. I did not expect to be driven beyond Beard, to lay greater stress than he did upon city

[10] Cecilia Kenyon, "Where Paine Went Wrong," *American Political Science Review*, XLV (1951), 1094, 1095, 1098, and "Men of Little Faith: The Anti-Federalists on the Nature of Representative Government," *William And Mary Quarterly*, third series, XII (1955), 3-43.

[11] Forrest McDonald, *E Pluribus Unum: The Formation of the American Republic*, 1776-1790 (Boston, 1965), pp. 235-236.

artisans, upon slavery, upon the role of ideas. These themes were imposed, one at a time, by the subject matter itself.

Beginning with the desire to defend Beard and the Progressive historians, I selected a microcosm in which class conflict was apparent: one of the Hudson River counties where tenant farmers in 1776 still enjoyed leases requiring grain to be ground at the lord's mill, the annual payment of certain "fat hens," and the yearly performance of work on the lord's land with cart and team. My hypothesis was that scrutiny of three events—the 1766 tenant rebellion, the confiscation of more than 200,000 acres from Loyalist landlords during the Revolution, and the division of the county in 1787-1788 over whether to ratify the United States Constitution—would demonstrate a continuity of protest in the heavily-tenanted southern and southeastern parts of the country. And so it proved, at least to my own satisfaction. Dutchess County appeared to bear out Carl Becker's thesis that a struggle over "who should rule at home" began before the war for independence and continued when the war was over. (See Essay 2).

To be sure, the political leaders who articulated Dutchess discontent were hardly social revolutionaries: they were rising "new men" who sought to compete with the great landed families for leadership of the Revolution. No matter, I argued that representatives need not be typical of the constituencies that elect them. I illustrated the point by studies showing that in the English Civil War, despite the underlying conflict of constituencies, leaders of both camps in the Long Parliament had similar socio-economic backgrounds.

But then difficulties arose. In southern Dutchess the landlords were Loyalist (the largest, Beverly Robinson, was an accomplice of Benedict Arnold) and the tenants were Whigs. In neighboring Albany County, however, the landlords were patriot Livingstons, and the tenants rose in support of British troops coming down from Canada in 1777. (See Essay 3). Both groups of tenants rioted and rebelled, but which side they supported evidently depended,

not on any Whig or Tory ideology of their own, but on the political
outlook of their landlords. Here was no simple correlation between
poverty and patriotism, as Beard and Becker often seemed to suggest.

A look at the urban poor made the Progressive view still less
plausible. The barest attempt to trace the continuity of workingmen's organizations and attitudes during the Revolutionary era
must at once encounter a massive paradox in the position of Progressive historians. The paradox is this: If (as Becker held) the city
workingmen were the most militantly revolutionary group in the
years 1763-1766, and if (as Beard maintained) the United States
Constitution was a counter-revolutionary coup d'etat, how is it that
the city workingmen all over America overwhelmingly and enthusi-
astically supported the United States Constitution? If Becker was
correct in believing that "the fear of British oppression was transformed into the fear of oppression by the national government,"[12]
surely the mechanics, foremost in the movement for independence,
should have shared the Antifederalist fear of centralization? But
they did not. In Boston, Philadelphia, Baltimore, and Charleston,
as well as in New York City, the workingmen were Federalist. In
New York City the case is particularly clear, because universal manhood suffrage and the secret ballot obtained in the election of delegates to the state ratifying convention, yet the Federalist ticket was
elected twenty to one. (Essays 4, 5).

Nothing revealed in the course of the New York case study dis-
proved the thesis that a domestic struggle for power accompanied
the War for Independence. On the contrary, provided that struggle
was understood as a contest for class dominance rather than discrete pecuniary gains, New York spectacularly exemplified it. The
brilliant New York conservatives grouped around the families of
Livingston and Schuyler functioned throughout the Revolution
as something very similar to an "executive committee of the ruling

[12] Carl L. Becker, *The History of Political Parties in the Province of New
York, 1760-1776* (Madison, 1909), p. 275.

class," consciously distributing themselves between state and national politics, deliberately implementing the appointment of Robert Morris as Financier and the movement for the Constitution thereafter. (See Essay 5). Yet Beard's dichotomy of "personalty" and "realty" led him to cast the Hudson Valley landlords as Antifederalists, and to dismiss the Constitution's artisan supporters as "politically non-existent."[13]

I digested these unforseen discoveries while beginning my first teaching job, at a Negro women's college. Living as we did on the campus of a Negro college, associating from day to day almost entirely with Negroes, and so insensibly absorbing something of what it means to be born into the Afro-American sub-culture, I became more conscious of the degree to which American historiography simply leaves the Negro out. One day, rereading Turner's essay on the significance of the frontier, my eye was caught by a sentence: "when American history comes to be rightly viewed it will be seen that the slavery question is an incident."[14] The idea suggested itself that Turner and Beard, concerned lest the conflict of Eastern capitalist and Western farmer be obscured by an outdated rhetoric of hostility between North and South, had minimized the role of slavery in American history before the Civil War. With this in mind I read through, first, the writing of Turner and Beard, and second, the letters of the Continental Congress and records of the 1787 Convention. The neglect of slavery in the former, the centrality of slavery in the latter, struck me as equally apparent. (Essays 6, 7).

Where did this leave one's understanding of the Revolution and the Constitution? Beard had interpreted the Constitution as a vic-

---

[13] As to the artisans, see Beard, *An Economic Interpretation*, pp. 24-26. In the 1935 reprinting of his book, Beard conceded that he had wrongly placed the landed aristocracy of New York among the Antifederalists (*ibid.*, pp. xv-xvi).

[14] *The Early Writings of Frederick Jackson Turner*, ed. Everett E. Edwards and Fulmer Mood (Madison, 1938), p. 213.

tory for mobile capital over capital invested in agricultural production. I began to suspect that, while small freeholders of the North and West were indeed unrepresented at Philadelphia, the Constitution was a compromise between capitalists like Robert Morris and the particular kind of farmers who owned Hudson River manors and southern plantations. I found this rough sense of what had happened confirmed by an epigram of Georges Lefebvre:

In England, after the revolutions of the seventeenth century, gentlemen and bourgeois joined to share power with the king; in the United States they dispensed with the monarch by common agreement . . .[15]

Attempting to examine in detail what took place at the Convention, I became intrigued with the coincidence that the Constitution's most dramatic concession to slavery, the so-called three-fifths compromise, occurred almost on the same day that the Continental Congress, meeting ninety miles away in New York, banned slavery from the Northwest Territory. Further scrutiny suggested that the two decisions had not seemed contradictory to contemporaries. Both were parts of a larger accommodation between the governing classes of North and South which could be termed "the compromise of 1787." (Essay 8).

It seemed to follow that the conflict between Jefferson and Hamilton represented, not (as Beard argued in his *Economic Origins of Jeffersonian Democracy*) a continuation of the conflict between Federalist and Antifederalist, but the break-up of the coalition which had made the Revolution and the Constitution. Far from originating as the defender of all agrarians, Jefferson's party was initially Southern in leadership and support. I developed the thesis that the Progressive historians' dichotomy between capitalist and farmer followed Jefferson's misreading of the 1790's as a contest between corrupt speculators and honest yeomen. The study of Dutchess Antifederalism had led me to the polemical manuscripts

[15] Georges Lefebvre, *The French Revolution from Its Origins to 1793*, tr. Elizabeth M. Evanson (London and New York, 1962), p. xviii.

of Albany Antifederalist Abraham Yates (see Essay 9); and as I worked on Yates's history of the movement for the Constitution and Jefferson's analysis of the 1790's I began to see Beard's history as the product of a radical tradition which went back, through Populism, to these men and beyond. When Turner compared the region of Populist strength a century later to the areas which went Antifederalist in 1787-1788, and Beard termed the period of Shays' Rebellion "Populism and Reaction," this vision of our history was "a latterday variant of the Jeffersonian mythos which saw nature's nobleman, the yeoman farmer, fleeced and oppressed by the paper speculators of the cities."[16] From Jefferson, too, and not from the muckraking style of the Progressive era alone, came the shallow economic interpretation that conceptualized opponents as conspirators interested only in personal power and profit.

Beard's history was Jeffersonian history. Seeking to demythologize Jeffersonian Democracy in a spirit of hard-headed Hamiltonian realism, Beard nevertheless failed to free himself from Jefferson's most characteristic habits of thought. In contrast, the picture presented in the following pages has been stimulated by two recent upheavals: the American civil rights movement, which suggested a fresh look at the importance of slavery in the Revolutionary era; and the worldwide colonial independence movement, which seemed to offer a new model for conceptualizing the Revolution and its relation to the Civil War. The resulting hypothesis seeks to incorporate what both the Beardian and anti-Beardian arguments have solidly established, while attempting to surmount what each argument has been unable to explain.

II.

Beard posited an essentially unchanging conflict throughout American history between capitalists and farmers. But the evidence is overwhelming that internal conflict was a secondary

---

[16] This passage is quoted from Essay 10, below, p. 247.

aspect of the revolution of 1776, which in fact was primarily a war for national independence. On the other hand, Beard's critics have generally maintained that the national unity they correctly perceive in the American Revolution continued to characterize the rest of American history. For them, then, the Civil War must be conceptualized as a tragic accident produced by a blundering generation: a model at variance with the very substantial body of evidence supporting Beard's thesis of the Civil War as a "Second American Revolution."[17] The way out of the dilemma is to synthesize Beard's view of the Civil War and the view of the American Revolution insisted on by Beard's critics.

Such a synthesis, so it seems to me, should include the following elements:

1. The American Revolution (like most colonial independence movements) was waged by a coalition of diverse social groups, united in the desire for American independence but with various additional aims that were in conflict.

2. The popular elements in this coalition—small farmers and city artisans—often clashed with their upper-class leaders, and fear of what the Declaration of Independence calls "convulsions

---

[17] Boorstin calls the Civil War one of the "most inexplicable . . . events of the modern era" (*Genius of American Politics*, p. 99) and Hartz, while insisting that the Civil War was "unique to America," concedes that it disrupted the liberal consensus which he considers the central theme of American history (*Liberal Tradition in America*, pp. 18-19, 43, 148, 172). Recent specialized studies accept Beard's theory of the Civil War in fundamentals while criticizing it in detail. Thus, for example, Robert F. Sharkey criticizes the Beards for picturing Northern capitalism as a "conceptual monolith" but adds, "with the overall dimensions of this interpretation I have no quarrel." (*Money, Class and Party: An Economic Study of Civil War and Reconstruction* [Baltimore, 1959], pp. 291-292, 299-306). Again, W. R. Brock rejects the contention that Northern businessmen had a unified economic program which they wished to promote but does not reject economic interpretation or the "overall" conception of the Civil War as a revolution. (*An American Crisis: Congress and Reconstruction, 1865-1867* [London, 1963], especially pp. 239-240).

within" and "domestic insurrections amongst us" was a principal motive for the formation of the United States Constitution.

3. The upper-class leaders of the Revolution were themselves divided into two basic groups, Northern capitalists and Southern plantation-owners, and the Constitution represented not a victory of one over the other but a compromise between them.

4. Serious conflict between North and South preceded the compromise of 1787, and in the 1790's—not in 1820 or 1850—the coalition of sectional leaders that had directed the Revolution and the movement for the Constitution almost at once broke down.

5. Thus (as in most colonial independence movements) a first revolution for national independence was followed by a second revolution which determined what kind of society the independent nation would become.

6. America therefore did have a bourgeois revolution comparable to the French Revolution, but it was directed not against England but against slavery and took place not in 1776 but in 1861.

These formulations retain Beard's emphasis on "personalty" (i.e., mobile capital, represented by investments in securities, commerce, manufacturing, bank loans, land speculation) while rejecting his conception of "realty" (i.e., capital invested in agricultural production). The Beardian category of "realty" obscures what happened both in the American Revolution and in the Civil War by blurring distinctions between different kinds of farmers, and most importantly, between freehold farmers of the North and West on one hand, and Southern plantation-owners on the other. The model presented here proposes that the Revolution and the formation of the Constitution expressed an alliance between Northern "personalty" and the particular form of "realty" which dominated the South (while in the late eighteenth century as in the mid-nineteenth, the political role of other forms of "realty"—for example, that of Midwestern wheat-growers during the Civil War—requires separate analysis).

As applied to the Civil War, the distinction between "person-alty" and "realty," capitalist and agrarian, emerges from the obvious facts: hence Beard's portrait of the Second American Revolution remains far more convincing than his analysis of the first. But here too, Beard's neglect of slavery as a force in American history seriously damaged his results. Thus Barrington Moore, Jr., for example, sees the Civil War as "the last revolutionary offensive on the part of what one may legitimately call urban or bourgeois capitalist democracy." But he differs from Beard in refusing to eliminate the issue of slavery. This is not because Moore believes that Southern slavery obstructed Northern industrial development. On the contrary, slavery may have been a stimulant. But "striking down slavery was a decisive step, an act at least as important as the striking down of absolute monarchy in the English Civil War and the French Revolution," for in the absence of emancipation, American capitalism might have come to maturity in an undemocratic political context, as was the case in Germany and Japan.[18] In contrast, Beard was led by his concept of agrarianism and realty to a view of the Civil War which came very close to that of the rural Southerners who fought in it.

As applied to the formation of the Constitution, Beard's distinction between personalty and realty was doubly unfortunate because it overlaid Orin Libby's more useful distinction between groups more and less involved in a commercial economy. Beard acknowledged Libby handsomely, and built his discussion of ratification on Libby's maps. But Libby, like Jackson T. Main more recently, did not draw the line between Federalist and Antifederalist at the boundary between city and country. For Libby as for Main the "commercial farmer" located on some large river which allowed him to export for distant markets, naturally inclined to Federalism. As Main says: "the struggle over the ratification of the Constitution

[18] Barrington Moore, Jr., *Social Origins of Dictatorship and Democracy: Lord and Peasant in the Making of the Modern World* (Boston, 1966), chap. III, especially pp. 112, 153.

was primarily a contest between the commercial and non-commercial elements in the population. This is the most significant fact, to which all else is elaboration, amplification, or exception." He specifies as to the division among farmers that

> the commercial interest was not just urban. The commercial centers were supported by nearby rural areas which depended upon the towns as markets and as agencies through which their produce was exported overseas. That is to say, the commercial interest also embraced large numbers of farmers . . . permeated the rich river valleys and bound the great planters and other large landowners in the commercial nexus.[19]

Thus the distinction (to use Libby's terminology) between "commercial" and "interior" farmers makes understandable what Beard's distinction between "personalty" and "realty" altogether fails to explain: how the Constitution could have been ratified by a society in which more than nine out of every ten adult white males were farmers. Above all, the Southern slaveholder stands forth in the Libby-Main framework, not (as Beard was forced to cast him) as an investor in land and government securities, but as the most substantial commercial farmer in the new nation's economy. The mere presence of so many large plantation owners at the Constitutional Convention suggests to common sense that there is something wrong with Beard's dichotomy. Beard was obliged to say: "The south had many men who were rich in personalty, other than slaves, and it was this type, rather than the slaveholding planter as such, which was represented in the Convention that framed the Constitution"; and to make his analysis fit ratification of the Constitution by that heartland of "realty," Virginia, he accepted Libby's assertion that Tidewater Virginia—of all places—was "the region of the large towns, and where commercial interests were predominant."[20]

As I see it, the United States Constitution represented, not the

[19] Jackson T. Main, *The Antifederalists: Critics of the Constitution, 1781-1788* (Chapel Hill, 1961), pp. 271, 280, following Orin G. Libby, *The Geographical Distribution of the Vote of the Thirteen States on the Federal Constitution, 1787-1788* (Madison, 1894).

[20] Beard, *Economic Interpretation*, pp. 30, 285.

triumph of capitalism over a landed aristocracy (like the French Revolution and the American Civil War), but a compromise or coalition between men of wealth in the cities and men of wealth on the land. Robert Brown is absolutely right when he states that "if Beard had based his thesis on *property* and not *personalty*, he would have been on much safer ground."[21]

Where Beard's analysis of the formation of the Constitution remains valid is in its stress on the initiating role of personalty. Forrest McDonald himself concedes that Beard's portrait of the Middle State capitalists grouped around Robert Morris of Philadelphia as "a consolidated group whose interests knew no state boundaries and were truly national in their scope," who (in McDonald's words) were "the greediest, most ruthless, and most insistent in demanding political action in their behalf," is a "perfectly accurate" description as of 1783.[22] But McDonald is right in maintaining that the movement which produced and ratified the Constitution in 1787-1788 was more broad than this. Well-to-do leaders both in New England and the South—especially in Virginia—had in the interim decided to throw their weight behind a movement for stronger national government. If personalty and Shays' Rebellion explain the former, they do not explain the latter. The dichotomy of "personalty" and "realty" fails to describe either the men who wrote the Constitution or the men who voted to ratify it.[23]

To reject an interpretation of the formation of the Constitution and the early Republic built on the antithesis between "personalty"

[21] Brown, *Beard and the Constitution*, p. 131.

[22] McDonald, *E Pluribus Unum*, pp. 34, 247.

[23] Lee Benson, in *Turner and Beard: American Historical Writing Reconsidered* (Glencoe, 1960), pp. 160-174, suggests that Beard and his principal critics all make the mistake of concentrating their attention on delegates to the Constitutional Convention and to the state ratifying conventions, as if those representatives were the electorate in microcosm. In reality, Benson insists, if Antifederalist delegates were almost as wealthy as their Federalist counterparts it would not disprove Libby's demonstration that a clear economic pattern appears in their constituencies. However, Beard is as much in error in overlooking the many poor men (commercial farmers and artisans) who *voted* for the Constitution, as he is in overlooking the rich "farmers" who helped to *draft* it.

and "realty" does not require abandoning an economic approach to the period. Beard's drama for villainous capitalist and virtuous farmer must make room for a more complex scenario which preserves his sense of the role of economic power.[24]

The slave, though he spoke few lines, should be moved front and center. If, as Beard said, there was a "large propertyless mass" which the Constitution "excluded at the outset," the one-fifth of the population in hereditary bondage better deserves that description than any group of whites; for few whites who began life without property failed to acquire it.[25] To whatever extent the Constitution betrayed the promise of the Declaration of Independence, it did so most of all for the Negro; surely John Alden says justly: "Had human slavery in the United States disappeared promptly as a result of the social ferment which was stimulated by the Anglo-American conflict, it would indeed be proper to think in terms of an Internal Revolution."[26]

Madison, from whose tenth Federalist Paper Beard claimed to derive his economic interpretation of history, put far more stress on

[24] E. James Ferguson sharply rejects Beard's distinction between "personalty" and "realty" while upholding the general validity of economic interpretation of the formation of the Constitution. In an exchange with Stuart Bruchey, Ferguson asserts that Beard's work "incorporates the idea that there were differences in attitude and interests between commerce and agriculture, between big property and small property, and among social classes, which led to political divisions, and that the classes of the nation possessing higher status and property were the driving force behind the movement for the Constitution." He goes on to say: "My initial reply to Mr. Bruchey would be that these concepts are not Beard's alone; that his work is not the sole test of their validity; that they infuse the sources for the period and constitute the operative hypotheses of a good many historical studies of it, old and new; and that subscribing to them does not necessarily make one a Beardian, unless indeed the name is given to anyone who deals with social and economic divisions as major causal factors." ("The Forces Behind the Constitution," *William and Mary Quarterly*, third series, XIX [1962], 434).

[25] "Out of twenty whites only one or two remained permanently poor." Jackson T. Main, *The Social Structure of Revolutionary America* (Princeton, 1965), p. 271.

[26] John R. Alden, *The South in the Revolution, 1763-1789* (Baton Rouge, La.; 1957), p. 348.

slavery than Beard himself did. He told the Constitutional Convention that "the States were divided into different interests not by their difference of size, but by other circumstances; the most material of which resulted partly from climate, but principally from the effects of their having or not having slaves." Madison insisted that "the institution of slavery & its consequences formed the line of discrimination" between the contending states.[27] But this was not the only conflict stressed by Madison. He did *not* say, as Robert Brown paraphrases him, that "the really fundamental conflict in American society at the time" was "the division between slave and free states, between North and South."[28] He only said that slavery was the basis of the most important conflict within the Convention. Rather than refuting a thesis of struggle between those with wealth and those without, what Madison did was to point out an additional division among men of wealth, based on slavery.

This becomes clear if one considers the earlier versions of Federalist No. 10, which Madison wrote for the more intimate audience of his colleagues at the Convention. Douglass Adair has argued that Beard, in citing Federalist No. 10, simply omitted that part of Madison's essay which described non-economic motives.[29] However, in the unpublished fragment on "Vices of the Political System of the United States" written just before the Convention, Madison himself paid relatively little attention to them:

All civilized societies are divided into different interests and factions, as they happen to be creditors or debtors—rich or poor—husbandmen, merchants or manufacturers—members of different religious sects—followers of different political leaders—inhabitants of different districts—owners of different kinds of property etc. etc.[30]

[27] The Records of the Federal Convention of 1787, ed. Max Farrand (revised edition; New Haven, 1937), I, 486; II, 10.

[28] Robert E. Brown, *Reinterpretation of the Formation of the American Constitution*, p. 48.

[29] Douglass Adair, "The Tenth Federalist Revisited," *William and Mary Quarterly*, third series, VIII (1951), 60, 60n.

[30] *The Writings of James Madison*, ed. Gaillard Hunt (New York, 1900-1910), II, 366-367.

The next version of the argument, in a speech at the Convention on June 26, emphasized even more the economic basis of politics:

In all civilized countries the people fall into different classes havg. a real or supposed difference of interests. There will be creditors & debtors, farmers, merchts. & manufacturers. There will be particularly the distinction of rich & poor.

Madison's concern in this speech was to urge the creation of constitutional checks against "a levelling spirit" which might lead to an "agrarian law."[31] Here he expressed the tension between the Convention as a whole and the small farmers unrepresented there, just as in other speeches he articulated the tension within the Convention between slave states and free.

Beard's fundamental plea for a "removal of the Constitution from the realm of pure political ethics and its establishment in the dusty way of earthly strife and common economic endeavor"[32] remains valid. But Beard's version of the nature of that strife requires revision. Northern capitalist and Southern planter joined hands in 1776 to win independence from England; united again in 1787 to create the United States Constitution; then drifted almost immediately, into sectional cold war. A showdown could be postponed, however, because each sectional society expected to augment its power from new states to be formed in the West. What Turner's frontier thesis explains is why Beard's second American revolution was so late in coming, and why the Jeffersonian ideology which rationalized slavery as "agrarianism" lingered too long.

III.

In the words of Professor J. H. Plumb of Cambridge University, "there are a number of signs that historical studies in America are about to take new directions. . . . A new

[31] *Records of Federal Convention,* I, 422-423 (Madison's notes), 431 (Yates's notes).

[32] Beard, *Economic Origins,* p. 3.

analytic materialism is putting down strong roots."[33] The new (perhaps New Left) American history emphasizes economic causes, while avoiding the caricature that limits "the economic factor" to conscious pursuit of pecuniary advantage.[34] It insists on a comparative approach to the revolutions of 1776-1783 and 1861-1865, without denying that American history has a variety of "exceptional" features. And it views history "from below" while not forgetting that, so far as the white community in America is concerned, class conflict has been less intense here than in Europe.

This book seeks to contribute to this new history.

[33] J. H. Plumb, review of Barrington Moore, Jr., *Social Origins of Dictatorship and Democracy*, in *The New York Times Book Review*, Oct. 9, 1966, p. 12.

[34] It has often been remarked that some passages in Beard's *Economic Interpretation* suggest a narrow "economic determinism" and others a more sophisticated theory of "economic influence." On the one hand, Beard says that the "direct, impelling motive" for the drafting of the Constitution "was the economic advantages which the beneficiaries expected would accrue to themselves first"; that the "first firm steps toward the formation of the Constitution were taken by a small and active group of men immediately interested through their personal possessions in the outcome of their labors"; and that the "members of the Philadelphia Convention which drafted the Constitution were, with a few exceptions, immediately, directly, and personally interested in, and derived economic advantages from, the establishment of the new system." On the other hand, at the beginning of the crucial chapter on "The Economic Interests of the Members of the Convention" Beard states:

"The purpose of such an inquiry is not, of course, to show that the Constitution was made for the personal benefit of the members of the Convention. Far from it. Neither is it of any moment to discover how many hundred thousand dollars accrued to them as a result of the foundation of the new government. The only point here considered is: Did they represent distinct groups whose economic interests they understood and felt in concrete, definite form through their own personal experience with identical property rights, or were they working merely under the guidance of abstract principles of political science?"

These quotations are from *An Economic Interpretation of the Constitution of the United States* (New York, 1913), pp. 17-18, 73, 324.

PART ONE

Class Conflict

2

Who Should Rule at Home?
Dutchess County, New York,
in the American Revolution

In the summer of 1831, one of the numerous
New York Livingstons told the inquiring Alexis de Tocqueville:
"All classes joined together in the Revolution. Afterwards the
strength of Democracy was so paramount that no one attempted
to struggle against it."[1] The two sentences point to a paradox in
the American Revolution which historians have never fully resolved. All classes did join together in the War for Independence.
Thus in Dutchess County the aristocratic landlord Robert R. Livingston,[2] who would lead off for the Federalists at the New York

[1] Alexis de Toqueville, *Journey to America*, ed. J. P. Mayer (New Haven,
1959), p. 20.
[2] The Livingstons of Clermont were the most powerful landlord family in
Dutchess in the third quarter of the eighteenth century. Their influence was
based on land acquired by strategic marriages with descendants of Henry

Reprinted from the *William and Mary Quarterly*, third series, XVIII
(1961), 330-359.

ratifying convention in 1788, and the plebeian entrepreneur Melancton Smith, the principal Antifederalist spokesman, were both good Whigs in 1776. But it is equally true that in Dutchess, as in New York state as a whole, the Revolution challenged "the aristocratic flavor which everywhere permeated society" before 1775.[3] "If one may judge anything by the number and the nature of the cases in Dutchess County courts," writes the county's most recent historian, "the period of the Revolution witnessed a conflict in society beginning twenty years earlier and lasting ten years longer than the actual hostilities of war."[4]

Contemporaries had no doubt that the War for Independence was accompanied by a struggle over who should rule at home. Fear of just such an internal revolution made Robert R. Livingston hesitate long on the brink of independence.[5] By the winter of 1777-1778, the historian William Smith observed that the New York Whigs were splitting into "the Popular & the landed Interest" and wrote with some smugness of the latter: "These People have had no Foresight of the natural Consequences of a republican Spirit in a poor Country, where Gentlemen of Fortune are but few. . . . They are losing their Significance every Day. They

---

Beekman, Sr., the largest landholder in early Dutchess history. The three most important Clermont Livingstons at the time of the Revolution were: Judge Robert Livingston, who died in 1775; his wife, Margaret Beekman Livingston; and their son, Chancellor Robert R. Livingston. They must be distinguished from two other branches, also involved in Dutchess affairs. Philip Livingston, Dutchess sheriff in 1775, belonged to the Livingstons of Livingston Manor, whose interests lay primarily in Albany (later Columbia) County. Robert G., Henry, and Gilbert Livingston belonged to a third and distinctly less prominent branch; their sphere of action was Dutchess County, and politically they often allied themselves with freeholders of the county opposed to the Livingston "interest."

[3] Carl L. Becker, *The History of Political Parties in the Province of New York, 1760-1776* (Madison, 1909), p. 14.

[4] Henry Noble McCracken, *Old Dutchess Forever! The Story of an American County* (New York, 1956), p. 234.

[5] George Dangerfield, *Chancellor Robert R. Livingston of New York, 1746-1813* (New York, 1960), Part ii, chaps. 1-3, especially pp. 60, 81-82.

will be happy if they can save their Estates."⁶ The financial crisis of 1779-1780, with its attendant clashes over price regulation and the confiscation of Loyalist lands, drew from Robert R. Livingston's mother a prayer for "Peace and Independence and deliverance from the persecutions of the Lower Class who I forsee will be as dispotic as any Prince (if not more so) in Europe."⁷ As the war drew to a close, Thomas Tillotson of Dutchess wrote forebodingly that New York had "a strong Democratic Spirit prevailing that will some day not far off give a stab to its happiness. . . . The people want nothing but to be a little more impoverished to prepare them for it. The first stroke would be at the Tenanted estates. . . ."⁸

This conflict perceived by contemporaries was real. The egalitarian "spirit" which Smith called republican and Tillotson democratic was not a figment of the Federalist imagination. Historians who so regard it often assume that pre-Revolutionary society was, in fact, substantially democratic.⁹ But whatever may have been the case in Massachusetts, Dutchess County before the American Revolution was a harsh, hierarchical community of which one complainant said with much justice that there was "no law for poor Men."¹⁰ It was a society in which an heiress married "under a crimson canopy emblazoned with the family crest in gold—a demi-

⁶ William Smith, *Historical Memoirs from 12 July 1776 to 25 July 1778 of William Smith*, ed. William H. W. Sabine (New York, 1958), pp. 280, 306.

⁷ Margaret Beekman Livingston to Robert R. Livingston, Dec. 30, 1779, Robert R. Livingston Papers, New-York Historical Society, New York City. Hereafter cited as R. R. Livingston Papers.

⁸ Thomas Tillotson to Robert R. Livingston, June 17, 1782, R. R. Livingston Papers.

⁹ E.g., Robert E. Brown, *Middle-Class Democracy and the Revolution in Massachusetts, 1691-1780* (Ithaca, N. Y.; 1955), *passim*; Louis Hartz, *The Liberal Tradition in America: An Interpretation of American Political Thought Since the Revolution* (New York, 1955), pp. 67-86.

¹⁰ Testimony at the trial of William Prendergast, leader of the tenant rebellion of 1766 (Irving Mark and Oscar Handlin, "Land Cases in Colonial New York, 1765-1767: The King v. William Prendergast," *New York University Law Review*, XIX [1942], p. 191). The court which condemned Prend-

lion crowned issuing from a coronet," and, "as on rent day, the tenants gathered before the manor hall to feast and wish happiness to the bride while within a lavish banquet was spread for the Van Cortlandts, Livingstons and other river families."[11] It was a society, too, in which the leader of a tenant rebellion on the lands of this same heiress was sentenced to be hanged, drawn, and quartered for high treason. At mid-century, Henry Beekman, Jr., had "ruled the rapidly growing population of Dutchess County almost as if he had been its manor lord," a state of affairs condensed in the fact that Beekman's rent-collector doubled as manager of his invariably successful campaigns for election to the New York Assembly.[12] Even after Beekman's son-in-law, Judge Robert Livingston of Clermont, had been defeated in the Assembly elections of 1768 and 1769, the chief appointive positions continued to go to the great landlords until the Revolution.[13]

---

ergast to death consisted "wholly of important landowners and land speculators" (*ibid.*, p. 167); for the attitude of the judges, see William Smith, *Historical Memoirs*, p. 40. The tenants petitioned the King that they had attempted to pursue their grievances by legal means, but had "found that every Attorney at law in that whole Province was previously retained on the other side" (brief of Daniel Ninham before Chancery, 1767, quoted in William S. Pelletreau, *History of Putnam County, New York* [Philadelphia, 1886], p. 80).

[11] Alice C. Desmond, "Mary Philipse: Heiress," *New York History*, XXVIII (1947), 26.

[12] Philip L. White, *The Beekmans of New York in Politics and Commerce, 1647-1877* (New York, 1956), p. 159. The correspondence of Henry Beekman, Jr., with his agent, Henry Livingston, is in the Henry Livingston Papers, Franklin Delano Roosevelt Library, Hyde Park, New York, and New York State Library, Albany, New York, and the Beekman Papers, N.-Y.H.S.; it is summarized by White, *ibid.*, pp. 191-207.

[13] The great landlords of Dutchess before the Revolution were, in the north, the intermarried Beekmans and Livingstons (note 2, above), and in the south, the heirs of Adolph Philipse. The latter were Philip Philipse, nephew of Adolph Philipse, and Roger Morris and Beverly Robinson, who married Adolph Philipse's daughters. In 1775 these families owned about one-half of the million acres in Dutchess County. The Philipse patent comprised 200,000 acres, while the whole of the present townships of Beekman and Pawling represented only a part of the holdings of Henry Beekman, Sr.

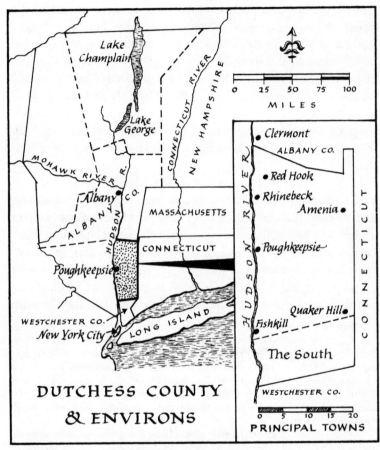

DUTCHESS COUNTY & ENVIRONS

PRINCIPAL TOWNS

Landlordism was stronger in some parts of the country than in others. In all parts of Dutchess men made a living by raising "good, sweet, merchantable winter wheat" (and, in the eastern section farthest from the Hudson, cattle) for the New York City market. Socially, however, north, south, and central Dutchess were distinct communities.

In northern Dutchess, resident large landlords set the social tone. They had their great homes or "places," in the eighteenth as in the nineteenth century, in the northwestern township of

Rhinebeck. Margaret Beekman Livingston, herself representing the union of two great families, owned six large houses and land assessed at £1500 in Rhinebeck, and at election time she sent her bailiff round to the tenants.[14] The social atmosphere in this part of the county is suggested by the Old Red Dutch Church, erected on the eve of the Revolution at Red Hook. It had special pews along the sides of the church for the landlords and their families, designed so that only the head of a seated occupant could be seen from the center of the building where the common people worshiped.[15]

In the south (the 200,000 acre region which later became Putnam County) the land and the people were poorer. "Mountainous and fit only for iron works," William Smith called the area in 1756.[16] The per capita tax assessment of the townships there, Frederickstown and Philipstown, was less than half that of Rhinebeck; taxpayers assessed at less than £5 made up over 90 per cent of the taxpaying population in Frederickstown and Philipstown, less than 40 per cent in Rhinebeck.[17] In contrast to the Germans

[14] For the houses, see "A Particular List or Description of Each Dwellinghouse . . . in Rhynbeck Town . . .," Gilbert Livingston Land Papers, New York Public Library, New York City. For the tax: Margaret Beekman Livingston to Robert R. Livingston, Dec. 30, 1779, R. R. Livingston Papers. For electioneering: Robert Livingston to James Duane, Apr. 30, 1788, Duane Papers, N.-Y. H. S.; Thomas Tillotson to Robert R. Livingston, Mar. 23, 1787, and Margaret Beekman Livingston to Robert R. Livingston, Apr. 1789, R. R. Livingston Papers.

[15] Philip Smith, *General History of Dutchess County from 1609 to 1876, Inclusive* (New York, 1877), pp. 382-383. An Antifederalist later made use of this manner of church design to exemplify the kind of society which, he thought, the United States Constitution would foster: see the allegory by "A Countryman" in the *New York Journal* (New York City), Dec. 6, 1787, with its description of the "large high pews for the better sort of people to sit in, so that they might not be troubled with the common people, or rabble as they fained to call them."

[16] William Smith, *The History of the Late Province of New-York, from its Discovery, to . . . 1762* (New York, 1829), I, 264.

[17] The total assessment and number of taxpayers for each township in 1771 are printed in James Smith, *History of Dutchess County, New York* (Syracuse,

and Dutch predominant in northern and central Dutchess, the
inhabitants in the southern part were almost entirely from New
England and Long Island.[18] They had come, said a Moravian
missionary, in search of "cheap farms, and . . . religious liberty."[19]
For a time they had found both, squatting on land which Adolph
Philipse claimed but had done nothing to develop. But in the
1750's the Philipse heirs had become more aggressive, ejecting
tenants who would not accept onerous leases; and it was here that
the formidable riots of 1766 had begun, when two thousand armed
tenants refused to pay rents, rescued comrades from the Poughkeepsie jail, marched on New York City for the same purpose, and
were finally dispersed only by redcoats with cannon. In 1775, all
of south Dutchess was held in tenancy rather than freehold.
Every officer of the Revolutionary militia in this section was a
tenant.[20]

The substantial freeholders of central Dutchess were—socially
and politically as well as geographically—a group intermediate between the landlords of Rhinebeck and the tenants of the south.
From Fishkill, Amenia, and Poughkeepsie came the popular politicians who courted tenant votes but who themselves belonged to

1882), p. 119. The percentages of taxpayers in different assessment categories
were computed from "Copy of Assessment Rolls of the Freeholders and Inhabitants of Dutchess County . . . 1786," N. Y. S. L.

[18] Regarding south Dutchess, McCracken states that in the 1800 Census
only 2 per cent of the names in the southern townships were Dutch (Mc-
Cracken, *Old Dutchess Forever!*, p. 471). As to northern Dutchess, Richard
Smith, traveling up the Hudson in 1769, landed at Henry Beekman's manor
in Rhinebeck and found no one who could speak English (*A Tour of Four
Great Rivers . . . in 1769*, ed. Francis W. Halsey [New York, 1906], p. 10);
while the historian of northeastern Dutchess states that before 1770 nine-
tenths of the inhabitants were Palatine Germans (Isaac Huntting, *History of
Little Nine Partners* . . . [Amenia, 1897], I, 133).

[19] Journal of Abraham Rhinke, quoted in Philip Smith, *Dutchess County*,
p. 112.

[20] Pelletreau, *Putnam County*, p. 120; Henry Lud[d]in[g]ton to George
Clinton, Feb. 20, 1778, *Public Papers of George Clinton* (New York and Albany, 1899-1914), II, 784-785. Hereafter cited as *Clinton Papers*.

"a rising middle-class of freeholders which disliked the domination of the landed aristocracy."[21] They included Dirck Brinckerhoff
(who had defeated Judge Livingston in the Assembly elections of
1768 and 1769), Ephraim Paine, Melancton Smith, Gilbert Livingston, and Zephaniah Platt. These were the men who in 1779-
1780 led the struggle for price regulation and the confiscation of
Loyalist lands, and in 1787-1788, the struggle against the United
States Constitution. From 1760 to 1790 and beyond, northern
Dutchess voted for the landlords' candidates and southern Dutchess against them, while central Dutchess oscillated between the
two.[22] In 1788, the leading men of northern Dutchess were Fed-

[21] White, *Beekmans*, p. 206. Whereas more than 90 per cent of the tax-
payers in southern Dutchess were assessed at £4 or less in 1786 (note 17,
above), Zephaniah Platt was assessed at £16 in 1771 and at £46 in 1786, besides heading a speculative group which bought up soldiers' claims to 30,000
acres of land near Lake Champlain; Dirck Brinckerhoff was assessed at £27
in 1786 and lent £7664 on mortgages between 1768 and 1785 (*Eighteenth
Century Records of . . . Rombout Precinct*, ed. H. W. Reynolds, Dutchess
County Historical Society, *Collections*, VI [Poughkeepsie, 1938], 55, 59, 71,
72, 73, 80, 81, 96, 97, 112, 128-131, 229, 270, 283); Gilbert Livingston
collected rents for his notorious uncle, Robert G. Livingston, and owned
at least £7540 worth of real estate (H. W. Reynolds, "James Kent," Dutchess
County Historical Society, *Yearbook*, VIII [1923], 23); Jacobus Swartwout
owned state and continental securities valued at approximately $7,600 (Forrest
McDonald, *We The People: The Economic Origins of the Constitution*
[Chicago, 1958], p. 307); Melancton Smith speculated in soldiers' warrants,
Loyalist lands, and in a number of the speculative projects of William Duer
(Israel Smith to Melancton Smith, Feb. 21 and 22, 1782, Daniel TerBoss to
Jonathan Lawrence & Co., Mar. 4, 1782, Lawrence and Smith Papers,
N.-Y. H. S.; Robert A. East, *Business Enterprise in the American Revolutionary
Era* [New York, 1938], pp. 94, 108, 117, 118, 146, 225, 275, 318).
The affluence of these popular leaders, however, was not in the same class
with that of landlords like Henry Beekman, Jr., who in 1760 was assessed at
£400 (McCracken, *Old Dutchess Forever!*, p. 73). The popular politicians were
indeed, as they described themselves, of a "middling" rank.
[22] See McCracken, *Old Dutchess Forever!*, pp. 447, 464, 472. A few examples: In the Congressional election of 1790, Rhinebeck went Federalist 215-
13, Philipstown and Frederickstown went Clintonian, 15-0 and 69-42; in the
Congressional election of 1800, Rhinebeck again voted Federalist 226-119,
Philipstown and Frederickstown again voted Clintonian, 110-19 and 75-3
(*New York Daily Advertiser* [New York City], May 21, 1790; New York

eralists; the two Dutchess delegates at the New York ratifying convention who voted against the Constitution came from the south; while the four delegates who were elected as Antifederalists but voted for the Constitution in the end, came from central Dutchess.

The still-smoldering tenant discontent in southern Dutchess helps to explain why, in the spring of 1775, the northern townships under the leadership of Judge Robert Livingston elected delegates to a provincial congress, while the south was "almost unanimously opposed."[23] British agents in the county, complained a Whig leader, "have corrupted the minds of many of the ignorant and baser sort of men among us, maliciously telling them the whigs were in rebellion; the King would conquer them, and their estates be forfeited; and if they take up arms against them, the King for their services will give them the whigs' possessions."[24] Two years later William Smith was told that the neighborhood of Quaker Hill, where the tenant rioters of 1766 had made their last stand, was forty to one "agt. Independency."[25] But not all tenants were Tories. Outright Toryism shaded off into Whig discontent. Later in the Revolution the Colonel of a regiment of Dutchess militia classified his men as "good Whigs," "Tories," and "middling Whigs." The last category was the largest.[26] Moreover, when the War for Independence began to develop social-revolutionary

---

Secretary of State, "Certificates of Election, 1799, 1800," Miscellaneous Records, XXV, N. Y. S. L.).

[23] Letters from Dutchess County correspondents to the *New-York Gazette: and Weekly Mercury* (New York City), April and May 1775, ed. Peter Force, *American Archives*, fourth series, II (Washington, D.C.; 1839), 304-305; Dangerfield, *Chancellor Livingston*, p. 57.

[24] Samuel Dodge to the President of the New York Provincial Congress, Dec. 5, 1775, *Journals of the Provincial Congress, Provincial Convention, Committee of Safety and Council of Safety of the State of New-York* (two volumes; Albany, 1842), II, 106. Hereafter cited as *Jour. Prov. Cong.*

[25] William Smith, *Historical Memoirs*, 118. See in confirmation Nathan Pearce to the Provincial Congress, Jan. 5, 1777, *Jour. Prov. Cong.*, I, 766-767.

[26] "Return of Delinquents in Col. Hopkins' Regiment . . . June 10, 1779," *Clinton Papers*, V, 71-73.

dimensions, allegiances wavered and changed. By 1779-1780 many landlords had become Tories or reluctant rebels, while tenants pressed for drastic measures to seize and distribute Loyalist estates.

I.

After Lexington and Concord a "coalition of parties" took place.[27] From 1775 to 1777, the Dutchess delegations to the Provincial Congresses and Convention were a mixed bag of men made up from the old governing group (including notorious landlords like Beverly Robinson and Robert G. Livingston, and James Livingston, the Dutchess sheriff at the time of the tenant rebellion) and the new, popular leaders. In these first years of the Revolution, there were few signs of the later division of the Whig leaders. Indeed, in the Convention debates over the proposed New York constitution in the spring of 1777, Gilbert Livingston and Zephaniah Platt voted with Robert R. Livingston against universal manhood suffrage in Assembly elections, and against the compulsory introduction of the secret ballot at the end of the war.[28]

As the war dragged on, future Federalists and Antifederalists labored together on a variety of overlapping Revolutionary committees in Dutchess. Striving to cope with endless administrative emergencies, they found themselves attacked from behind, as it were, by a rising popular discontent. The discontent involved a series of grievances painfully interlocked. High taxes, frequent militia duty, and the burden of refugees from southern New York were singled out by Robert R. Livingston in a letter to George Washington. In 1781 the New York legislature, in a letter to its

[27] Letter from Dutchess County to *New-York Gazette: and Weekly Mercury* (New York City), May 15, 1775, *American Archives*, fourth series, II, 305.

[28] *Jour. Prov. Cong.*, I, 867, 891-892.

constituents, mentioned "the Weight of Taxes, the rigorous Measures that have been used to restrain the Disaffected, Exertions oppressive to Individuals by which Supplies have been obtained, the Wants of the Army, the Calls upon the Militia, and the Destruction of our Frontiers. . . ."[29]

In these first years of the war, militia duty was perhaps the heaviest burden. Conservative Whigs viewed the militia with some distrust from the outset. James Duane wrote to Robert Livingston (the Lord of Livingston Manor) in 1775:

I am much pleased that young Mr. Livingston is raising a company in the Manor. I wish he may extend his View's further, in the only plan, which, independent of the grand Contest, will render landed property Secure. We must think in Time of the means of assuring the Reins of Government when these Commotions shall subside. Licenciousness is the natural Object of a civil [here the word, "war," was crossed out by Duane in the manuscript] discord and it can only be guarded against by placing the Command of the Troops in the hands of Men of property and Rank who, by that means, will preserve the same Authority over the Minds of the people which they enjoyed in the time of Tranquillity.[30]

But the men of property and rank did not control the militia in Dutchess. The highest-ranking officer in the county, Jacobus Swartwout, was the son of a tenant. Colonel Henry Luddington, commanding the south Dutchess regiment, was a tenant himself, as were all his officers. The Whig leaders in Dutchess, wrote William Smith in 1776, had a "general Suspicion of the lower Classes of the People" and no great confidence in the militia.[31]

[29] Robert R. Livingston to George Washington, Jan. 8, 1781, R. R. Livingston Papers; *Votes and Proceedings of the Senate* (Fishkill, 1781), p. 71.

[30] James Duane to Robert Livingston, June 7, 1775, quoted in Beverly McAnear, "Mr. Robert R. Livingston's Reasons against a Land Tax," *Journal of Political Economy*, XLVIII (1940), 76.

[31] William Smith, *Historical Memoirs*, pp. 27, 34.

If the officers were uncertain, the men were much more so. The chairman of the Dutchess Committee of Safety, writing eleven days after the Declaration of Independence, warned that the county's militia was untrustworthy and should not be called out. Of the four hundred militiamen in Rhinebeck, one hundred had been disarmed for suspected disloyalty, and he doubted whether there were two townships in the county with less disaffection. He concluded: "We have always thought we should be happy if we were capable of combating our internal foes, and leave those from without to be resisted in some other way."[32]

The reason for the soldiers' dissatisfaction is not far to seek. A private received $6.66 a month. Bounties promised to supplement the basic pay were late in coming. In August 1776, Zephaniah Platt wrote that "there is great complaints amongst the troops concerning their bounty, many of them having no money to purchase necessaries, having left at home what little they had for the use of their families."[33] A year later Governor George Clinton protested that "the Continental Pay and Rations being far below the wages given for ordinary Labor the Difference becomes a Tax rendered by personal Service and as the Train Band List from the Exemptions arising from Age Office & other Causes consists chiefly of the Middling & lower Class of People this extraordinary Tax is altogether paid by them."[34] Frequent advertisements for the apprehension of deserters appeared in the Dutchess newspapers.

The "tax" of militia service bore with particular severity on the

[32] Egbert Benson to the New York Provincial Convention, July 15, 1776, *Jour. Prov. Cong.*, II, 309.

[33] Willis Fletcher Johnson, *Colonel Henry Luddington: A Memoir* (New York, 1907), p. 19; Zephaniah Platt to the New York Provincial Convention, Aug. 24, 1776, *Jour. Prov. Cong.* II, 279.

[34] George Clinton to the Committee of Safety of the Continental Congress, July 31, 1777, *Clinton Papers*, II, 142-143. On the difficulty of recruiting because of low militia pay, see also Egbert Benson to the New York Committee of Safety, Mar. 19, 1776, *Jour. Prov. Cong.*, I, 384-385.

poor tenant militiamen of south Dutchess. Their colonel, Henry Luddington, complained that "at best the Regiment are very poor when compared with other Regiments and are call'd on to raise an eaquil number with the others, when I can affirm that ten farmers in Coll. Brinckerhoff's Regiment is able to purchase the whole of mine. In this uneaquil way, I have been obliged to turn out my men untill they are so much impoverish'd that they almost dispair."[35] This was written in 1781; but as early as the spring of 1777, the commissioners for detecting conspiracies were laboring to enforce discipline in Luddington's regiment, and one Captain Delavan told the Provincial Convention that southern Dutchess was largely disaffected. At the same time a traveler reported to William Smith that "the Drafts in Dutchess were few and would not serve [because] the People were wore out last year. Those in the Army lost the opportunity of seeding their Ground and were now starving for Bread."[36]

II.

The Provincial Convention which heard these disquieting reports in early 1777 was also attempting to draft New York's Revolutionary constitution. Abraham Yates, Jr., of Albany, antiquarian and future Antifederalist, believed that discontent in the militia had much to do with the democratic features of the new government. "The Yeomanry of the Country," he wrote, "were wanted to fight and the Militia Duty which equally affected the poor and the rich (a Man of £10 had the same Duty as the one of £10,000) upon the Principal of Personal Service was Become very Burthensome to the yeomanry and if the Rich Intended the

[35] Henry Lud[d]in[g]ton to George Clinton, May 1, 1781, *Clinton Papers*, VI, 817.

[36] "General Jacobus Swartwout," Dutchess County Hist. Soc., *Yearbook*, XIII (1928), 68; *Jour. Prov. Cong.*, I, 910; William Smith, *Historical Memoirs*, p. 119.

other should continue to fight for there Estates it was Necessary
to show that they did not make any Difference but w[h]ere it was
unavoidable."[37] While the Convention defeated the proposal to
give the franchise in Assembly elections to all taxpaying resident
freeholders over twenty-one years of age, the property requirement
for the vote was decreased. Perhaps even more significant were the
institution of annual rather than septennial Assembly elections
and certain changes in electoral procedure. Whereas elections to
the colonial Assembly and to the Provincial Congress and Convention had been held at the county seat by viva-voce voting, the
gubernatorial election of June 1777 was held at five different
places in Dutchess County, and in at least one precinct by secret
ballot. That precinct was Rhinebeck, the stronghold of landlord
influence, and the election inspector was Melancton Smith![38]

It has recently been suggested that the absence of the secret
ballot in pre-Revolutionary New York may not have seriously im-
paired democracy.[39] If this were so, why did John Morin Scott
fight for the secret ballot in all elections at the New York Convention? Why did Charles DeWitt charge the Livingstons that
"when the DeLanceys were to be quelled down they were Advocates for Elections by Ballot and now their Power was broke were

37 "Notes on Early History of New York, etc.," Abraham Yates Papers,
Box 3, N. Y. P. L.

38 On voting in colonial New York, see Michael N. D'Innocenzo, "Voting in
Colonial New York" (Master's thesis, Columbia University, 1959); on voting
for the Provincial Congresses and Convention, Becker, *New York*, pp. 227,
252; on the Convention's provision for the gubernatorial election of 1777,
Jour. Prov. Cong., I, 918; and on the way the election was actually conducted
in Rhinebeck, William Smith, *Historical Memoirs*, pp. 159-160. Smith says
that the instructions of the Convention as to voting were ambiguously worded,
and that Melancton Smith interpreted them to require the use of the secret
ballot. In 1778 the legislature made it clear that voting for governor was to be
by ballot, and "not by counties but by boroughs towns manors district and
precincts . . ." (First Session, chap. 16).

39 Milton Klein, "Democracy and Politics in Colonial New York," *New
York History*, XL (1959), 231-232.

opposed to it"?[40] Yates, again, testified eloquently to what the late Sir Lewis Namier, speaking of England in 1760, called "the inevitable result of open voting by people in dependent positions."[41] "What material difference is there," Yates asked, "whether one elector by his own voice sends a Member to parliament, or a manour settled with a hundred or a thousand Tenants, under the influence of one Person (and moved by his insinuation, nod or at least a letter . . . the Tenant [gives] his vote against his inclination, against his most intimate friend or relation, to a person the landlord was pleased to nominate)." If the "landed Gentlemen" agreed on a candidate, Yates continued, the election was a foregone conclusion; if not, "the public houses in every quarter were opened and a trial made who had the most influence and the largest purse."[42]

[40] So Peter R. Livingston and John Morin Scott reported to William Smith (William Smith, *Historical Memoirs*, pp. 129, 157). Smith also states that Thomas Tredwell of Suffolk voted against the constitution of 1777 because it did not require the ballot in all elections *(ibid.*, p. 121). A draft of the Constitution providing for the secret ballot in Assembly elections is in the Abraham Yates Papers, Box 2, N. Y. P. L. Both Tredwell and Yates were Antifederalists in 1788.

[41] Lewis Namier, *The Structure of Politics at the Accession of George III*, second edition (London, 1957), p. 70.

[42] "Speeches to Delegates in Congress, 1786," Abraham Yates Papers, Box 4. The importance assigned to the introduction of the secret ballot is supported by contemporary sources. But it would seem that, even before the Revolution, an intense popular feeling sometimes expressed itself at the polls despite all obstacles. Thus in the Assembly election of 1768, following close on the heels of the tenant rebellion of 1766, Judge Livingston "had so far lost the esteem of the Freeholders in that County, that he gave up before half the Freeholders then present had given in their votes, tho' he had every thing in his favour, which power could give him" (Cadwallader Colden to the Earl of Hillsborough, Apr. 25, 1768, in *Documents Relative to the Colonial History of the State of New York*, ed. E. B. O'Callaghan [Albany, 1856-1887], VIII, 61). When he lost again in the following year, he was said to have been defeated by the votes of tenants "notwithstanding all the pains was taking with them" (Peter R. Livingston to Philip Schuyler, Feb. 27, 1769, quoted in Dangerfield, *Chancellor Livingston*, p. 40).

The common folk of Dutchess, as they went to the polls in June
1777, must have pondered the fact that in the earlier, viva-voce
voting for Dutchess delegates to the Provincial Congress, univer-
sally-hated landlords like Beverly Robinson and Robert G. Livingston had been returned.[43] For in this first election after the
creation of the new Constitution, politics in Dutchess took a sharp
swing to the left. George Clinton was decisively elected Governor.
In Dutchess his margin was 206-132.[44] William Smith was told that
resentment toward the Livingstons was the dominant passion behind the vote: Philip Schuyler, he noted just before the elections,
"says Dutchess and Ulster are jealous of the Livingstons who have
already got all the valuable Places and that they will not vote Ph: L
[Philip Livingston, Sheriff of Dutchess County] for Govr. . . .";
another informant told him that "the People of Dutchess and
Ulster were perswaded in chusing a Govr. to name no Livingston
nor any in Connection with that Family & hence Clinton was preferred to Jay & Schuyler."[45]

The election of Clinton was indeed a blow to the Livingstons'
control over the Revolutionary ferment. On the eve of election,
Robert R. Livingston had argued "the propriety of swimming with
a stream, which it is impossible to stem." Contrasting the position
of the Pennsylvania conservatives with that of his own group in
New York, he continued: "Wilson will remember that I long ago
advised that they shd. yield to the torent if they hoped to direct
its course—you know that nothing but well timed delays, inde-

[43] For the reputation of these landlords, see McCracken, *Old Dutchess
Forever!*, p. 433. Beverly Robinson was the most active of the Philipse heirs in
prosecuting ejectments in southern Dutchess in the 1760's; for the tenants'
feeling about him, see page 47, below.

[44] N.Y. Secretary of State, *Calendar of Historical Manuscripts Relating to
the Wars of the Revolution in the Office of the Secretary of State*, two volumes
(Albany, 1868), II, 242, reprinting "Canvas of Votes for Governor and Lieu-
tenant-Governor of New York, 1777," from Miscellaneous Papers, XXXVII,
225-233. Professor Alfred Young kindly called these returns to my attention.

[45] William Smith, *Historical Memoirs*, pp. 151, 326.

fatigable industry, & a minute attention to every favourable circumstance could have prevented our being exactly in their situation."[46]
After Clinton's election, it began to seem that Pennsylvania and
New York might not be so different. In August 1777, Livingston
wrote Gouverneur Morris concerning the first signs of a popular
movement which was to bulk large in Dutchess two years later:
"You have seen the attempts of the county of Albany to imitate
the Philadelphia Committee in [price] regulations etc. tho' they
have not been followed by the other Counties yet they have excited a spirit that will be troublesome." By early 1778 his tone
had become acid. No doubt thinking of the Dutchess situation at
his doorstep as well as of Governor Clinton, Livingston wrote
Morris that "the ignorance of some, & the wickedness of others are
hourly perverting the constitution," and, "you know too much of
some people in power here to think the State safe in their hands."
In April, Livingston lamented to Morris that the legislature wanted to regulate prices, prohibit the export of flour, and lay "a most
unprecedented tax . . . on all Traders & Manufacturers who have
made more than £1000." In the same letter, less than a year after
his philosophical reflections on swimming with the stream, he
announced that he was considering retirement from New York
politics.[47]

Thus the events of 1777—the adoption of a compromise but still
significantly more democratic constitution, Clinton's victory, Livingston's dismay—marked the first decisive fragmentation of the
Whig coalition in New York. In the state, Yates and Scott aligned
themselves against Rensselaer, Schuyler, and Livingston. In Feb-

[46] Robert R. Livingston to William Duer, June 12, 1777, R. R. Livingston
Papers.

[47] Robert R. Livingston to Gouverneur Morris, Aug. 8, 1777, Jan. 1778,
Jan. 29, 1778, and Apr. 6, 1778, R. R. Livingston Papers. Morris attempted
to rally Livingston to action: "Take a Survey of the Ground you have to act on.
Where are the Eminences? They must be gained—*They* must be *gained* . . . .
Will not some of their Forces revolt? . . . Take Ceres Bacchus and Minerva to
your Aid" (Morris to Livingston, Jan. 21, 1779, R. R. Livingston Papers).

ruary 1778, William Smith noted that there was "a Severence between the Popular & the landed Interest and they will mutually pull each other down." In Dutchess, the landlords ceased to seek election. Robert G. Livingston, a member of the Dutchess delegation to the second Provincial Congress, became a passive Tory, and when the British fleet sailed up the Hudson to Kingston and burned the manor houses of Rhinebeck, Livingston's was left conspicuously untouched. Beverly Robinson, a delegate at the same Congress, became an active Tory, an officer in the British army. *His* house was Benedict Arnold's base of operations in the spring of 1780. As for Robert R. Livingston, he, together with Duane, John Jay, Duer, Gouverneur Morris, and Schuyler, began a powerful, co-ordinated campaign to strengthen and to capture the national government.

III.

Conservative Whigs had hoped that the creation of a state constitution would put an end to the irregular activities of local committees—what William Smith called an "Infinity of Lawgivers"[48]—and restore an orderly political and judicial structure which they could control. But just as discontent in the militia had influenced the politics of 1777, so now new grievances rose up from below to push the popular leaders on to still more extreme positions and ultimately, in 1779-1781, to call forth a revival of the local committees. As Scott, Platt, and Brinckerhoff made proposals to regulate prices and to sell confiscated and unappropriated lands, "the basis of their popularity,"[49] Robert R. Livingston and his friends could only strive to undo at Philadelphia what was enacted at Albany. In March 1780, when the New York legislature finally passed a bill to sell the Loyalist lands, the Congress in Philadelphia staved off price regulation and took the first step in the

[48] William Smith, *Historical Memoirs,* p. 149.

[49] Robert R. Livingston to Gouverneur Morris, Sept. 10, 1778, R. R. Livingston Papers.

conservative financial program by devaluing the Continental currency. This was the last act of a drama which had begun in the winter of 1777-1778, when John Morin Scott introduced bills in the New York legislature to regulate prices and wages, and to confiscate Loyalist lands.[50]

In Dutchess, pressure for price regulation and land confiscation rose with the cost of living. Figures in the papers of the Dutchess Commissioners of Sequestration suggest the magnitude of price inflation: a Negro slave girl sold for £50 on December 23, 1777, and for £3,680 on October 5, 1780; on August 16, 1780, a pair of oxen was sold for £1,040. As currency depreciated and prices rose, taxes and requisitions became ever heavier. Some Dutchess farmers left their wheat unground rather than accept the worthless quartermasters' certificates. Looking back years later on the hardships of those days, a group of Dutchess tenants recalled that while some had fled to the enemy, they themselves had "remain'd stedfast on . . . determined to defend the right of [our Co]untry as well as our own Property." They had suffered particularly, they said, from the nearness of the troops, "who were constantly Cantoned & encamped around us, notwithstanding our willingness at all times to supply their reasonable wants but how inadequate was our little property to the Support of an Army often hungry, Naked and distressed for the necessary Comforts of life, which consequently, at times, by living so contiguous to them Reduced us to the same predicament."[51]

The common man personalized his grievances and blamed financial distress on the malevolence of speculators. Henry Luddington and others inveighed against the "wicked, mercenary

[50] *Votes and Proceedings of the Senate* (Fishkill, 1777), pp. 17, 199.

[51] Papers of the Commissioners of Sequestration, Dutchess County, N.-Y. H. S.; Ephraim Paine to Robert R. Livingston, Feb. 12, 1779, and Robert R. Livingston to John Penn, Jan. 28, 1780, R. R. Livingston Papers; petition of tenants on the "Water Lotts," Dutchess County, Sept. 6, 1784, New York Assembly Papers, XXVI, N. Y. S. L.

intrigues of a number of ingrossing jockies, who have drained this
part of the State of the article of bread to that degree, that we
have reason to fear there is not enough left for the support of the
inhabitants."[52] The "petition of the freeholders and inhabitants
of Dutchess County" told the New York legislature that speculators were selling provisions to the enemy for specie and refusing
to sell to Whigs for paper, and asked for action against "a vile set
of Men whose God is their Gain. . . ."[53]

To many a perplexed householder, not only in New York but
throughout all the struggling states, the revival of local committees
seemed, ultimately, to be the way to check the monopolistic prac-
tices of merchants and the dishonesty of public officials. Direct
action on the spot, so ran the argument, would check what no
mere law was competent to prevent. "At length," proclaimed a
correspondent to the Poughkeepsie newspaper, "is the virtuous part
of the community alarmed, and the old and true friends to their
country again step forth to remedy evils the laws cannot reach, by
the exertion of Committees, the terror of all villains. . . . As soon
as the authority of your Committees ended, knavery shewed its
head, villains of every class came forth and practiced with impunity. . . . Let no time be lost then, my countrymen, in forming
your Committees."[54]

Before the castastrophic year 1779, in which the Continental
currency sank from about one-eighth to about one-fortieth the
value of specie, the Dutchess committees were somewhat diffident
in taking direct action without approval from above. The chairman
of the Rhinebeck committee wrote to the president of the New

[52] Henry Luddington and others to the New York Council of Safety, Dec.
3, 1776, *Jour. Prov. Cong.*, II, 355.

[53] "The Petition of the Freeholders and Inhabitants of Dutchess County,"
undated, N. Y. S. L.

[54] *New York Journal* (Poughkeepsie), Aug. 16, 1779. The price-fixing movement in the various states and the Continental Congress is described by Richard B. Morris, "Labor and Mercantilism in the Revolutionary Era," *The Era
of the American Revolution: Studies Inscribed to Evarts Boutell Greene*, ed.
Richard B. Morris (New York, 1939), pp. 76-139.

York Convention in March 1777 that a local speculator was debasing the currency but that the committee did not know whether it was authorized to act; in November he complained of the high price of Robert Livingston's iron and the revival of horse racing, adding, it "is not as we recollect in our power to prevent it."[55] Far different was the manner of the Dutchess committees revived in 1779 in response to Philadelphia's call for committees "in every State and county."[56] The committee of Rombout precinct, chaired by future Antifederalist Jacobus Swartwout, announced that traders were to buy goods only at prices fixed by the committee and sell them only at designated rates of profit, after invoices had been exhibited to the committee or its chairman. The committee of Poughkeepsie, under the chairmanship of future Antifederalist Gilbert Livingston, called for the immediate confiscation and sale of forfeited estates. A county-wide committee, meeting in August 1779, resolved to "diligently inquire into the conduct of all public officers."[57] At the same time the committees recognized the need for more centralized action by the state legislature and the Continental Congress. When Governor Clinton addressed the legislature in August 1779, he acknowledged the flood of local petitions concerning price and currency problems by referring to "the Sense that your Constituents loudly express of the Necessity of applying some suitable Remedy to this growing Evil."[58]

Meantime an even more controversial issue had loomed up. In the same issues of the newspapers which told of price-fixing com-

[55] Herman Hoffman to the President of the New York Convention, Mar. 17, 1777, and Jacob Heermane to the President of the Council of Safety, Nov. 21, 1777, *Jour. Prov. Cong.*, II, 409, 457.

[56] *New York Packet* (Fishkill), July 15, 1779.

[57] *Ibid.*, Sept. 16, 1779; *New York Journal* (Poughkeepsie), Aug. 9, Aug. 16, 1779.

[58] Speech of Aug. 24, 1779, *Clinton Papers*, V, 210. The price-fixing movement alarmed and frightened the conservative New York Whigs. See, for example, Gouverneur Morris to Robert R. Livingston, Mar. 27, 1778: "Is it possible my friend that the State of New York can think of passing a *regulating Act*. How hath this madness got hold upon them" (Livingston-Bancroft Transcripts, II, N. Y. P. L.); John Sloss Hobart to Robert R. Livingston, Nov.

mittees started in Philadelphia, Boston, and Williamsburg in 1779, Dutchess farmers read of the confiscation of Loyalist lands in Pennsylvania, New Jersey, and Vermont. John Morin Scott had introduced a bill for this purpose in the New York Senate the year before, and dark rumors had begun to circulate in Dutchess. William Smith was told that "a Man in the Secrets of the Leaders" of the Dutchess and Ulster Clintonians had commented—on the Tory literature promising the estates of Whig landlords to their tenants—that it "was half right but the Tenants would not get the Lands in that Way meaning from the Crown but that when the Independency is established the Manors would be parcelled out to such Tenants as were in Favor with the New established Government."[59] In October 1778, "the respectful address and petition of the freeholders and others, inhabitants of the county of Dutchess" made it plain that tenant unrest as well as the government's need for money underlay the agitation for confiscating and selling Loyalist lands. Pleading with the legislature to speed passage of such a bill, the petition warned: "The delay of this act to another session is big with uncertainty of its passing at all, and therefore of the most dangerous consequences to this State. Especially as it will occasion universal uneasiness and in all probability produce tumults and insurrections, and tend to a domestic tyranny and confusion as much to be dreaded as the evils brought upon us by our connections with Great Britain."[60]

15, 1779: "The liberty of acquiring property is, probably, the greatest incentive to action in the whole moral system.... Man is, by nature, a lazy beast.... Exert yourself therefore to prevent our resolves [the resolves of the Hartford Convention, favoring a general limitation of prices] from obtaining the sanction of congress, let there be no convention at Philadelphia" (R. R. Livingston Papers).

[59] William Smith, *Historical Memoirs*, p. 326.

[60] This petition is quoted by Johnson, *Luddington*, pp. 153-156. It could not be located at the N. Y. S. L., and was presumably destroyed in the great fire there, which totally consumed several volumes of petitions that had been removed from the Assembly Papers. The reception of the petition is noted in the Assembly and Senate Journals.

For if Whigs throughout the county saw in Loyalist property a potential prop to Revolutionary finance, the tenants of southern Dutchess had their own reasons for wanting the confiscation and sale of Loyalist estates. Two-thirds of south Dutchess belonged to Beverly Robinson and Roger Morris, attainted by the act of October 1779. The tenants had been reluctant rebels in 1775-1776, but the opportunity of acquiring their farms as freeholds would appear to have worked mightily on their convictions. For Simon Calkins and other south Dutchess tenants whom Beverly Robinson had dispossessed in the 1760's, the legislation to confiscate and sell Loyalist lands was an opportunity to rehearse the history of their grievances and to lay claim to their inheritance. They had, they told the legislature in a 1779 petition,

settled a wild uncultivated Tract of Land . . . and turned it into comfortable Habitations [with an] Expectation of Reaping the Benefit, and enjoying [the fruits of] their Labour and Toil in the Decline of Life; being [confident] . . . that whoever should be the proper Owner . . . would have Justice Goodness and Compassion . . . to allow them the Priviledge of enjoying those Habitations [and] Farms which they had made comfortable and in some measure profitable by the sweat of their Brows, upon their paying an equitable and reasonable Rent.— But contrary to this . . . as soon as their farms were in any measure made comfortable convenient or profitable by their Industry, one Beverly Robinson instigated by his associates Philip Philipse and Roger Morris, and assisted by a Banditti of Kings Troops . . . in the Year 1766 . . . obliged them to quit their Houses and Farms and commit themselves naked unto Providence. . . .

Therefore, this much-charred and barely-legible document concludes, they desired the legislature to "enact such Laws or adopt Measures as may effect the Restoration of these your Petitioners. . . ."[61]

[61] Petition of Simon Calkins and others, Sept. 2, 1779, New York Assembly Papers, XXVI, N. Y. S. L. The continuity of the spirit of tenant unrest in Dutchess County from 1766 to 1780 is illustrated by a comparison of this petition with those of the 1760's, for example, "A petition for a Confirmation of our inheritance together with our associates," Nov. 10, 1763, Miscellaneous Manuscripts—Dutchess County, N.-Y. H. S.

The course of the Revolutionary War brought to the tenants of the Dutchess Highlands not only the opportunity of acquiring freeholds, but the threat of being dispossessed from what precarious tenure they had already achieved. This much-troubled region was the southern boundary of the area controlled by the New York Revolutionary government and hence, the natural place for the Whig refugees from southern New York to accumulate. In March 1777, the legislature created Commissioners of Sequestration to sell the personal effects of Loyalists "under moderate rent from year to year to persons friendly to the cause of America," giving first priority to refugees.[62] This meant that a tenant of a Loyalist landlord like Beverly Robinson could himself be dispossessed to make way for a refugee. To those tenants who, like James Cox, received letters from the Commissioners ordering them to remove for this reason, the spirit of '76 may have suddenly seemed less important, and the spirit of '66 more real.[63]

By the fall of 1779 a formidable tremor of unrest was shaking the ground beneath the feet of the Whig leaders. Tenants, at least in Dutchess County, had passed from the withholding of rents[64] to mutterings about more aggressive action. "The people have be-

[62] For the steps leading up to this legislation, see Harry B. Yoshpe, *The Disposition of Loyalist Estates in the Southern District of the State of New York* (New York, 1939), pp. 13-15. [The work of the Dutchess Commissioners of Sequestration is described at length in my *Anti-Federalism in Dutchess County, New York* (Chicago, 1962), chap. IV.]

[63] Theodorus Van Wyck to James Cox, Jan. 26, 1779, Papers of the Commissioners of Sequestration, Dutchess County, folder 1. Needless to say there were two sides to the situation. John Campbell wrote to Van Wyck, Jan. 31, 1780: ". . . those two Families have Twelve Children the Oldest not Eleven Years old and to my knowledg one of those Families have been six weeks this winter without Bread—and when the small remains is gone I brought out of New York this must be my situation unless you relieve me" (*ibid.*, folder 2).

[64] For the widespread withholding of rents, see Robert R. Livingston to the Trustees of Kingston, Mar. 1, 1778, R. R. Livingston Papers; the advertisements of Robert G. Livingston, *New York Journal* (Poughkeepsie), Jan. 4, Aug. 16, 1779, and *New York Packet* (Fishkill), Aug. 19, Sept. 2, 1779, directed "to those tenants in arrears, from four, eight or ten years in particu-

come very licentious," Thomas Tillotson wrote Robert R. Livingston in December.[65] In the same month Livingston's mother, Margaret Beekman Livingston, capped a complaint about oppressive taxes (levied by another future Antifederalist, John DeWitt) with the prayer for deliverance from the "persecutions of the Lower Class" already quoted.[66] Not only in Dutchess but all over America, it would seem, the pressure on legislative bodies from the people "out of doors" reached a high point in this winter of 1779-1780. October 1779, when the New York legislature enacted the permanent confiscation (though not yet the immediate sale) of Loyalist estates, was also the month when resentment against profiteering culminated in the "attack on Fort Wilson" in Philadelphia.

The grave state of civilian morale was more than duplicated in the military. The commanding general of the northern army, William Heath, wrote in quiet desperation that the troops had been eight days without bread, "a universal uneasiness" prevailed, and mutiny seemed imminent. On December 16 he wrote that two-thirds of one Dutchess regiment had simply gone home, but he recommended leniency for the mutineers because of the shortage of food.[67]

As the legislators struggled through unprecedented snows and

---

lar"; Henry B. Livingston to Robert R. Livingston, May 1775: "The Tenants here are Great Villains. Some of them are resolved to take advantage of the times & make their Landlords give them Leases forever" (quoted in Bernard Mason, "Organization of the Revolutionary Movement in New York State, 1775-1777" [Doctoral dissertation, Columbia University, 1958], p. 60).

[65] Thomas Tillotson to Robert R. Livingston, Dec. 13, 1779, R. R. Livingston Papers.

[66] Two years later Mrs. Livingston was still complaining of DeWitt's taxes (Margaret Beekman Livingston to Robert R. Livingston, July 16, 1782, R. R. Livingston Papers). It is evident from her letters that this great absentee owner was for the first time being assessed for holdings in eastern Dutchess and for the Dutchess poor tax.

[67] William Heath to George Clinton, Dec. 3 and Dec. 16, 1779, Jan. 25, 1780; Clinton to Heath, Dec. 23, 1779, *Clinton Papers,* V, 396-398, 421-422, 429-430, 463-467. See Dangerfield, *Chancellor Livingston,* p. 119.

temperatures as low as eighteen degrees below zero to reach the
January session in Albany, politicians of both parties voiced alarm.
"I have not felt equal Distress at the Situation of our Affairs at
any Period since the commencement of the War," wrote Clinton;
"the Garrison of Fort Schuyler," echoed Philip Schuyler, "has been
on half allowances, that of Fort George so distressed they have
been on the point of Evacuating"; and John Sloss Hobart summed
up what all felt in the phrase: "this winter . . . is the most important to us of any that will fall within our age."[68]

Screwed to this pitch of tension, what bonds of confidence
remained between the radical and the conservative New York
Whigs were stretched and snapped. In this 1780 session of the New
York legislature, when the immediate sale of Loyalist lands was
enacted,[69] one sees in full operation the opposing parties which, in
1787-1788, would take the names Federalist and Antifederalist.
Egbert Benson of Dutchess, himself already under attack in the
Dutchess County newspapers for Tory sympathies, wrote at the

[68] George Clinton to Robert R. Livingston, Jan. 7, 1780; Philip Schuyler
to Robert R. Livingston, Jan. 18, 1780; John Sloss Hobart to Robert R. Livingston, Feb. 15, 1780, R. R. Livingston Papers. Two years later the contractor
Jacob Cuyler referred to the year "Seventy nine Eighty when they were ready
to Disband for want of Provisions" (Jacob Cuyler to James Duane, Aug. 31,
1782, Duane Papers).

[69] The long struggle over Loyalist lands can be properly understood only
when it is divided into three stages. First, Loyalist lands were sequestered
(Mar. 1777); then confiscated (Oct. 1779); and then sold (Mar. 1780). Each
step in this process provoked a separate legislative battle. More property was
sequestered than confiscated, and more confiscated than sold. In Poughkeepsie, for example, the personal belongings of 45 persons were sold under the
sequestration law, but only 1 of the 45 lost his land (Edmund Platt, *The
Eagle's History of Poughkeepsie from the Earliest Settlements, 1683 to 1905*
[Poughkeepsie, 1905], p. 301); and that one, Bartholemew Crannell, recovered his land in the late 1780's with the help of his Whig son-in-law, Gilbert
Livingston. George Clarke, with large holdings in northeastern Dutchess, went
to England and "not wishing to lose this vast landed property . . . sent his
son to America to take charge of it and at the same time to profess deep
sympathy with the Whig element" (James Smith, *Dutchess County*, p. 214).

end of the session that it had "been the most disagreeable and troublesome one I have known; almost a continual Wrangle from first to last. It certainly is the first in which I have known either Men or Measures lay under the Imputation of Disaffection. At our first sessions the Debates ran high . . . but we still believed each other Whigs and so far there was a perfect Confidence; at the last Meeting however our Proceedings were poisoned by a Distrust, and without Cause, if not of Toryism at least of cool dispirited Whiggism, equally injurious."[70] Benson's statement confirms the judgment of Allan Nevins and E. Wilder Spaulding that it was at this time, and over this issue, that "the patriots were clearly divided into moderate and extremist factions."[71]

It was symbolic that Benson, the future leader of Dutchess Federalism, led the fight in the Assembly against sale of the confiscated estates, while the favoring faction was guided by Dirck Brinckerhoff, the anti-landlord champion of 1768 and 1769. In September 1779, Benson moved to delay the sale of forfeited lands until the next meeting of the legislature and to prohibit the sale of unimproved lands in the confiscated estates. In each case Brinck-

[70] One correspondent accused Benson of saying in 1779 that "for two years past, the Whigs have done the State more damage than the Tories" (*New York Journal* [Poughkeepsie], Mar. 15 and Mar. 22, 1779). This would tend to confirm the chronology suggested by the text: 1775-1777 as the period of Whig unity; 1777-1779 as the period of developing tension; 1779-1780 as the moment of open division.

Benson's remarks on the session are in Egbert Benson to Robert R. Livingston, Mar. 20, 1780, R. R. Livingston Papers. Livingston commented to Duane: "I was this day distressed by a letter from Benson, in which he mentions the mad lengths to which a party spirit arising, as far as I can find, from no real cause, has hurried our Legislature. It is much to be lamented that internal factions should break out before we had driven the enemy from our doors" (to James Duane, May 2, 1780, Duane Papers).

[71] The phrase quoted is from Allan Nevins, *The American States During and After the Revolution, 1775-1789* (New York, 1924), p. 268. E. Wilder Spaulding says: "The Confiscation Act for the first time aroused a conservative Whig opposition to the extreme measures of the government" (*New York in the Critical Period, 1783-1789* [New York, 1932], p. 122).

erhoff and the majority of the Dutchess delegation voted against Benson. But the bill was sent back to committee and came up for final action at the next session.[72]

The committee reported out on February 4, 1780, stating that memorials had been received from several counties imploring the speedy sale of confiscated lands. Again the Assembly voted on whether to proceed to immediate sale; again Brinckerhoff and most of the Dutchess delegation were in favor, again Benson was opposed. The crucial division came on March 10, when the Senate returned the bill to the Assembly, urging that sales be postponed until further attempts had been made to raise money by loan: a third time Benson voted for delay by supporting the Senate suggestion, and a third time Brinckerhoff and the bulk of the Dutchess representatives joined the now-victorious majority.[73]

What lay behind these votes was not a contest of good men and bad men. On February 25, at the same Assembly session, a bill was introduced which provided that slaves who voluntarily enlisted for three years with the consent of their masters should thereby become free. Brinckerhoff moved to reject; Benson voted in favor.[74] What distinguished Benson from Brinckerhoff in the crisis of 1779-1780 was a different relation to the popular movement for land confiscation and price regulation. Benson came from the conservative constituency of Rhinebeck. Throughout the session he consulted Robert R. Livingston, who thought the confiscation law "a most ill judged" bill: "never," Livingston wrote, "was there a greater compound of folly avarice & injustice."[75] Behind Brinckerhoff, who lived in Fishkill, stood the agitated voters of southern Dutchess, searching the newspapers for their representatives' votes,

[72] *Votes and Proceedings of the Assembly* (Fishkill, 1779), pp. 26, 28.

[73] *Ibid.*, pp. 95, 150.

[74] *Ibid.*, p. 127.

[75] Egbert Benson to Robert R. Livingston, Feb. 20, Mar. 20, June 28, July 8, 1780; Robert R. Livingston to John Jay, Mar. 4 and Apr. 20, 1779, R. R. Livingston Papers.

in order "to know before every new election, by the votes of the old one, in what manner they have acquitted themselves, and how well they are entitled to our future choice, which surely no one can have the least pretension to who voted against the confiscation bill."[76] Whatever his personal views may have been, Brinckerhoff, like Scott, bent with the storm and courted the good opinion of local committeemen like Gilbert Livingston and Peter Tappen.[77] It paid off at the polls. In 1781 Benson, hitherto the dominant figure in the legislature,[78] lost his Assembly seat and did not recover it until 1787. Brinckerhoff, on the other hand, served in five of the eight Assemblies which preceded the adoption of the United States Constitution.

Democratic in its origins, the confiscation law was also democratic in its results. Of the 496 forfeited lots sold under the law of March 10, 1780, in Dutchess County, 455 were in southern Dutchess, and 414 had belonged to Beverly Robinson and Roger Morris.[79] The 455 lots were sold directly to 401 persons: rarely, obviously, did a purchaser acquire more than one farm. Almost without exception the lots sold were small, under the five-hundred-acre maximum specified by the law. Moreover, not only were the lots

[76] "A Country Man" in the *New York Journal* (Poughkeepsie), May 18, 1779.

[77] See Robert R. Livingston to John Jay, Apr. 20, 1779, with its reference (crossed out in the manuscript) to "Scotts desire to satisfy the ship carpenters of Poughkeepsie" (R. R. Livingston Papers). The "ship carpenters of Poughkeepsie" were Gilbert Livingston and Peter Tappen, who were building ships for the Revolutionary government.

[78] Alexander Hamilton later called Benson the pre-eminent figure in the Assembly during the Revolution (writing as "H——— G———" in the *New York Daily Advertiser* [New York City], Mar. 12, 1789); Walter Livingston wrote to Robert R. Livingston on Jan. 7, 1781, of Benson as the man who "is supposed to govern the politicks of this State" (R. R. Livingston Papers).

[79] Except where indicated, the facts in this paragraph are derived from the Abstract of Forfeited Lands for Dutchess County, N.-Y. H. S. This volume corresponds exactly with Ledger A of Deeds in the basement of the county clerk's office at Poughkeepsie, New York.

small and shared among many hands, but in almost half the sales the purchasers were tenants in possession of the land at the time of confiscation. Of the 401 purchasers of forfeited farms in south Dutchess, 166 had paid taxes in these townships in 1777.[80] Of forty tenants actually in possession of a group of Robinson's lots offered for sale in July 1780, twenty purchased the land that they were farming.[81] William Pelletreau is certainly very near the mark in his conclusion that "in a large number of cases, in fact a majority, the lands were sold to the parties who were already in possession of the various farms, as tenants of Beverly Robinson and Roger Morris."[82] As in the case of the tenanted estates of Westchester County, the confiscation of Loyalist lands in Dutchess County helped to democratize the structure of society.[83]

[80] The assessment rolls for southern Dutchess in 1777 are printed in Pelletreau, *Putnam County*, pp. 121-128.

[81] *New York Journal* (Poughkeepsie), July 24, 1780.

[82] Pelletreau, *Putnam County*, p. 93. This is not to deny either that tenants were often cruelly dispossessed, or that speculators acquired many of the farms. The former is suggested by a petition, Jan. 15, 1781: "We the subscribers beg leave to represent the circumstance of Daniel Hunt who is now eighty-seven years of age. He lives on a small farm that did belong to Col. Robinson not more than twenty acres of improved land. He has always been friendly to the country he has lived on the place twelve years. If you will be pleased to order that the place may not be sold but let him continue the few days he has to live it can't be long and he is not able to buy it . . ." (Miscellaneous Manuscripts—Dutchess County, N.-Y. H. S.). Speculation is well illustrated by that prince of speculators, William Duer, who bought two of Robinson's farms for himself and Robert Morris, assuring his partner that since the purchase could be made in money worth only 1/22 of its face value, they could expect a profit of 4 per cent on the investment in rent and a 200 per cent profit when they sold out (East, *Business Enterprise*, p. 112). Radical politicians like John Lamb, Zephaniah Platt, John Morin Scott, Jacobus Swartwout, Mathew Patterson, and Melancton Smith each picked up a farm or two. See also note 96 below.

[83] Yoshpe, *Loyalist Estates*, p. 115, concluded that in the Southern District "patriotic profiteers contrived to get the bulk of the loyalist estates into their own hands." But Spaulding, in reviewing Yoshpe's book, correctly pointed out that Yoshpe slighted his own evidence that many tenants on the Philipse

IV.

After the passage of the confiscation legislation, the popular ferment continued, but that legislation remained its most significant concrete achievement. Almost a year later Robert R. Livingston wrote that "the people are clamorous [;] the whole County of Dutchess have chosen precinct & County committees to instruct their members." At the same time he wrote to George Washington of the unrest among the common people: "sore and dissatisfied [,] their discontents begin to break out in complaints against their rulers in committees and instructions."[84] After still another year, Margaret Beekman Livingston worried that wheat continued at the low price of five shillings a bushel: "I know not what will become of our farmers";[85] and Thomas Tillotson, as quoted earlier, wrote that "the people want nothing but to be a little more impoverished to prepare them" for violent action. But by 1781-1782 the radical program for meeting the financial emergency had (in its decentralized form of local committee action) been shown impractical, and (in its centralized aspect at the Con-

---

Manor in Westchester acquired their farms (this evidence is at *ibid.*, pp. 50-59; Spaulding's review is in *The American Historical Review*, XLV [1939-1940], 899-900). The entire literature on confiscation in New York is crisply summarized by Catherine Snell Crary, "Forfeited Loyalist Lands in the Western District of New York—Albany and Tryon Counties," *New York History*, XXV (1954), 239-258. The Dutchess and Westchester evidence, considered as a whole, suggests that where confiscation involved large, tenanted estates, the results may have been substantially democratic, while speculators found their pickings primarily in scattered, urban, or unoccupied parcels.

[See now Beatrice G. Reubens, "Pre-Emptive Rights in the Disposition of a Confiscated Estate. Philipsburgh Manor, New York," *William and Mary Quarterly*, third series, XXII (1965), 435-456, which supports the generalization that confiscation of large Hudson valley estates substantially democratized land ownership.]

84 Robert R. Livingston to Gouverneur Morris, Jan. 18, 1781, and to George Washington, Jan. 8, 1781, R. R. Livingston Papers.

85 Margaret Beekman Livingston to Robert R. Livingston, Dec. 22, 1781, R. R. Livingston Papers.

tinental Congress) been defeated. What remained of the radical
impulse was not a practical program for the nation, but a seedbed
of stubbornly democratic attitudes which the 1780's would vainly
try to cultivate and bring to harvest.

Then, amid the cut and thrust of controversy over the adequacy
of the Confederation, rival mythologies of what happened in the
Revolution were perfected. Both Federalists and Antifederalists
claimed to be the exclusive inheritors of the American Revolution.
In 1787, Robert R. Livingston, in an Independence Day oration
to officers of the Cincinnati, more than a little implied that the
true Whigs of '76 had all become Federalists. On the other side,
Abraham Yates, Jr., argued that "the Characters that Now are
called Aristocratic were then called high prerogative Gentlemen."
"It is admitted," Yates went on, "that there are poor as well as rich
Tories . . . yet we know by experience that there would not have
been a Tory in fifty in our late struggles if they had not been disaffected by the rich."[86]

These mythologies linger on in rival historical interpretations of
the Revolutionary era, but the reality would appear to be different
from either version. Neither the Federalist nor Antifederalist leaders of Dutchess had been Tories. Politicians of democratic and
aristocratic bent could join in support of independence because the
American Revolution as a social movement was not intended or
foreseen. It developed as a pragmatic outcome of the practical crises
which had to be surmounted if the war was to be won. As Merrill
Jensen and Oscar and Mary Handlin, writing from different stand-
points, agree, the new forces which arose in the years after Lexington "were the products of the problems of those years."[87]

And yet that is only half of the story. The responses evoked by

[86] Draft of oration to the Society of the Cincinnati, given New York, July
4, 1787, R. R. Livingston Papers; "Speeches to Delegates in Congress, 1786,"
Abraham Yates Papers, Box 4.

[87] The phrase quoted is from Oscar and Mary Handlin, "Radicals and Conservatives in Massachusetts after Independence," *New England Quarterly*,
XVII (1944), 355. For Jensen's argument that "the American Revolution was
a democratic movement, not in origin, but in result," see his "Democracy and
the American Revolution," *Huntington Library Quarterly*, XX (1956-1957),
321-341.

the successive Revolutionary crises, for example the alternate programs brought forward to cope with the financial emergency of 1779-1780, had deep roots in the colonial past. The antagonisms which rose to the surface of Dutchess politics as the war went on were long-standing and familiar. Far from springing full-grown from the brow of revolution, these antagonisms centered on the old conflict between the ruling families of the landed aristocracy and the tenants and small freeholders of the county. It was this linkage of the concrete wartime struggles over militia service and Revolutionary finance to traditional and easily-mobilized popular sentiments that made it certain democracy would emerge from the struggle, as de Tocqueville was told, paramount.

Such at least is the model suggested by the events of the Revolution in Dutchess County, New York. For a few years after Lexington and Concord, landlord-tenant conflict was partially overlaid by the concord in Whiggery of all Dutchess political leaders, aristocratic and popular. While their future constituents were refusing to form Revolutionary committees or to elect delegates to the Provincial Congress, Zephaniah Platt was defending a liberty pole erected in Poughkeepsie, and Melancton Smith, an ardent Whig since the 1760's, was raising the first Revolutionary militia company in Dutchess.[88] But by 1777-1778, still more by 1779-1780, the old alignments had revived. And when, at the New York ratifying convention of 1788, Melancton Smith rose to confront Robert R. Livingston and defend the participation in politics of the middling and humble sort of people,[89] he only echoed the poem of a twelve-year-old boy, written in the heated elections of the late

[88] For Smith's political views before 1775, see his letters of Dec. 2, 1769, and Jan. 2, 1771, Melancton Smith Papers, N. Y. S. L.

[89] The famous exchanges between Smith and Livingston laid particular stress on the question: From what socio-economic groups should the legislative representatives of a republic be recruited? At one point Livingston asked Smith if he intended to go out among the hedgerows and enlist the blind, sick, and lame as representatives; at another, switching tactics, he proclaimed, "We are all aristocrats." This theme, underlying the entire debate, is brilliantly characterized by Dangerfield, *Chancellor Livingston*, pp. 222-233. Far from being rhetorical, it was the essential point at issue in Dutchess politics throughout the Revolutionary era.

1760's, which told the Livingstons that "not a vote would you get if it wan't for your land."[90]

Not that the popular leaders—Melancton Smith, Dirck Brincker-hoff, Zephaniah Platt, Gilbert Livingston, Jacobus Swartwout, Ephraim Paine, and their like—were typical of the poor farmers who elected them. On the contrary, they were well-to-do and represented (to borrow a term from another controversy) the "entrepreneurial" element in the Dutchess democracy.[91] But these men chose, no doubt in part because of their own humble origins, to ride rather than to contend with the whirlwind of popular feeling. Whereas Robert R. Livingston, in George Dangerfield's fine phrase, stood for the "politics of privilege," the Smiths, Platts, and Brinckerhoffs of Dutchess politics represented the "politics of opportunity."[92] While never entirely at ease with the presence in politics of the really poor, these popular leaders developed a democratic philosophy of politics which called for the election to office of men of a "middling sort," frequent elections, rotation of office, small election districts, and a large representative branch.[93] Their brief hour of

---

[90] This little verse, which begins, "One night in my slumbers, I saw in a dream/Judge Livingston's party contriving a scheme," will be found in "A Packet of Old Letters," Dutchess County Hist. Soc., *Yearbook*, VI (1921), 36n.

[91] See note 21, above.

[92] Dangerfield, *Chancellor Livingston*, p. 88.

[93] See the program of a meeting of Amenia freeholders *(Poughkeepsie Country Journal*, Dec. 22, 1785), which also calls for paper money and the repudiation of debts to Tories.

The attitude prompting these proposals is well suggested by Melancton Smith's notes for a speech at the New York ratifying convention: "The Senate will be a small Body, distant from ye people in a situation not to be observed by them—Men are apt in this condn. to forget their dependence—to lose their sympathy—to contract selfish habets . . . A Senator will be most of his time from home—will associate with none but his own class—will become a stranger to the condn. of the people—He should return and be obliged to live with the people. . . ." (Melancton Smith Papers). In view of the frequency with which Antifederalists expressed democratic sentiments of this sort, it is difficult to avoid the conclusion that Cecelia Kenyon's study of the Antifederalist ideology ("Men of Little Faith: The Anti-Federalists on the Nature of Representative Government," *William and Mary Quarterly*, third series, XII [1955], 3-43) presents a very one-sided picture.

dominion over Dutchess politics foreshadowed the decline of the aristocracy in the politics of New York a generation later.

Looking back, it is easy to underestimate the meaning of the confiscation and sale of Loyalist estates, the major legislative achievement of Dutchess County's internal revolution. No doubt the confiscation laws only accelerated a long-run trend toward freehold tenure. Hard-bitten landlords like Robert G. Livingston still sold off a farm here, a farm there, finding it more convenient to hold mortgages on freeholds than to try to control a tenant's management of the land.[94] The Revolution did not "abolish the leasehold system."[95] Even in south Dutchess, where the bulk of the confiscations occurred, many farms purchased by tenants slipped out of their hands again in the 1780's as they failed to meet payments and were forced to resell.[96] With the coming of peace, landlords like

[94] "Only let the farm year to year because I will sell them both as soon as possible"; "If any body would be in earnest about it I would agree about the price for I had better sell them almost at any rate than to have them out for they want repairs" (Robert G. Livingston to Gilbert Livingston, Apr. 6, 1773, and Mar. 22, 1775, Gilbert Livingston Papers, Box 1, N. Y. P. L.).

[95] This is the judgment of the distinguished Dutchess antiquarian Helen W. Reynolds, "The Story of Dutchess County," Dutchess County Hist. Soc., *Yearbook,* XVIII (1933), 32; and of McCracken, *Old Dutchess Forever!,* pp. 425, 430, 433. But it is refuted by the electoral census of 1790, which lists 1115 40 s. tenants along with 2780 £20 and £100 freeholders (*New York Daily Advertiser* [New York City], Jan. 15, 1791), figures which if anything underestimate the extent of tenancy, since tenants were often classified as freeholders for electoral purposes. The correct generalization is that of David Maldwin Ellis, *Landlords and Farmers in the Hudson-Mohawk Region,* 1790-1850 (Ithaca, N. Y.; 1946), p. 28: "Dutchess County . . . presented a checkered pattern of land tenure with numerous leaseholds interspersed among the predominant freeholds."

[96] For a struggle between mortgage lenders to gain ownership of a confiscated Dutchess farm, see Henry G. Livingston to Gilbert Livingston, Mar. 4, 1781, Gilbert Livingston Papers, Box 1. Several petitions of tenants who had made deposits on their farms but could not meet the installment payments are in the New York Assembly Papers, XXV, XXVI, N. Y. S. L. Provision for installment payments was not included in the confiscation legislation in order to benefit speculators. On the contrary, the Council of Revision twice warned that unless a provision for installment payments were included, the lands would be monopolized by speculators, who alone had quantities of ready cash (*Votes and Proceedings of the Senate* [Fishkill, 1777], p. 214;

Robert G. Livingston and his son Henry took the oath of loyalty and resumed their trade: "I have wrote several letters to William Devine [a tenant]. . . . I must order him to be arrested please to write him a line threaten him perhaps that may prevail on him to do something"; "Dirck has run off and left his son in possession. . . . Poppy desired me to turn him off as he used him ill by sending him insolent Messages such as refusing him rent and saying he would pay to the King etc. etc."[97] The county's economy had not been revolutionized.

So it seems looking back. But to contemporaries, living through the event and making it, the confiscation of Loyalist lands had a more comprehensive significance. It was the first major breakthrough of the independence struggle into social change. It brought to political expression the trend toward freehold tenure which, in time, would destroy the neofeudal society of the Hudson Valley.

The best objective measure of the change wrought by the Revolution in the county is the disappearance of the old ruling families from political office. Thus Beverly Robinson was replaced as first judge by Ephraim Paine, a self-taught lawyer who dressed so plainly

---

Votes and Proceedings of the Assembly [Fishkill, 1779], pp. 144-145). But many tenants were so short of cash in the mid-1780's that they petitioned to pay part of their payments in wheat and beef.

Another difficulty faced by the south Dutchess tenants in attempting to purchase their farms was that the confiscation legislation required tenants to pay all arrears of rent. This was a heavy burden: on May 1, 1777, Beverly Robinson's tenants had owed him £2753, two-and-a-half times their total annual rent. The tenants contended that the requirement to pay back rent prevented them, "a very few excepted," from purchasing their farms. See the petitions of Reuben Ferris and 93 others, June 26, 1781; Alexander Kidd and 102 others, Mar. 1782; and 61 residents of Philipstown, Mar. 1782 (New York Senate Papers, X, Box 2, and XI, Box 1); for the arrears of rents on Robinson's farms, see Frederick C. Haacker, "Early Settlers of Putnam County, New York" (1946), typescript at N. Y. S. L., 2. A law of Apr. 14, 1782 (Fifth Session, chap. 45) eased the tenants' situation by permitting them to pay half of their arrears in securities rather than specie.

[97] Robert G. Livingston to Gilbert Livingston, Oct. 26, 1785, Henry G. Livingston to same, Feb. 1, 1785, Gilbert Livingston Papers, Box 1.

he was often mistaken for a laborer; Sheriff Philip Livingston gave way to Melancton Smith, who had clerked in a retail store and was a mere "Mister" among a flock of "Esquires" in the Dutchess delegation to the first Provincial Congress.[98] Between 1777 and 1788 not one member of the old ruling families held an important elective or appointive position in Dutchess County.[99] For a decade it seemed that the Revolution had settled not only the question of home rule, but also—and just as decisively—the question: Who should rule at home?

[98] For Ephraim Paine, see Newton Reed, *The Early History of Amenia* (Amenia, 1875), pp. 72, 102-103, and Philip H. Smith, *Dutchess County*, pp. 121-122. For Melancton Smith, see "Committee of Dutchess County to the New-York Congress," *American Archives*, fourth series, II, 834.

[99] Franklin B. Hough, *The New York Civil List* (Albany, 1861), pp. 62-65, 74, 109-111, 122-130, 183-193, 420, 446, 457. Henry and Gilbert Livingston might seem exceptions to this generalization. But they belonged to the non-propertied branch of the Livingston family descended from Gilbert, one of the three sons of the first Robert. Whereas for the Manor and Clermont Livingstons politics was an avocation, "for the Gilbert line . . . local public offices tended to be a means of livelihood": the clerkship of Dutchess County was perennially in this family (Joan Gordon, "Kinship and Class: The Livingstons of New York, 1675-1860" [Doctoral dissertation, Columbia University, 1959], pp. 264-265).

3

The Tenant Rising
at Livingston Manor,
May 1777

The New York tenant rebellion of 1766 is one of the most dramatic examples of internal social conflict during the era of the American Revolution, and the "tin horns and calico" tenant riots 75 years later prove that class conflict in the Hudson Valley outlasted the struggle for national independence. But it has not been recognized that tenant disturbances also occurred in the midst of the Revolutionary War. In his classic study of agrarian conflict in colonial New York, Irving Mark commented on the difficulty of determining the extent of anti-rent agitation during the Revolution.[1] The present paper will establish the fact that in the spring of 1777, coinciding with the completion of New York's Constitution, about five hundred tenants on Livingston

---

[1] Irving Mark, *Agrarian Conflicts in Colonial New York, 1711-1775* (New York, 1940), p. 15*n*.

Reprinted from *The New-York Historical Society Quarterly*, XLVIII (1964), 163-177.

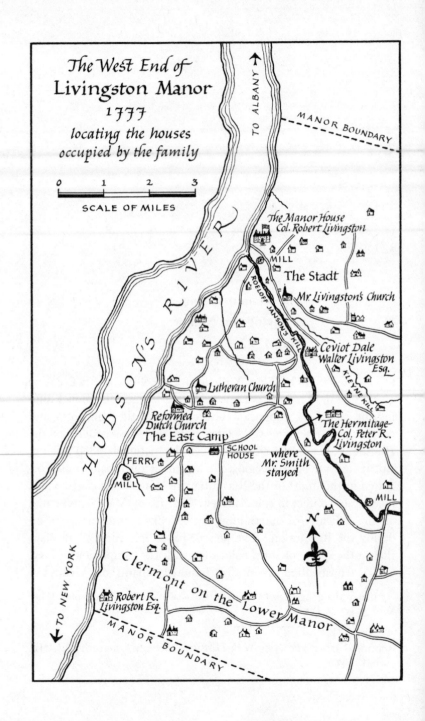

The West End of
Livingston Manor
1777
locating the houses
occupied by the family

0   1   2   3
SCALE OF MILES

TO ALBANY

MANOR BOUNDARY

HUDSON'S RIVER

The Manor House
Col. Robert Livingston

MILL

The Stadt

Mr. Livingston's Church

ROELOFF JANSON'S KILL

Ceviot Dale
Walter Livingston
Esq.

KLEYNE KILL

Lutheran Church

Reformed
Dutch Church
The East Camp

The Hermitage
Col. Peter R.
Livingston

where
Mr. Smith
stayed

SCHOOL
HOUSE

FERRY

MILL

MILL

N

TO NEW YORK

Clermont on the Lower Manor

Robert R.
Livingston Esq.

MANOR BOUNDARY

Manor took arms to aid the British in the hope that a British victory would lead to their obtaining freehold title to their farms.

The Livingston Manor rising affords a revealing glimpse of the
decay of aristocratic authority in Revolutionary New York. The
Livingston family had provided leadership for the state's patriot
party. When the rising occurred Robert R. Livingston, Gouverneur
Morris, James Duane, John Jay, and other New York conservatives
were preparing to back fellow-landlord Philip Schuyler in his contest with George Clinton and John Morin Scott for the office of
governor. Two months later, with the rising suppressed and the
election over, Schuyler would blame his defeat on the fact that
disgruntled tenants had stayed away from the polls.

Tenant unrest on the 160,000 acres of Livingston Manor was two
generations old in 1777. It was here, on the east bank of the Hudson River south of Albany (the present Columbia County), that
indentured servants from the German Palatine settled to make tar
from the pitch pine. In 1711 Governor Robert Hunter ordered
130 soldiers to the vicinity of "the East Camp" to awe and disarm
the mutinous tenants there.[2] In the early 1750's manor tenants
near the Massachusetts border refused to pay rents, petitioned the
Massachusetts legislature for title under that colony, and resisted
with arms the attempts of the third Lord of the Manor to eject
them.[3] In 1762 the third Lord, Robert Livingston, Jr., wrote his
son-in-law James Duane about "the Club who have for these five
years plagued me in the back part of my Mannor."

They are all a pack of Vagabonds who are fled from their Creditors &
gott together in the mountains & want my flatt Lands to Settle on, but
Chiefly to Sell & pay their debts, for they cannot live any longer in the
mountains as they have nothing left to support on.[4]

[2] *Ibid.*, pp. 111-112.
[3] See correspondence of Robert Livingston, Jr. with his Massachusetts agent
Jacob Wendell, 1751-1755, Livingston Papers, Museum of the City of New
York; Oscar Handlin, "The Eastern Frontier of New York," *New York
History*, XVIII (1937), 50-75.
[4] Robert Livingston, Jr. to James Duane, Feb. 15, 1762, Duane Papers
New-York Historical Society. For extensive documentation of rioting on the

The same part of the manor, most distant from the commerce of the Hudson and closest to the freehold farmers of New England, would be the last to lay down arms in 1777; would go strongly Antifederalist in 1788 because of "the ill fated Controversies about their Lands";[5] and would be the scene, in 1791, of the shooting of Columbia County sheriff Cornelius Hageboom, in retaliation for attempted evictions.

The quasi-feudal character of Livingston Manor leases explains this persistent discontent. The leases of the third Lord of the Manor "were for 75 to 100 acres with the tenant obligated to clear two acres a year, plant one hundred fruit trees, pay rent in winter wheat at the rate of approximately eighteen bushels for 75 acres, give the lord of the manor two days of work a year and four 'fatt' hens."[6] In the Lower Manor, the portion of Livingston Manor which belonged to the so-called Clermont branch of the family, headed by Robert R. Livingston, typical leases in 1762 called for a tenth part of the tenant's wheat, a day's riding with horse and team, and an obligation on the part of the tenant to get any boards he needed from the manor sawmill.[7] The Revolution effected little change: an English visitor to Clermont in 1794 commented that these leases "mark more of the spirit of feudal aristocracy" than he had expected to find on the land of leaders of the Republican Party;[8] and in 1795 the manor tenants themselves complained that

manor near the Massachusetts line in the 1750's, see *The Documentary History of the State of New York*, ed. E. B. O'Callaghan (four volumes; Albany, 1850), III, 826-828.

[5] Peter Van Schaack used this phrase in predicting Federalist defeat in eastern Columbia County in a letter to Philip Schuyler, April 3, 1788, Schuyler Papers, New York Public Library.

[6] Joan Gordon, "Kinship and Class: The Livingstons of New York, 1675-1860" (Doctoral dissertation, Columbia University, 1959), p. 133.

[7] Robert R. Livingston, Sr., to Robert R. Livingston Jr., March 12, 1762, Robert R. Livingston Papers, N.-Y.H.S.

[8] William Strickland's diary (manuscript collection, N.-Y.H.S.), quoted in

their leases were "oppressive and burthensome to the last degree, unfriendly to all great exertions of Industry and tending to degrade your Petitioners from the Rank the GOD of Nature destined all Mankind to move in, to be SLAVES and VASSALS." While the manor store provided the tenants with a diet of "molasses, rice and limited spices," the Livingston family enjoyed "such delicacies as sweet oil, raisins, currants, cloves, cinnamon, cheeses, oysters, mint wafers, figs, olives and capers."[9]

Tenant unrest on the manor prior to the Revolution reached a climax in the general rising of 1766. The British officer Captain John Montresor noted in his journal that two hundred tenants had "turned Levellers," armed themselves, and "marched to murther the Lord of the Manor and level his house, unless he would sign leases for 'em agreeable to their form. . . ." The tenants were dispersed by 40 armed men led by Walter Livingston, future Speaker of the New York Assembly and member of the Treasury Board of the Continental Congress.[10]

After independence Livingston Manor became a microcosm of the struggle over who should rule at home. The landlords were the traditional leaders of the anti-British party in the state; the tenants were New York's most obdurate malcontents. Where landlords were Tories, as in neighboring Dutchess County, tenant unrest could be harnessed to the Revolution by the confiscation of Loyalist lands.[11] But on Livingston Manor, where the landlords were prominent Whigs, the tenants became vigorous Tories.

There were signs of coming trouble on Livingston Manor long

George Dangerfield, *Chancellor Robert R. Livingston of New York, 1746-1813* (New York, 1960), p. 6. For a description of Clermont leases in the 1790's, see *ibid.*, p. 190.

[9] *Documentary History of New York*, III, 838; Gordon, "Kinship and Class," p. 148.

[10] *The Montresor Journals*, ed. G. D. Scull (New York, 1882), pp. 366, 375-376.

[11] [For wartime tenant unrest in Dutchess County, see Essay 2.]

before May 1777. In 1775 Robert R. Livingston of Clermont wrote
to his good friend John Jay:

I told you some time before I left you that many of our Tenants here
refused to sign the association, & resolved to stand by the King as they
called it, in hopes that if he succeeded they should have their Lands.
Since troops have been raised in the province & two of my Brothers have
got commissions they have been frighted & changed their battery. In
order to excuse themselves they assert that they can not engage in the
controversy since as their leases [are] not for lives their families must
want when they are killed.
   To deprive them of all excuse, my father [*Robert R. Livingston, Sr.*]
has declared to them that a new lease shall be given to the family of
every man who is killed in the service & Mrs. Livingston [*the writer's
mother and the owner of much land in her own name*] has come to
the same resolution. Notwithstanding which the scoundrels have as we
are informed sent in a petition to the [New York Provincial] Congress replete with falsehoods & charges injurious to the memory of my
Grandfather & Mrs. Livingston.

Jay must be sure to rebut the tenants' charges, Livingston concluded, for the tenants "will if they meet with the least encouragement throw the whole country into confusion." At about the
same time, Henry B. Livingston was writing to Robert R. Livingston from the Upper Manor: "The Tenants here are Great Villains. Some of them are resolved to take advantage of the times &
make their Landlords give them Leases forever."[12]

By the fall of 1776 a tenant rising was openly feared. Peter R.
Livingston, heir to the Upper Manor and President of the Provincial Congress, was told that the disaffection on the manor was increasing daily; that many tenants were hiding in the woods; that
the militia was not reliable. A week later William Smith noted in
his diary that the manor regiment had been ordered to march
against Burgoyne, but that Henry Livingston, the commanding

12 Robert R. Livingston to John Jay, July 17, 1775, Jay Papers (Columbia
University); Henry R. Livingston to Robert R. Livingston, quoted in Bernard
Mason, "Organization of the Revolutionary Movement in New York State,
1775-1777" (Doctoral dissertation, Columbia University, 1958), p. 60.

officer, would disobey the order on the advice of Robert R. Livingston, "it being the Opinion of both, that not above 50 will move ... & that there is Danger of a Rising if the Whigs go ... agt their Families and especially agt the Members of the Committee."[13]

The phrase, "a Rising ... agt the Members of the Committee," seems strange at first, for scholars have accustomed us to thinking of the committees of safety and correspondence in Revolutionary New York as instruments of popular radicalism. But, although elections were annual and open to all inhabitants, the Livingston family maintained tight control over the Manor Committee of Safety throughout the war. Tenants figure in its records not as committeemen but as suspected Loyalists.[14]

In September 1776 the Manor Committee was informed that one Jury Wheeler had said that if he had to go to the army, the first person he would shoot would be his captain. The next month, witnesses testified that a number of disaffected persons had gathered in the southeastern corner of the manor and "Intend to Strike some Blow, the Very first favourable Opportunity." Also in October 1776 Andries Reese reported having heard Adam Cillmer say that "if the Regulars should come up in the Country they would be rejoiced." Several persons, Reese continued, had signed something called the "Kings Book," saying that if they could "come to

[13] Samuel Ten Broeck to Peter R. Livingston, Oct. 9 and 10, 1776, *Journals of the Provincial Congress, Provincial Convention, Committee of Safety and Council of Safety of the State of New-York* (two volumes; Albany, 1842), II, 319-320; William Smith, *Historical Memoirs*, ed. William H. W. Sabine (two volumes; New York, 1956-1958), II, 26.

[14] E.g., Carl L. Becker, *The History of Political Parties in the Province of New York, 1760-1776* (Madison, 1909). The Manor Committee somewhat resembled a parish vestry in the South. Its leaders, such as chairman Samuel Ten Broeck, were continually reelected, and the nature of these elections is suggested by the fact that in 1778 there was only one voter in attendance (Smith, *Historical Memoirs*, II, 293-294). It is interesting to note that contrary to a widespread impression, the Committee did not cease to function when a new government was formed in 1777, but existed until 1783 (*New York Packet*, Jan. 18, 1781 and June 7, 1783).

The Two Branches of the Livingston Family

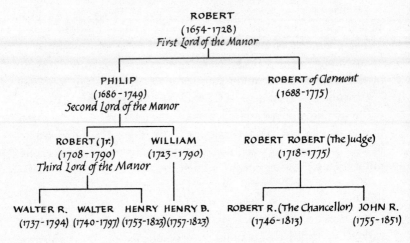

the Kings people" they would all fight for the King as long as they had blood.[15]

Meanwhile, the tenants of other manors were restless, too. In the late autumn of '76 there was trouble in Rensselaerwyck, where four hundred men were said to be in arms.[16] The following April, just before the manor rising, correspondents reported to Philip Schuyler from Albany that Toryism had increased amazingly and "become very predominant." The militia was deserting in bodies. It was impossible to procure a team anywhere in the countryside, and an attack on the jail by six or eight hundred men was expected.[17]

[15] "The Minutes of the Committee of Safety of the Manor of Livingston, Columbia County, New York, in 1776," *New York Genealogical and Biographical Record*, LX (1929), 325, 326, 328-329.

[16] Alice P. Kenney, "The Albany Dutch: Loyalists and Patriots," *New York History*, XLII (1961), 340.

[17] Richard Varick to Philip Schuyler, April 14, 16, and 21, 1777; Bartholemew Wells to Schuyler, April 21, 1777, Schuyler Papers, N.Y.P.L.

Such discontent might have remained dormant save for the great British offensive of 1777, which attempted to cut New York in two by launching one army up the Hudson from New York City and a second down the lakes from Montreal. Indeed, could the tenants have waited until the fall, when Burgoyne was near Albany and Clinton had forced his way up the Hudson far enough to burn Kingston, a tenant rising might have changed the outcome of the Battle of Saratoga. But the tenants acted upon misinformation about the military situation. One can trace the spread of false rumors among them in successive reports to the Manor Committee. In October 1776 an informant reported that, "last Week at the Burying at Peter Habers there was some Men together, who said that they had heard that our Army was defeated at Fort Washington" [a full month prior to the actual event]. Later a report came from one tenant, who had "gone to Harme Bests to Enquire for News," that if the rumored presence "of the Kings Troops" at Poughkeepsie were confirmed, "he did not Intend to go to the Committee." Late in November false intelligence that "the Kings Troops or Regulars are Just by" was passed on to the Committee. More sophisticated men than the tenants, about half of whom were illiterate, were often just as much in the dark. Thus in April 1777, when the Livingston tenants (so the Manor Committee was told) were wondering whether the fleet off Boston was French or English, Richard Varick passed on to Philip Schuyler a rumor that British frigates had reached Peekskill, but four days later wrote again to say that the rumor of frigates was unfounded. By then, however, the manor tenants, perhaps misled by the same tidings, had risen.[18]

[18] "Minutes of the Committee of Safety of the Manor of Livingston," pp. 331, 332, 335, 341; Varick to Schuyler, April 28, 1777, Schuyler Papers, N.Y.P.L. Evidence of the tenants' illiteracy is the high percentage of marks among the signatures to the 1795 petition cited in note 9. In assembly debates of 1787 on the secret ballot, both Alexander Hamilton and William Malcolm stated that in some parts of the state illiteracy reached 50 per cent. (*New York Daily Advertiser*, Jan. 29 and 31, 1787.)

The rising consisted of a series of skirmishes extending through the first week of May, in which the tenants never brought their full force to bear because they expected momentarily British military aid that never materialized. William Smith, under house arrest at Livingston Manor as a suspected Tory, had an ideal observation post. One local informant told him that the rising started when new men were selected for the militia by officers rather than (as was apparently customary) by ballot. Smith conjectured, however, that hostilities were touched off by the arrival on the manor of the Claverack militia, which led the tenants to suspect the discovery of their conspiracy. We know from the Tory press of New York City that at about this time a brush took place between 40 inhabitants of the manor and patriot soldiery escorting prisoners by order of the Albany Committee. In this incident the prisoners were freed one day and recaptured the next, at the cost of five lives.[19]

In an atmosphere charged with rumor and counter-rumor, it may well be that the hostilities spread spontaneously from such local incidents. Nevertheless, there can be no doubt that an elaborate conspiracy, embracing almost all the manor tenants, existed. The commission for detecting conspiracies, appointed by the Provincial Convention, found the number of conspirators "infinitely greater than we could have conceived."

Almost every body in the upper manor, particularly the eastern part of it, appears to have engaged with the enemy, first by taking an oath of secrecy, and then an oath of allegiance to the King of Great Britain; it appears to have been their design to have waited till the enemy came up, when they were to rise and take the whigs prisoners.[20]

Smith's account parallels that of the commissioners. He estimated that the conspirators included four hundred Upper Manor tenants

---

[19] Smith, *Historical Memoirs*, II, 133; *The Royal American Gazette*, May 15, 1777, and *The New-York Gazette*, May 19, 1777.

[20] Robert R. Livingston, Zephaniah Platt, and Mathew Cantine to the Provincial Convention, May 8, 1777, *Jour. Prov. Cong.*, I, 918-919.

of Robert Livingston, Jr., sixty Lower Manor tenants of Robert R. Livingston, plus fifty non-tenants of the community—figures which correspond closely to the total number of farms and militiamen on the manor. As to the goals of the conspiracy, Smith said that many had sworn "to join the Regulars & deliver up the Whiggs. . . . They were to expect the Regular Army up by the first Inst. . . . The Sworn were to have Pay from the Time of the Junction & each 200 Acres of Land."[21]

The tenants never had a chance. Their arms were improvised: powder and ball borrowed from neighbors under pretext of deer hunting; several hundred pounds of powder stolen from the Livingston mill at Rhinebeck; lead extracted from the nets strung across the Hudson to block the British ships.[22] Mustered against the conspirators were a hundred Claverack militiamen under Robert Van Rensselaer and John R. Livingston, who had "Orders to fire upon every Man fleeing before them"; 200 Dutchess County militiamen and some New England troops at the eastern end of the manor. Also available for call as a last resort, were troops under Alexander McDougall and George Clinton. As early as May 5th "certain of the Tenants in Arms" approached Henry, Peter, and Walter Livingston, offering to surrender to their father, Robert Livingston, Jr., if the tenants might be guaranteed against eviction from their farms. Before long, however, the Commissioners were concerned, not with putting down an uprising, but with lack of prison space. On the 12th Varick reported to Schuyler that "many miscreants" at the manor "give themselves up, saying they have been deluded," and that a dozen were condemned to die "as soon as a Jack Ketch can be procured."[23] At most six tenants died in

---

[21] Smith, *Historical Memoirs*, II, 130, 132; Gordon, "Kinship and Class," 133.

[22] Smith, *Historical Memoirs*, II, 195; *The New-York Gazette*, May 19, 1777.

[23] *Jour. Prov. Cong.*, I, 909-910; Smith, *Historical Memoirs*, II, 127-130; Varick to Schuyler, May 12, 1777, Schuyler Papers, N.Y.P.L. The British nickname for a public executioner was "Jack Ketch" after John Ketch who held

the skirmishing; there is no record of how many were executed.[24]

More than three hundred prisoners were dispersed to Kingston, Albany, and various spots in Dutchess County. The three commissioners could not possibly sift each case individually: as the Provincial Convention wrote to them (in a letter drafted by John Morin Scott), "though the harvest will be large the laborers are few." One out of every ten was held hostage, while those who seemed "penitent and ignorant" were dismissed after swearing loyalty to the patriot cause. For some time after, the Livingstons were deluged with requests for amnesty from women whose husbands were still hiding in the woods.[25]

For the Livingstons of Livingston Manor this week in May 1777 revealed with a shock how shaky was the basis of their power. William Smith lived with them, and he tells of a distraught aunt summoning Philip Livingston home from the Continental Congress; of Peter Livingston making up packets of provisions, in case flight proved necessary; of the Lord of the Manor, Robert Livingston, Jr., afraid to leave his own house. The latter, indeed, was beside himself. According to Smith:

He did not utter a Sentiment which he did not contradict and frequently in express Terms, except his Execrations upon his Tenants— His Fears have driven him to Temerity. He exclaims agt. setting up any Governt. at this Juncture . . . Poor Gent—He says his Tenants owe him £10,000—He can't bare the Thought that his Indulgences shew that he has no Influence upon them—Much less that they are in such a Temper as to prevent him from riding about in his own Manor— and seeing no Safety but in their Expulsion hints his Wishes that they may be all hanged and their children starved.

Behind all this hostility, as Smith perceived, was fear. Walter Liv-

that post from 1663 to 1686 and bungled the beheading of both William, Lord Russell (1683) and the Duke of Monmouth (1685).

[24] Smith, *Historical Memoirs*, II, 127, 132, 134, 136. Smith in one place says between two and six tenants were killed, and at another says three.

[25] Provincial Convention to Cantine, Platt, and Livingston, May 5, 1777, Robert R. Livingston to Peter R. Livingston, May 7, 1777, *Jour. Prov. Cong.*, I, 912; II, 475.

ingston explained that the rioters were treated gently "for Fear of starving their Families & exasperating the Multitude." Smith himself reflected that "if the Discontented grow more numerous and exasperated what a horrible Scene must open on the Ascent of Genl. [William] Howe [from New York City] or a Descent of Sir G[uy] Carleton [from Canada]."[26]

Burgoyne, by arriving upstate too late with too little, spared the Hudson Valley landlords a conjunction of rebel tenants and Redcoats, and the menace of armed rebellion was soon stilled. But there was no avoiding the political consequences of the tenant rising. The Lord of Livingston Manor lamented to William Smith that "he could formerly carry 400 Voters to an Election—but by our new Govt was Nothing—Nay that his Tenants were agt. him." Indeed they were. On May 24th, the annual election for members of the Manor Committee took place in a quasi-military atmosphere, with 20 soldiers guarding the polls. Evidently no tenants voted, for Smith commented in his diary: "considering the late Disturbances how can it be expected that the Tenants will attend." When from June 16th to 19th the first elections under the new state constitution took place, Smith noted explicitly that no one from the manor attended.[27]

These abstentions may well have cost Philip Schuyler, the conservative candidate for governor, the election. On June 20th John Jay wrote to Schuyler that the elections in the "middle district" had gone well, and that "a tolerable degree of unanimity . . . in the upper counties" should make Schuyler victorious.[28] But in Albany County, where formerly Robert Livingston, Jr. alone had commanded four hundred votes, Schuyler polled less than six hundred and blamed his defeat on the low vote in that county.[29] Little

[26] Smith, *Historical Memoirs*, II, 128, 131-134, 136.

[27] *Ibid.*, 136, 146, 163.

[28] John Jay to Philip Schuyler, June 20, 1777, in *The Correspondence and Public Papers of John Jay*, ed. Henry P. Johnston (four volumes; New York, 1890-1893), I, 142.

[29] Schuyler received 589 votes in Albany County, Clinton 125. [For the

love was lost between the tenants of Livingston Manor and George
Clinton, who told Smith in 1778 that he wished the manor tenants
could be hanged. But they were the enemies of his enemies, and by
making possible his election they helped to convert Revolutionary
New York from the "politics of privilege"—political control by
the wealthy, landed families—to the more democratic and representative "politics of opportunity."[30]

The sullen Toryism of the manor tenants lasted throughout the
war, and the political contest between "Demo and Aristo" continued into the peace.[31] Never again could the votes of the manor
tenants be taken for granted. We hear in the 1780's of "Letters &
Lists contending . . . and every subterfuge invented by both
parties"; of manor tenants who lacked the legal minimum of £100
freehold to qualify as voters for Governor and Senators nevertheless casting ballots to fill these offices; of a division of the manorial
election district with the aim "of collecting the tenants together as
little as possible & thus checking the influence of mischievous
persons"; of Antifederalist charges that the third Lord used "Com-
pulsive Measures . . . to lead the Tenants"; and of Federalist re-
grets that he did not "personally interfere [sufficiently to] inter-
pose his *Authority*." The gentleman himself confessed to sending
his sons from polling-place to polling-place in order to combat "a
number of emisaryes daily going about to poison the Tenants."[32]

---

source of this statistic see Essay 2, p. 40n.] For Schuyler's analysis of the returns, see Schuyler to William Duer, July 3, 1777, Schuyler Papers, N.Y.P.L.

[30] Smith, *Historical Memoirs*, II, 417; Dangerfield, *Chancellor Livingston*,
p. 88.

[31] Before William Smith left for New York City in mid-summer of 1778,
he recorded such incidents as the departure of 68 men to join Burgoyne in the
fall of 1777, and widespread draft-dodging and desertion in the spring of
1778 (*Historical Memoirs*, II, 225, 267, 307, 366, 385). In August 1777 the
manor tenants were repudiating the oath of loyalty to the Revolution which
they had taken the preceding May (*Jour. Prov. Cong.*, I, 1039). The phrase
about "Demo and Aristo" occurs in a letter from Henry to Walter Livingston,
April 24, 1785, R. R. Livingston Papers.

[32] For the electoral contest on the manor in 1785, see Henry to Walter

Here clearly was a change of atmosphere from the bleak defiance
of the Livingston landlords in 1766, when Robert R. Livingston
of the Lower Manor had written to Robert Livingston, Jr., of the
Upper Manor, "if you give anything by compulsions of this sort
you must give up everything."[33] Just as Carl Becker said:

> The great families, the traditional leaders, found it necessary . . . to
> modify their methods of political management. They found it increas-
> ingly necessary to win over their "interest" to every measure and to
> every ticket by force of reason, or what passed for reason.[34]

Yet the case of Livingston Manor also shows that past studies
have too often identified socio-economic radicalism with forward-
ness in the cause of independence. Precisely because they were so
radical economically, the tenants of Livingston Manor opposed
their Whig landlords politically. Their situation did not allow
them to look farther than the primary issue of "hearth and
home";[35] and like the slaves of the South, the tenants felt their
hope lay with the King.

Livingston, April 24, 1785, R. R. Livingston Papers, N.-Y.H.S.; for 1786 and
1787, Abraham G. Lansing to Hendrick Gardiner, April 19, 1786, and Abraham Yates to ————, June 2, 1787, Abraham Yates Papers, N.Y.P.L.; for 1788,
Cornelius Wynkoop, Jr., to Peter Van Gaasbeck, May 5, 1788, Van Gaasbeck Papers (Franklin Delano Roosevelt Library, Hyde Park, N.Y.), also
Peter Van Schaack to Philip Schuyler, April 3, 1788, Schuyler Papers, N.Y.P.L.,
and Robert Livingston, Jr., to James Duane, April 30, 1788, Duane Papers,
N.-Y.H.S.

[33] Letter of May 14, 1766, Redmond-Livingston Manuscripts, quoted in
Mark, *Agrarian Conflicts*, p. 140n.

[34] Becker, *The History of Political Parties in the Province of New York*,
p. 17.

[35] Peter Van Schaack to Philip Schuyler, April 3, 1788, Schuyler Papers,
N.-Y.H.S.

4

The Mechanics in New York
Politics, 1774-1785

For Carl Becker, the mechanic was the revolutionary democrat *par excellence*. When Becker spoke of the
American Revolution as not only a struggle for home rule, but also
a struggle over who should rule at home, he saw the city artisan as
the principal protagonist in the internal struggle. Becker's teacher
Frederick Jackson Turner believed that the democratization of
American politics and society began on the frontier. Becker, in
contrast, relegated protest among upstate tenants to the wings and
brought the urban workingman front and center. He called the
extra-legal committees of the American Revolution the "open door"
through which the politically-excluded "pushed their way into the

---

The first section of this essay originally appeared as part of a joint introduction by Alfred Young and Staughton Lynd to their articles: "The
Mechanics in New York Politics, 1774-1788" and "The Mechanics and
the Jeffersonians: New York, 1789-1801." The remainder of this essay
is drawn from "The Mechanics in New York Politics, 1774-1788." Reprinted by permission from *Labor History*, V (1964), 215-246.

political arena," and it was above all "the unfranchised mechanic and artisan" whom Becker saw striding through the door. He discerned in their demands "the germs of those opposing tendencies which, after the war was over," would divide the patriot party into radical and conservative wings. The rivalry of Federalist and Republican parties in the 1790's, Becker suggested, was "merely the revival, in a slightly different form, of the fundamental party divisions which had existed from the time of the stamp act."[1]

Becker's portrait of the mechanic as a young democrat was accepted by scholars as late as World War II.[2] More recently it has been severely criticized, on the ground that the Revolutionary "mechanic" was a small businessman, not a laborer, as well as on the ground that the mechanic, contrary to Becker, could vote and, insofar as he exercised this right, staunchly supported upper-class leaders.[3] Meantime, however, interest has grown as to the part played by the inarticulate in the politics of late eighteenth-century Europe. George Rudé, Albert Soboul, Robert R. Palmer and others suggest that the "mobs" who supported John Wilkes in England and formed the revolutionary clubs in Jacobin Paris were extremely heterogeneous in their social and economic composition, but never-

[1] Carl L. Becker, *The History of Political Parties in the Province of New York, 1760-1776* (Madison, 1909), pp. 5, 11, 22, 256, 275.

[2] Specialized studies which confirmed Becker's portrayal of the underprivileged and radical mechanic included Arthur M. Schlesinger, Sr., *The Colonial Merchants and the American Revolution, 1763-1776* (New York, 1918); Oscar T. Barck, Jr., *New York City During the War for Independence: With Special Reference to the Period of British Occupation* (New York, 1931), chap. 1; Herbert Morais, "The Sons of Liberty in New York," *The Era of the American Revolution*, ed. Richard B. Morris (New York, 1939), pp. 269-289; Eugene P. Link, *Democratic-Republican Societies, 1790-1800* (New York, 1942); Richard B. Morris, *Government and Labor in Early America* (New York, 1946), especially pp. 188-189.

[3] See e.g., Milton M. Klein, "Democracy and Politics in Colonial New York," *New York History*, XL (1959), 221-245, and Walter Hugins, *Jacksonian Democracy and the Working Class: A Study of the New York Workingmen's Movement, 1829-1837* (Stanford, 1960).

theless (particularly in the case of France) played a genuinely au-
tonomous role in pushing middle-class reformers toward radical
acts.[4]

There is a further circumstance which lends special interest to
reexamination of the Revolutionary mechanics. While Becker regarded the city mechanics as the most revolutionary and democratic of social groups in the years before the Revolution, his fellow
Progressive, Charles Beard, wrote of the mechanics after the Revolution that they had not "developed a consciousness of a separate
interest or an organization that commanded the attention of the
politicians of the time." In the dramatic struggle over ratification
of the Constitution which occupied a key position in his classic
work, *An Economic Interpretation of the Constitution*, the mechanics to Beard were "politically non-existent."[5]

I.

"Contemporary Englishmen," writes Carl Bridenbaugh, "defined the mechanic arts 'as such Arts wherein the
Hand and Body are more concerned than the Mind'."[6] The term

[4] See particularly Robert R. Palmer, "Popular Democracy in the French
Revolution: Review Article," *French Historical Studies*, I (1960), 445-469.
According to Georges Lefebvre in revolutionary Paris journeymen and apprentices customarily acted politically with their employers (*The Coming of
the French Revolution*, tr. Robert R. Palmer [Princeton, 1947], p. 98). E. P.
Thompson comments that English radicals Thomas Hardy and Francis Place
were journeymen at one stage in their careers and master craftsmen at another (*The Making of the English Working Class* [London, 1963], p. 20).

[5] Charles A. Beard, *An Economic Interpretation of the Constitution of the
United States* (New York, 1913), pp. 24-26.

[6] Carl Bridenbaugh, *The Colonial Craftsman* (New York, 1950), p. 155.
[For an elaborate discussion of the contemporary meanings of the terms
"mechanic," "artisan," and "tradesman" see now Charles S. Olton, "Philadelphia Artisans and the American Revolution," (Doctoral dissertation, University of California at Berkeley, 1967), pp. 3-16. This dissertation on the
largest and most radical group of revolutionary artisans confirms the conclusion
of the present essay with respect to the mechanics and the suffrage. See pp. 137,
137n., and 367.]

"mechanic" was used to refer not only to skilled artisans, but to all groups below the rank of merchants and lawyers. This included, at one end of the occupational spectrum, the unskilled laborer on the docks and, at the other extreme, the master craftsman who owned his shop, employed a dozen journeymen and apprentices, was taxed more than many merchants, and might do some general retailing on the side.[7] In between were a numerous body of cartmen or draymen (some 300 in 1788, 1,000 in 1800), petty retail tradesmen, and stallkeepers. Contemporaries also were careful to draw distinctions within the working population as is suggested by such phrases in common usage as "mechanics, laborers and cartmen," or "the substantial mechanics" and "the lowest order of mechanics." Taken together, the mechanics were a large group; by Bridenbaugh's estimate, about one-half the population of Revolutionary Charleston, and two-thirds the population of Boston, Newport, New York City, and Philadelphia belonged to the mechanic class. Benjamin Labaree's figures for Newburyport, where over half the adult males (in 1773) were artisans and laborers, suggests that mechanics were a majority in smaller cities, too.[8] We may conclude that the mechanics of the American Revolution were—as Robert Palmer describes the Parisian *sans culottes*—"the people . . . without the frosting."[9]

The best known of Revolutionary mechanics, Paul Revere, illustrates the diversity of the group. Revere had a brother and a cousin who were silversmiths, two sons-in-law who were house carpenters,

[7] For example, William Goforth (one of the mechanics elected to the New York Assembly in 1785) is described in book after book as a "shoemaker" but also sold rum and dry goods (*New York Journal*, Dec. 2, 1784). William Gilbert, Anthony Post, and Thomas Ivers, three other mechanic politicians, owned property assessed at £5500, £3500, and £2000, respectively ("Tax-Payers of the City and County of New York, 1796," New-York Historical Society).

[8] Carl Bridenbaugh, *Cities in Revolt: Urban Life in America, 1743-1776* (New York, 1955), p. 283; Benjamin W. Labaree, *Patriots and Partisans: The Merchants of Newburyport, 1764-1815* (Cambridge, Mass.; 1962), pp. 4-5.

[9] Palmer, "Popular Democracy," p. 453.

a nephew who was a tailor, and another cousin who built ships. Besides his skilled and lucrative metal work, Revere imported hardware, cloth and paper. Himself the employer of many workmen and (to use his own words) "very well off for a tradesman," Revere permitted his daughter to marry an apprentice.[10]

There can be little doubt that most of those known as "mechanics" were below the level of master craftsmen. The prevailing mode of production in colonial towns was a small workshop in which a master employed one to four journeymen and apprentices.[11] Many enterprises were even larger. The New York City printer Rivington employed sixteen men, and one master carpenter employed twenty-three.[12] Shipyards and ropewalks, Richard Morris estimates, employed at least five and sometimes as many as twenty-five workmen; distilleries, breweries, and candle works were also substantial enterprises.[13] Some indication of the relative strength of different types of mechanics emerges from the figures reported for two trades in a New York City parade of 1788. Among the cabinet-makers there were sixteen master workmen, twenty journeymen, and thirty apprentices; among the coopers 138 master workmen and journeymen, and fifty-five apprentices.[14]

The term "mechanic" does not imply unanimity on all issues, since clearly it was a diverse grouping. Witness, for instance, the existence of economic action of journeymen against employers. Such action was rare, but not unknown in large trades such as

[10] Esther Forbes, *Paul Revere and the World He Lived In* (Boston, 1942), pp. 371-373, 396, 400, 416, 458-459.

[11] Bridenbaugh, *Colonial Craftsman*, p. 129; Morris, *Government and Labor*, p. 42.

[12] Barck, *New York City*, p. 140.

[13] Morris, *Government and Labor*, p. 40. The New York Provincial Convention excused from military duty seventeen men at each furnace for melting iron into pigs; ten anchor-makers, four carriers and a bellows-man at the anchor forge in Orange County; two master-workmen and two attendants at each paper mill; and two master-workmen and six laborers at each salt works (*New-York Gazette*, Aug. 26, 1776).

[14] *New York Packet*, Aug. 5, 1788.

printing, shoemaking, and house carpentry.[15] Post-war economic trends—the shift from custom-made to wholesale order work, the decline of apprenticeship and indentured servitude, the emergence of a factory district in the suburb which is now New York's lower east side[16]—coincided with the influx of poor immigrants to intensify the conflict between employer and employee, as well as between the mechanics *en masse* and the city's merchants.

The mechanic of the American Revolution was well-paid when compared to his European counterpart;[17] "nearly all craftsmen were literate";[18] and, as we shall see in a moment, more than half of the mechanic class could vote. Yet the mechanic was hardly a first-class citizen. Before 1776, Noah Webster noted, the "principal families" of New York City "by associating, in their public amusements, with the middling class of well-bred citizens, render[ed]

[15] See Morris, *Government and Labor*, pp. 150-152, 156-166, 196-201. An illuminating incident occurred in September 1785. Journeymen carpenters employed in building a house for radical leader Isaac Sears publicly thanked him for continuing their wages at the "usual rate" notwithstanding "the ungenerous attempts of the Master-Carpenters to reduce them." In the next issue of the same newspaper the master-carpenters complained of Sears' partiality (*New York Packet*, Sept. 12 and 15, 1785).

[16] For characterization of New York City neighborhoods, see T. E. V. Smith, *The City of New York in the Year of Washington's Inauguration, 1789* (New York, 1889), and Frank Monaghan and Marvin Lowenthal, *This Was New York: The Nation's Capital in 1789* (Garden City, N. Y.; 1943).

[17] Franklin said of American workmen in the 1780's that they "all demand and obtain much higher wages than any other part of the world would afford them," and Tom Paine stated in *The Crisis*, No. 10, that the "income of a common laborer, who is industrious, is equal to that of the generality of tradesmen in England" (Benjamin Franklin, "The Internal State of America," ed. Verner W. Crane, *William and Mary Quarterly*, third series, XV [1958], 225; *The Complete Writings of Thomas Paine*, ed. Philip Foner [New York, 1945], I, 203). Monaghan and Lowenthal estimate that in 1789, when bread cost three cents a pound and beef three-and-a-half cents, a skilled workman in New York City earned fifty cents a day, an unskilled workman half as much (*This Was New York*, pp. 77, 80). Averages, of course, can be misleading: then as now there was an "other America."

[18] Bridenbaugh, *Colonial Craftsman*, p. 169. Franklin testifies to the same effect in "The Internal State of America."

their rank subservient to the happiness of society." But the war, Webster continued, "operated to diminish the sociability of the citizen of New York."[19] The Reverend Manasseh Cutler, passing through the city in the mid-1780's, observed likewise that "the several classes of people mix very little."[20] A decade later the French traveler, La Rochefoucauld, very aptly sketched the paradox of quasi-equality in the midst of hierarchy:

In balls, concerts, and public amusements, these classes do not mix; and yet, except the laborer in ports, and the common sailor, everyone calls himself, and is called by others, a *gentleman*; a small fortune is sufficient for the assumption of this title, as it carries men from one class to another. They deceive themselves very much who think that pure Republican manners prevail in America.[21]

There was economic exclusion, too. In eighteenth-century America, as in seventeenth-century England, the "provision of capital" was "the fundamental question" on which the craftsman's status depended.[22] Mechanics, like merchants, required access to capital, and the bank wars of the 1780's and 1790's were as important to the mechanic as was the issue of political recognition.

Carl Becker and the scholars who followed him took it for granted that mechanics, lacking social and economic recognition, also lacked the vote. So far as New York City is concerned, this was too sweeping a conclusion. The mechanics, said a New York

---

[19] Noah Webster, "Description of New York," *New York Directory* (1786), p. xv.

[20] *Life, Journals and Correspondence of Rev. Manasseh Cutler, L.L.D.* (Cincinnati, 1888), I, 309.

[21] Duc de Francois A. F. Rochefoucauld Liancourt, *Travels Through the United States of America* (London, 1799), II, 672.

[22] H. N. Brailsford, *The Levellers and The English Revolution* (London, 1961), p. 128. Franklin, remembering his own beginnings, provided in his will for a loan fund for young tradesmen; similarly Paine, in *Agrarian Justice*, proposed that the state give £15 to every young person reaching the age of twenty-one (Carl Van Doren, *Benjamin Franklin* [New York, 1938], pp. 762-763; *Complete Writings of Paine*, ed. Foner, I, 612-613, 618).

pamphleteer in 1783, had ever had it in their power to carry an election; and a newspaper correspondent in 1785 confirmed this testimony, remarking that the mechanics "undoubtedly constitute a great majority of the citizens."[23] On the other hand, comparison of the electoral statistics in a rich and poor ward suggests that among the poorer class of mechanics less than half could vote for state Assemblymen (see Table). In the East ward, where most of the great merchants lived, assessed property valuation per head of family in 1790 was more than five times the comparable figure for the Out ward, known as a factory district and a residential area for the poor. In 1790 the proportion of voters among free white males over twenty-one was 74 per cent in the East ward and only 42 per cent in the Out ward.[24] The suffrage bottle thus may be viewed as half full or half empty;[25] any generalization that all or most mechanics could not vote or that virtually all mechanics could vote[26] is inadmissible.

[23] *To the Worthy and Industrious Mechanics of this State* [Dec. 1783], broadside, N.-Y.H.S.; *New York Packet*, Feb. 24, 1785.

[24] The tax assessments by ward in 1790 are given in *The Iconography of Manhattan Island* ed. Isaac N. Phelps Stokes (six volumes; New York, 1915-1928), V, 1259. The figures for 1793 are comparable: East Ward £837,445; Out Ward £243,728 ("Tax-Payers of the City and County of New York, 1793," N.-Y.H.S.). Voters (by which is here meant persons qualified to vote for state assemblymen) in 1790 are enumerated in the electoral census of that year, *New York Daily Advertiser*, Jan. 15, 1791.

[25] See Michael D'Innocenzo, "Voting in Colonial New York" (Master's thesis, Columbia University, 1959), Appendix A, p. 78. We have no electoral census for the colonial era. In 1768, 1924 voters cast ballots in New York City, or 52 per cent of the adult males over 21; in 1769, 1515 or 40 per cent of the adult males voted. Assuming that not all the eligible voters cast ballots, D'Innocenzo concluded that 50 to 60 per cent of the adult men were eligible to vote. [See also Roger J. Champagne, "Liberty Boys and Mechanics of New York City, 1764-1774," *Labor History*, VIII (1967), 123-133, for an analysis of the 1768-1769 poll lists which concludes that two-thirds of the city's adult white males could vote and that one-half of these were mechanics.]

[26] See, on the one hand, Becker, *History of Political Parties*, p. 11, and Beard, *Economic Interpretation of the Constitution*, p. 67; and in opposition,

PROPERTY VALUATION AND VOTERS, NEW YORK CITY, 1790

WARD	Heads of families	Assessed valuation	Valuation per head of family	Free white males over 21	Voters	Voters as % of free white males
East	582	£630,000	£1083	773	575	74%
Out	1089	£186,000	£171	1189	504	42%

(For the sources of these statistics, see note 24.)

In Becker's presentation, then, it would appear that the suffrage question was too much emphasized. He was not wholly wrong in suggesting that mechanics were kept from voting: many were. But the sense of political exclusion embraced many more issues than the suffrage. The suitability of mechanics for elective office, the voter's ability to instruct and control his representatives once they were elected, the administration of justice, the ability to elect officers who had traditionally been appointed, were as important in the period considered as the right to vote.

In Philadelphia, the largest American city, such grievances were agitated well before the War for Independence. Thus, for example, Philadelphia mechanics complained in 1770 that

it has been customary for a certain company of leading men to nominate persons and *settle the ticket* for assemblymen, commissioners, assessors, etc., without even permitting the affirmative or negative voice of a mechanic to interfere, and, when they have concluded, to expect the Tradesmen to give a sanction thereto by passing the ticket; this we have tamely submitted to so long that those gentlemen make no scruples to say that the Mechanics (though by far the most numerous, especially in this county) have no right to be consulted, that is, in fact have no right to speak or think for themselves.[27]

Robert E. Brown, *Charles Beard and the Constitution: A Critical Analysis of "An Economic Interpretation of the Constitution"* (Princeton, 1956), pp. 63-64, and Klein, "Democracy and Politics," p. 237.

[27] "A Number of Tradesmen," *Pennsylvania Gazette*, Sep. 27, 1770, quoted by Charles H. Lincoln, *The Revolutionary Movement in Pennsylvania, 1760-1776* (Philadelphia, 1901), p. 80n.

In New York, it was 1774 before such grievances, expressed by mechanic organizations, began to be heard. And though interrupted by the wartime British occupation, they rose to a crescendo through the decade which followed.

II.

The mechanics appeared as an independent and organized force in New York politics in the spring of 1774. During the previous decade "one group, the mechanics, was uniformly identified with the Sons of Liberty."[28] But the Sons of Liberty in New York were always controlled by merchants, and it was not until 1774, apparently, that the General Committee of Mechanics was formed.

Carl Becker himself believed that this Committee "was virtually a continuation of the organization of the *Sons of Liberty*," and that "ostensibly representing the mechanics only, this committee was in fact the chief instrument through which the radical leaders" continued their agitation.[29] Evidence for this assertion is lacking. On the contrary, one finds that of six chairmen of the pre-Revolutionary Committee of Mechanics, those whose occupations can readily

---

[28] Roger J. Champagne, "The Sons of Liberty and the Aristocracy in New York Politics" (Doctoral dissertation, University of Wisconsin, 1960), p. 3. In a dissertation on the role of sailors in pre-Revolutionary New York politics, Jesse Lemisch contends that as early as 1765 lower-class elements advocated a distinct "radical" policy of carrying on trade without stamps, while "liberal" merchants espoused non-importation. However, the generalization that workingmen followed mercantile leadership until 1774 is not invalidated if one accepts Lemisch's argument; for he agrees with previous scholars that the Stamp Act mobs followed ship captains such as Isaac Sears and Alexander McDougall. See L. Jesse Lemisch, "Jack Tar vs. John Bull: The Role of New York's Seamen in Precipitating the Revolution" (Doctoral dissertation, Yale University, 1962).

[29] Becker, *Political Parties*, p. 120. [See now Bernard Mason, *The Road to Independence: The Revolutionary Movement in New York, 1773-1777* (Lexington, 1966), pp. 15n., 21n., 23n., 27n., for additional evidence that the Mechanics Committee was not simply a continuation of the Sons of Liberty,

be identified were a sailmaker and a cooper;[30] that the Committee
of Mechanics was regularly distinguished by contemporaries from
the organizations of merchants; and that, in the spring of 1776,
when the principal radical merchants had left the city or become
politically inactive, the Committee of Mechanics operated more
vigorously than ever.[31]

When early in May 1774, the Boston Port Bill reached New
York City, "a number of merchants and the Body of Mechanics"
of the city nominated a committee of correspondence.[32] In a famous letter of May 20, the young conservative Gouverneur Morris
described the public meeting at which the list of fifty-one nominees was presented to the general populace for its approval. "I
stood in the balcony," Morris wrote,

and on my right hand were ranged all the people of property, with
some few poor dependents, and on the other all the tradesmen, etc.,
who thought it worth their while to leave daily labour for the good of
the country. . . . The mob begin to think and reason. Poor reptiles! it
is with them a vernal morning; they are struggling to cast off their
winter's slough, they bask in the sunshine, and ere noon they will bite,
depend upon it. The gentry begin to fear this. . . . I see, and I see it
with fear and trembling, that if the disputes with *Great Britain* continue, we shall be under the worst of all possible dominions; we shall
be under the domination of a riotous mob.

and represented the assumption by mechanics of a more independent role in
politics.]

[30] I have found six chairmen of the Committee of Mechanics during 1774-
1776: Jonathan Blake, Daniel Dunscomb, Nathan Tylee, Christopher Duyckinck, Lewis Thibou and Malcolm McEwen (Becker, *Political Parties*, pp. 120n.,
165n.; *New York Journal*, Apr. 11, 1776; *New York Packet*, Apr. 11, 1776;
New-York Gazette, June 10 and 17, 1776). Duyckinck was a sail-maker and
Dunscomb a cooper (*New-York Gazette*, July 23, 1770; *New York Packet*,
Aug. 5, 1788). A revolutionary group in Boston on the eve of Independence,
the "Loyal Nine," included a printer, a jeweler, two distillers, two braziers, and
a master mariner (Bridenbaugh, *The Colonial Craftsman*, p. 175).

[31] Isaac Sears and John Lamb had left, Alexander McDougall was absorbed
in military duties (see Champagne, "New York Politics and Independence,
1776," *New-York Historical Society Quarterly*, XLVI [1962], 281-282).

[32] Becker, *Political Parties*, p. 113n.

Like Becker, Morris believed that one issue between the "people of property" and the "mob" was domestic: "they fairly contended about the future forms of our Government, whether it should be founded upon aristocratic or democratic principles."[33]

"Most if not all" of the committee of fifty-one were merchants or lawyers,[34] and from its inception this committee was under pressure from the Committee of Mechanics. In May 1774, the mechanics decided that "they would try the committee of 51 and if they misbehaved they would be removed."[35] In June 1774, a radical commentator wrote from Boston:

Those worthy members of society, the tradesmen, we depend on, under God, to form the resolution of the other ranks of citizens, in Philadelphia and New York. They are certainly carrying all before them here. . . . This will insure a non-importation in this province, whether messieurs les marchands, will be graciously pleased to come into it or not.[36]

In July 1774, when the committee of fifty-one nominated delegates to attend the first Continental Congress, the Committee of Mechanics complained that "the Committee of Merchants did refuse the Mechanics a representative on their body, or to consult with their committee, or offer the names of the persons nominated to them for their concurrence."[37] In the end, however, the committee of fifty-one agreed that the election in each ward should be supervised by two of its own members and two members of the Committee of Mechanics. For a time it seemed, too, that the committees would offer rival slates of delegates, but the Committee of Me-

[33] Gouverneur Morris to Mr. Penn, May 20, 1774, *American Archives*, ed. Peter Force, fourth series, I (Washington, D.C.; 1837), 342-343.

[34] Champagne, "New York and the Intolerable Acts, 1774," *New-York Historical Society Quarterly*, XLV (1961), 204n.

[35] Political memorandum of May 20, 1774, Alexander McDougall Papers, New-York Historical Society, quoted in Champagne, "New York and the Intolerable Acts," p. 206.

[36] Thomas Young to John Lamb, June 19, 1774, Lamb Papers, N.-Y.H.S.

[37] Broadside of July 6, 1774, quoted in Becker, *Political Parties*, p. 123n.

chanics finally withdrew its own list when the merchants' nominees
pledged themselves to press for complete non-importation at the
forthcoming Congress.[38]

Whether (as Becker thought) the idea of a Continental Congress
originated with the conservative merchants or whether (as Roger
Champagne, Becker's reviser, argues) the idea came from radicals
Sears, Lamb and McDougall,[39] when the first Continental Congress adopted the radical program of non-importation and non-
exportation in the fall of 1774 the mechanics at once became identified with the embryo federal government. As Arthur M. Schlesinger, Sr. put it, radicals at the first Continental Congress

> had defined—nationalized—the issue at stake in such a manner as to
> afford prestige to radical groups, wherever they were to be found, and
> to weaken the hold of the moderate elements, on the ground that the
> latter were at variance with the Continental Congress.[40]

Becker makes the same point. After this first Congress, he writes:

> the old factions, based upon differences of opinion as to how and by
> whom the resistance to English measures should be conducted, grad-
> ually gave place to parties asserting allegiance to different authorities.
> . . . The ultra-radicals, although asserting in words their allegiance to
> Great Britain, were more and more inclined to regard any refusal to
> submit to the decrees of Congress as a treasonable desertion of the
> American cause.[41]

The New York mechanics were prominent in welcoming the work
of the Congress, and in enforcing its authority by obstructing the
movement of supplies and workingmen to the British troops in

[38] See *ibid.*, pp. 119-136.

[39] Contrast *ibid.*, 118n. with Champagne, "New York and the Intolerable
Acts," pp. 200-201. Champagne is almost certainly correct; and the point is of
some importance, for it indicates that a national government was promoted
by radicals rather than—as Becker may have wanted to suppose—by conservatives.

[40] Schlesinger, Sr., *The Colonial Merchants and the American Revolution*,
p. 432.

[41] Becker, *Political Parties*, pp. 155-156.

Boston.[42] Thus fourteen years before the adoption of the United States Constitution the mechanics were acting on the premise that strong national government and democracy were complementary, not in conflict.

An important result of the first Continental Congress was that the committee of fifty-one was dissolved by agreement between itself and the Committee of Mechanics, and a new Committee of Inspection was created to carry out Congress' non-intercourse policy. The sixty members of the Committee of Inspection were chosen from two lists of 100 names separately proposed by the committee of fifty-one and the Committee of Mechanics.[43] In April 1775, the Committee of Inspection was enlarged to 100, including Daniel Dunscomb, chairman of the Committee of Mechanics, and three other members of the mechanics' committee.[44] Yet the officers of the Committee of Inspection remained merchants, albeit radical merchants,[45] and the Committee of Mechanics stayed in existence to needle its mercantile counterpart.

In the climactic spring of 1776 the Committee of Mechanics functioned as the most popular link in the chain of *ad hoc* bodies which had taken over government from the British. Ultimate authority rested with the Committee of Safety of the New York Provincial Congress. In New York City the Committee of Inspection held power. The Committee of Mechanics suggested new measures to the higher bodies, ran its own candidates for elections, insisted on the sovereignty of the "people at large," and attempted to clear a direct channel of communication between the general

[42] *Ibid.*, p. 161*n.*, pp. 162-163.

[43] *Ibid.*, pp. 165-168.

[44] *Ibid.*, p. 198. The other three were Abraham Brasher, Theophilus Anthony and Jeremiah Platt.

[45] In the spring of 1776 the officers of the Committee of Inspection were: chairman, Henry Remsen; deputy chairman, John Broome; secretary, Joshua Winter. The Sub-Committee of Secrecy and Inspection consisted of William Mercier, Daniel Phoenix, Anthony L. Bleecker, Garret Abeel, James Alner, John Stagg. (*New-York Gazette*, Feb. 12 and Mar. 11, 1776).

populace and the Continental Congress. Like its European counterparts as described by Robert Palmer, the mechanics' committee
laid more emphasis upon democracy, in the sense of "the delegation of authority and the removability of officials," than upon the
extension of the suffrage.[46] Indeed, in addressing the Provincial
Congress and the Committee of Inspection the Committee of Mechanics described itself as "part of your constituents," "part of the
Electors for this city and county";[47] and asked, not that its members be given the ballot, but that the mandate of their votes be
heeded.

On occasion the Committee of Mechanics simply registered
assent to actions taken at higher levels. Thus on March 14, 1776,
"about 6 or 700 of the Mechanicks of this city" escorted their Committee to the Exchange, where an address was delivered thanking
the Committee of Inspection for regulating the prices of articles
of general consumption imported from the West Indies.[48] More
often, however, the mechanics urged the merchants to new action.
On April 1, the Committee of Mechanics memorialized the Committee of Inspection regarding the "unwarrantable stretch of
power" by the Provincial Congress in asserting that it, rather than
"the people at large," should elect New York's delegates to the
Continental Congress. The memorial thanked the Committee of
Inspection for appointing deputies to attend a public meeting on
this issue called by the mechanics. Then it concluded: "Gentlemen,
if you agree with us, we make no doubt but every necessary step
will be taken, and that letters of advice will be sent to each
county."[49]

[46] Robert R. Palmer, *The Age of the Democratic Revolution: A Political
History of Europe and America, 1760-1800*, I (Princeton, 1959), 4-5.
[47] Address of the General Committee of Mechanics to the Provincial Congress, May 29, 1776 and address of the General Committee of Mechanics to
the Committee of Inspection, Apr. 1, 1776, *New-York Gazette*, June 10 and
Apr. 8, 1776.
[48] *Ibid.*, Mar. 18, 1776.
[49] *Ibid.*, Apr. 8, 1776.

Again on April 6, the General Committee of Mechanics informed the General Committee of Inspection that the mechanics
had resolved to accept the paper money of Massachusetts and
Rhode Island so as to strengthen national unity. This address ended
by saying: "[We] call on you, Gentlemen of the General Committee of Inspection, and pray that you will be pleased, as soon as
convenient, to resolve and order that same may take place throughout your jurisdiction."[50]
The mechanics were ever-ready to back up their good advice with
direct action. On March 18, the printer Samuel Loudon advertised
for sale a pamphlet criticizing Tom Paine's *Common Sense*, which
had been published two months earlier. Loudon was at once sum-
moned before the Committee of Mechanics by its chairman, Christopher Duyckinck. Loudon asked that the matter be referred to the
Committee of Safety of the Provincial Congress. The mechanics
agreed, but only after locking up the printed sheets of Loudon's
pamphlets. Loudon appeared before the Committee of Safety on
March 19 and agreed to stop printing the offending pamphlet; but
at ten that night Duyckinck, with a "large company" of "unautho-
rized men," broke into Loudon's home, took the printed sheets, and
burned them on the Common.[51]
The defense of *Common Sense* was a congenial task for the mechanics because Paine, himself a former staymaker, voiced a political philosophy which the mechanics of New York City shared.
As Paine sought to push America toward independence, so on May
29 the "General Committee of Mechanics in Union," meeting in
"Mechanicks Hall," asked the Provincial Congress to instruct New
York's delegates in the Continental Congress to press for immediate independence.[52] As Paine recommended a Continental Conference, a majority of whose delegates should be elected by the
"people at large," so the New York mechanics employed the same

[50] *New York Journal*, Apr. 11, 1776.
[51] *New York Packet*, Apr. 11, 1776.
[52] *New-York Gazette*, June 10, 1776.

phrase in asking that the state's delegates to the Continental Congress should be popularly elected.[53]

Paine's ideas were everywhere that spring of 1776. Between January and July almost every issue of the city's three weekly newspapers carried some lengthy discussion on "the different kinds of government." Universal adult suffrage, annual elections, rotation of office, equal apportionment, the secret ballot, popular election of all local officials, complete religious tolerance, and the abolition of slavery, were repeatedly discussed.[54]

The mechanics' request that the Provincial Congress instruct the state delegates (in Philadelphia) for independence was carried to the Congress by Lewis Thibon, Committee of Mechanics chairman. The Provincial Congress coldly rebuked the messenger. "We consider the mechanics in union as a voluntary association," ran the Congress reply. "[We believe] that neither that association, nor their committee, will claim any authority whatsoever in the public transactions of the present time." The Provincial Congress letter ended by refusing to instruct its delegates to the Continental Congress.[55]

[53] *Ibid.*, June 17, 1776.

[54] Among the political propositions of Paine's *Common Sense* are the following: That representative government is necessary in large societies but should approximate as closely as possible a direct democracy in which each citizen participates; that representatives should be apportioned equally, and rotated by frequent elections; that governments should be limited by written constitutions, providing for the security of persons and property and "above all things, the free exercise of religion." Paine helped to draft the most democratic state constitution of the Revolution, Pennsylvania's. He called it "an open constitution . . . which considers mankind as they came from their maker's hands—*a mere man*, before it can be known what shall be his fortune or his state." (*Complete Writings of Paine*, II, 283, 285). For discussion of these ideas in the New York City press in the spring of 1776, see e.g., "Independent Whig" and "Essex" in the *New York Journal*, Feb. 22, 29, Mar. 7, 14, 28, Apr. 4, 1776; "The Interest of America" in *ibid.*, June 6, 13, 20, 1776; "To the Freeborn Sons of America," "On the different Kinds of Government," "To the Printer of the New-York Packet," *New York Packet*, Mar. 21, 28, Apr. 18, 1776; and the essays of "Cato" and "Cassandra" in the *New-York Gazette*.

[55] *New-York Gazette*, June 10, 1776.

Ten days after this rebuff the mechanics again addressed the Congress, this time turning the logic of republicanism from the question of home rule to the question of who should rule at home. Independence was imminent. It would mean the formation of a new state government. The language of the June 14 memorial signed by Malcolm McEwen, as Committee of Mechanics chairman, recalled the phrases of *Common Sense* and anticipated those of the Declaration of Independence. The mechanics' address demanded that the people ratify the new state constitution. "Inhabitants at large," it said, "exercise the right which God has given them, in common with all men, to judge whether it be consistent with their interest to accept, or reject, a Constitution framed for that State of which they are members. This is the birthright of every man [who] is, or ought to be, by inalienable right, a co-legislator with all the other members of that community." Not all men were qualified to draft constitutions, the letter continued,

but that share of common sense which the Almighty has bountifully distributed amongst mankind in general, is sufficient to quicken every one's feeling, and enable him to judge rightly, what degree of safety, and what advantages he is likely to enjoy or be deprived of, under any Constitution proposed to him. For this reason, should a preposterous confidence in the abilities and integrity of our future Delegates, delude us into measures which might imply a renunciation of our inalienable right to ratify our laws?

Warning against either "foreign or domestic oligarchy," the mechanic memorial went on to insist that the people must also have power to amend their Constitution with ease. "This power necessarily involves that of every district, occasionally to renew their deputies to committees and congresses, when the majority of such district shall think fit; and therefore, without the intervention of the executive, or any other power, foreign to the body of the respective electors."[56]

The Declaration of Independence, when it appeared, voiced ap-

[56] *Ibid.*, June 17, 1776.

prehension of "convulsions within" and "domestic insurrections amongst us." It would seem that the government-from-below evident in the ideas and actions of the New York Committee of Mechanics in the spring of 1776 was a sample of just what the drafters of the Declaration feared. Roger Champagne, the most recent scholar to survey New York City politics in these months, concludes that "only the timely invasion of Long Island by the British saved the aristocrats from a political crisis of an explosive character."[57]

III.

Something like half of New York City's population of almost 25,000 fled the city in the summer and fall of 1776. These refugees faced seven lean years of exile between September 1776, when the British occupied New York City, and November 1783, when General Washington and his army led the returning natives down Broadway.

We see little of the mechanics during the war, but those few glimpses are significant. Cooper Daniel Dunscomb and silversmith Abraham Brasher were among the nine men appointed by the Provincial Convention to represent the New York City refugees in the new state Assembly. Blacksmith Robert Boyd, chairman of the General Society of Mechanics and Tradesmen after the war, made axes for the Continental Army[58] and also served two years in the Assembly as a representative for Ulster County. Ropemaker Thomas Ivers, active in the Sons of Liberty since the Stamp Act crisis and a controversial candidate for alderman after the return to New York City, was prominent in a 1779 petition campaign.[59] The votes and activities of these mechanic leaders are suggestive as to the thinking of the larger body of mechanics during the war years.

[57] Champagne, "Sons of Liberty," p. 508.
[58] As to the axes, see Timothy Pickering to Philip Schuyler, Nov. 18, 1783, Schuyler Papers, New York Public Library.
[59] See note 65 below regarding these petitions of 1779.

"Radicalism" during and after the War for Independence is commonly associated with the confiscation of Loyalist lands, renunciation of debts to Loyalists, and the emission of paper money. Mechanic legislators opposed all these measures. When in the spring of 1779 the Council of Revision vetoed a bill for the confiscation of Loyalist lands, Brasher and Dunscomb were among the handful of Assemblymen who voted to sustain the veto. A year later Brasher, Boyd, and Dunscomb all voted against speedy sale of confiscated lands, and Brasher and Dunscomb were two of the five members of the Assembly who voted to uphold the Council of Revision's veto of this bill. In 1782, Dunscomb opposed a bill to permit persons owing debts to Tories to discharge their obligation by paying one-fortieth of the sum into the state treasury: he moved that the law be entitled, "An Act for the Payment of one fortieth Part of the Debts due to Persons within the Power of the Enemy." Boyd was again a member of the Assembly in 1786, when a bill for the emission of bills of credit (paper money) passed the New York legislature, and he was one of seven persons who opposed this law.[60]

Yet, to borrow a phrase from Eric Williams, there was method in their badness. The difference between rural extremists like Brinckerhoff of Dutchess[61] and the refugee legislators from New York City was not that one group was "radical" and the other not, but that they espoused different kinds of radicalism. Rural radicals favored a syndrome of measures designed to avoid taxation by means of confiscation. City radicals, during and after the war, favored heavy taxation to enable the state to meet its obligations to Congress.[62] Thus Boyd, as a member of the Assembly's paper cur-

[60] Votes and Proceedings of the Assembly, various places and dates, for Mar. 15, 1779; Feb. 4 and Mar 8, 1780; Mar. 9, 1782; Mar. 3, 1786.

[61] [On rural radicalism in New York during the War for Independence, see Essay 2.]

[62] It was the easier for New York City refugees to advocate heavy taxation while the war was in progress since their own property was behind the British lines and could not be taxed.

rency committee in 1779, recommended heavy taxes and price-fixing rather than new emissions, and in that same session sponsored
an act "to prevent monopoly and extortion, and to regulate
trade."[63] A rural member, Thomas Palmer, charged in the press
that

> a wicked party, with the Refugee Members, and Boyd at their head,
> determine to ruin the State by tax and otherwise. They had brought in
> a bill for seizing all the wheat for the army, except one bushel per head
> per month to each family.

Palmer went on to assert that Boyd "with those of his opinion, has
made up a majority against" confiscating lands and taxing appropriated lands of persons outside the state. Boyd replied, stressing
the importance of fulfilling the state's obligations to Congress.[64]

There were other refugees who favored confiscation, however. In
October 1779 five petitions with 143 signatures were presented to
the Assembly by refugees from New York City. The name of mechanic Thomas Ivers was at the head of two of the petitions. The
petitions asked that elections be held to replace the Senators and
Assemblymen appointed to represent New York City; that a confiscation law be passed immediately; that New York's delegates to
the Continental Congress be changed each year; that a school be
established in Dutchess County for the instruction of the refugees'
children, under the direction of trustees chosen annually by ballot.[65] The political demands of these petitions, as well as the suggested manner for governing the refugees' school, were entirely
congruent with the demands of the Committee of Mechanics in
the spring of 1776. The petitions were no doubt formulated in
meetings of the refugees from New York City and from Long and
Staten islands in the summer of 1779. According to Alexander

[63] *Votes and Proceedings of the Assembly* (Fishkill, 1779) for Sept. 18, Oct.
9, 1779.

[64] *New York Packet*, Apr. 13, 20, 1780. I am obliged to Mr. Robin Brooks
for calling these passages to my attention.

[65] *Votes and Proceedings of the Assembly* (Fishkill, 1779) for Oct. 17, 1779.

Hamilton, these meetings had as their "ostensible object to choose representatives for those places in Assembly," but he expected they might also plant "the seeds of a future reformation" of the New York state government.[66]

Again in the summer of 1783, with independence secure but New York City still occupied by the British, the city refugees met several times and produced two fiery memorials threatening revenge and confiscation to the Tories in the city.[67] The refugees set up a committee of arrangements to plan their triumphal parade into the city which included upholsterer Henry Kipp, silversmiths William Gilbert and Ephraim Brasher, and hatters Thomas LeFoy and Henry Bicker, with the latter as chairman.[68] Mechanic influence was evident in New York City's first postwar election in December 1783. After a spirited exchange of broadsides—in which "Juvenis" recommended the election of merchants since "the prosperity of the Mechanic depends on that of the Merchant," and "A Citizen" replied by advising "that the various Classes should as far as is practicable, be immediately represented"—the entire slate of Assemblymen nominated by a "general meeting of the Committee of Mechanicks" was elected by a four-to-one landslide.[69]

[66] Alexander Hamilton to John Jay [June 26, 1779], *The Papers of Alexander Hamilton*, ed. Harold C. Syrett, (New York, 1961–), II, 82.

[67] Brutus, *To All Adherents to the British Government and Followers of the British Army Commonly called Tories* . . . (Poughkeepsie, Aug. 15, 1783) and *The Memorial of the Subscribers, in Behalf of Themselves and Others, the Refugee Citizens of New-York* (Newburgh, Sept. 1, 1783), broadsides, N.-Y.H.S. The British officers and Tory inhabitants of New York City, as well as the more well-to-do refugee Whigs, feared during the summer and fall of 1783 that "the lower Classes" would take advantage of the return to the city to seize and plunder property (see chap. VII of my "The Revolution and the Common Man: Farm Tenants and Artisans in New York Politics, 1777-1788" [Doctoral dissertation, Columbia University, 1962]).

[68] *Independent New York Gazette*, Nov. 22, 1783.

[69] Juvenis, *To the Mechanicks and Free Electors of the City and County of New-York* (Dec. 23, 1783) and A Citizen, *To the Electors of the City of New-York* (Dec. 26, 1783), broadsides, N.-Y.H.S. The nominating meeting of the Committee of Mechanics on Dec. 27 is described in another broadside at

As in the spring of 1776, so in the spring of 1784 it was the Committee of Mechanics not the Sons of Liberty which met most frequently.[70] After 1784 the Sons of Liberty are no longer heard from but the Committee of Mechanics continues, nominating its own ticket in each annual election.[71]

In January 1784 a committee of "late exiled Mechanics, Grocers, Retailers and Innholders" was formed to instruct the city's Assemblymen. Hatter Henry Bicker was chairman, and among the members were tallow chandler Hugh Walsh, saddler John Young, and pewterer William Ellsworth. The committee's instructions began with payment of the public debt, one more indication of the me-

---

N.-Y.H.S. The results of the election, according to the *New York Packet*, Jan. 1, 1784, were:

Marinus Willett	249	Peter V. B. Livingston	35
John Lamb	239	Comfort Sands	31
Henry Rutgers	231	James Beckman	25
Isaac Sears	223	John Morin Scott	17
John Stagg	215	Henry Remsen	11
William Malcolm	212	John Broome	5
Robert Harpur	209	Samuel Broome	5
Peter P. Van Zandt	204	Alexander Hamilton	4
Hugh Hughes	180	Gulian Verplank	3
		Samuel Dodge	2
Daniel Dunscomb	53	John Berrien	2
Evert Bancker	51	Daniel Phoenix	1
Thomas Randall	47	Isaac Stoutenburgh	1

The election took place by show of hands at City Hall (*New York Gazetteer*, Dec. 10, 1783). Alexander Hamilton said later that few besides those who had been refugees voted in this election. He also implied that all refugees were permitted to vote upon swearing an oath of loyalty because "if the returning citizens were not at this juncture gratified, tumults were by some apprehended" (*A Second Letter from Phocion to the Considerate Citizens of New-York* [New York, 1784], p. 22).

[70] Meetings of the Committee of Mechanics are reported in *New York Packet*, Jan. 15, 1784; *New York Journal*, Mar. 18, 1784; *Independent Journal*, May 12, 1784; *New York Packet*, May 31, 1784.

[71] *New York Packet*, Apr. 25, 1785 and Apr. 24, 1786; *New York Journal*, Apr. 26, 1787.

chanics' concern that the national government fulfill its obligations. The program recommended by the committee also included duties on imported manufactures, especially luxuries, to encourage native industries; denial to England of all commercial privileges not accorded by England to the United States, with a recommendation that Congress make such regulations general; support for public education; easy naturalization; and a variety of restrictions against Loyalists who had spent the war in New York City.[72] The same concern for strengthening the Federal government appears in an Address to the Continental Congress by "the Artificers, Tradesmen and Mechanics" of New York City in February 1785. The address was signed by prominent mechanics, including blacksmiths Robert Boyd and Edward Meeks, silversmith John Burger, and hatter Henry Bicker. "We sincerely hope," said the address, "our Representatives will coincide with the other States, in augmenting your power to every exigency of the Union."[73]

Although they agreed in desiring a stronger national government, on other issues New York City's mechanics and merchants were as much at odds after the war as before it. The importer of English goods who flooded the American market with products which destroyed the American mechanic's livelihood was already half a Tory in the mechanic's eyes. When in addition the merchants' Chamber of Commerce met in January 1784 with three of the five officers elected under British rule in attendance, when later that spring the Bank of New York was created with one Tory merchant as Treasurer and two others on the Board of Directors, the city mechanics found it easy to identify merchants with Loyalism, to view the refugee artisan as Whiggery's sole defender, and to pronounce particular anathemas on Alexander Hamilton for giving legal aid to Tory merchants who had "fattened" on the "spoils" of war.[74] "A Bat-

[72] *Independent Gazette*, Jan. 29, 1784.

[73] *New York Journal*, Feb. 24, 1785.

[74] For the speed with which Tory merchants regained their economic footing after the British evacuation, compare the lists in *Colonial Records of the New*

tered Soldier" penned a broadside to "the Whig Mechanicks" that ran:

on your Union, depends the future Fate of the Whig Interest in this City and County. And if you fail herein, you may depend on it, that you and your Children, will soon become Hewers of Wood, and Drawers of Water, to the Tories in this State.[75]

During the early months of 1784 the "late exiled Mechanics, Grocers, Retailers and Innholders" protested the licensing of Tory businessmen; and the Sons of Liberty (including the chairman of the Committee of Mechanics, Henry Bicker) called on their Assembly representatives not only for political disfranchisement of Tories, but also for their exclusion from "advantages of trade and commerce."[76]

An economic issue of particular importance to the mechanics

York Chamber of Commerce, 1768-1774, ed. John A. Stevens (New York, 1867), pp. 295, 306, and see Oscar Zeichner, "The Loyalist Problem in New York after the Revolution," *New York History,* XXI (1940), 301. William Seton was the Loyalist Treasurer of the Bank of New York, and Daniel Mc-Cormick and Joshua Waddington its Loyalist Directors (*New York Packet,* Mar. 18, 1784). "We never had so much to fear from their arms, as from their influence and wealth," a newspaper correspondent warned. "They hope by their influence in a Bank, to lay the foundation of power, whereby they may not only aid each other in commercial matters, but silence every Whig character who applies to them for aid." (*Independent Gazette,* Mar. 11, 1784). For his role in aiding such Tories, a "Mechanic" attacked Alexander Hamilton in the spring of 1784 as "the confidential or ridiculous earwig of our late worthy General . . . the little, pompose, stripling delegate—the Jack-Daw of public affairs . . . Fox instead of Phocion" (*New York Journal,* Mar. 25, 1784). "Phocion" compounded his sins in mechanic eyes by opposing trade unions as monopolies. A *Letter from Phocion to the Considerate Citizens of New York* (New York, 1784), p. 11.

[75] A Battered Soldier, *To the Whig Mechanicks of the City and County of New-York* (Dec. 27, 1783), broadside, N.-Y.H.S. A Friend to Mechanics replied in kind: "In all countries, it is no uncommon practice for men, grasping at power, to call first upon the Mechanicks, and endeavour to use them as mere Ladders to their ungovernable ambition" (*To the Worthy and Industrious Mechanics of this State,* broadside, N.-Y.H.S.).

[76] *Independent Gazette,* Jan. 24, 1784; *New York Gazetteer,* Mar. 31, 1784.

was that of access to capital. Here again the New York City mechanic found himself at odds with the city's merchants, whether Whig or Tory. All agreed that credit should be expanded: the President, Director, and Stockholders of the Bank of New York, for example, petitioned the New York legislature that "a Scarcity of Specie for a long time to come may be expected. This defect must be supplied by an Artificial Medium."[77] The question was how credit should be expanded, and by whom. The Whig merchants of New York City—including the old radical leaders Lamb, Sears and Willett, and the future Antifederalist Melancton Smith—joined in petitioning the legislature for Alexander Hamilton's Bank of New York.[78] No prominent mechanics signed that petition, nor were any among the Bank's first customers.[79] Artisans repeatedly expressed their distrust of private banks.[80] Instead, the mechanics sought to create a modest loan fund of £3,000 by incorporating their old Committee of Mechanics as the General Society of Me-

---

[77] Petition of Oct. 8, 1784, Papers of the Bank of New York, New York City. The petition observed that before the Revolution the common remedy had been bills of credit, but that after the experiences of the war, bank paper was more likely to command confidence.

[78] Petition of Feb. 10, 1785, Papers of the Bank of New York. There were other reasons for the estrangement between Sears, Lamb, and Willett and their old mechanic followers. Sears had grown wealthy during the war and when he returned to New York City moved into No. 1 Broadway, the home which had been occupied by the British commander, Sir Henry Clinton (Robert J. Christen, "Isaac Sears: Radical in Rebellion" [Master's thesis, Columbia University, 1953], p. 50). In 1784 Lamb was appointed Collector of Customs for the Port of New York and Willett was appointed Sheriff for the City and County of New York; thus they became, unnaturally for them, duty-bound to oppose riots.

[79] The Bank of New York's earliest ledger-book of customers, for 1787-1788, shows the names of such radical merchants as John Broome, Peter Curtenius, David Gelston, Nathaniel Hazard, Isaac Ledyard, Brockholst Livingston, Henry Rutgers, Paschal Smith, [Melancton] Smith and Wyckoff, Marinus Willett and Wynant Van Zandt, but so far as I could tell no prominent mechanics (Papers of the Bank of New York).

[80] *New York Journal*, May 13, 1784 and "Mechanic," *ibid.*, Mar. 25, 1784.

chanics and Tradesmen.[81] Mercantile opinion hovered between the fear that incorporation would enable the mechanics to raise their wages and give them governmental power, "in this city at least," and the thought that "it is less dangerous to incorporate a body of men by law, than suffer them to *cement* with an idea of having received injustice."[82] The Council of Revision vetoed the incorporation bill, and one old Son of Liberty wrote to another:

I should like to know whether these gentlemen . . . would consider themselves endanger'd by a Combination of the Mechanicks to extinguish the Flames of their Houses, were they on fire, or if any one of the Faith was drowning whether he would reject a Mechanick's hand to save him?—And are not those honest Men, the very Persons, who *principally* extinguish all Fires, and, in Conjunction with the Country, have saved the State?[83]

As the mechanics saw the matter, equal economic opportunity was an integral part of the larger vision of equality suggested by the emblem of the General Society of Mechanics and Tradesmen: "An aged woman, with a pair of scales in one hand, and a nest of swallows in the other, fed by the old one."[84] Along with their economic concerns went the demand, social and political at the same time, that mechanics be elected to office.

[81] Lending money was one of the five purposes of the General Society of Mechanics and Tradesmen (*New York Packet*, Feb. 17, 1785). Originally the mechanics asked for a loan fund of £3000; the legislature whittled the sum to £1500 before sending the bill to the Council of Revision, where it was vetoed (Charles Tillinghast to Hugh Hughes, Feb. 26, 1786, Lamb Papers). Nevertheless the General Society went ahead and loaned sums of not less than £100, giving preference to members, on three-fold security in New York City real estate; in December 1787, the minimum loan was lowered to £50 (*Annals of the General Society of Mechanics and Tradesmen of the City of New-York from 1775 to 1880*, ed. Thomas Earle and Charles T. Congdon [New York, 1882], p. 11; minutes of the General Society of Mechanics and Tradesmen, library of the Society, Dec. 14, 1787).

[82] *New York Packet*, Feb. 24, 1785.

[83] Hugh Hughes to Charles Tillinghast, Mar. 7, 1785, Lamb Papers.

[84] *Annals of the General Society*, p. 12.

"An exiled Mechanic" suggested in April 1785 the importance of choosing representatives who would favor incorporation of the General Society of Mechanics and Tradesmen: "we have a powerful mercantile interest to struggle with, and we should be extremely careful of adopting a single measure that will tend to support it."[85] Why not mechanics, then? another newspaper correspondent asked. "Being of the opinion that the pedantic lawyer, the wealthy merchant, and the lordly landholder, have already had their interests sufficiently attended to, and think[ing] the respectable mechanics and carmen are not only adequate, but entitled to the reins of government," this author concluded by naming twenty-six mechanics whom he thought suitable timber for Assemblymen.[86] In the ensuing election two mechanics, Robert Boyd and William Goforth, were in fact successful.[87] The next year, correspondents to the merchants' newspaper, *The New York Daily Advertiser*, unleashed a pre-election barrage against the idea of class representation. "Nobody" opined:

We ought to invest no man at this critical period with that important trust, but such whose firmness, integrity and ability are sufficiently ascertained. I am very sensible that the application of reasoning of this nature will have little avail, if the mechanics of the city are solely al-

---

[85] *New York Packet*, Apr. 7, 1785.

[86] *Ibid.*, Apr. 14, 1785.

[87] The successful Assembly candidates were (*New York Journal*, May 5, 1785):

William Malcolm	666	William Duer	624
William Denning	663	Robert Boyd	623
John Stagg	661	Evert Bancker	623
William Goforth	660	Isaac Sears	574
Robert Troup	641		

With the exception of Troup, all these men had been nominated by the Committee of Mechanics. Interestingly enough, however, the previous year Goforth and another mechanic, Daniel Dunscomb, had run on a conservative slate which triumphed over the Sons of Liberty candidates headed by Sears (for the votes by ward of the 1784 election, see *Independent Journal*, May 1, 1784).

lowed to fill up the appointments of statesmen. That they are a respectable body of men I willingly grant, and ought to have their due weight, but it is unreasonable for them to ask more.[88]

"Somebody" took up the same theme four days later:

Men who have spent the prime and vigour of their days in reading and contemplating the rise, progress and declension of states and empires;—men who study Grotius, Puffendorf, Montesquieu and Blackstone. . . . Away with such legislators! we will neither be able to comprehend the laws they may make, nor to practice them when they are made. But the laws of the mechanics, like the makers of them, will be simple and unperplexed. . . . Therefore let us have mechanics, and mechanics only for our legislature.[89]

In 1774 the Loyalist Miles Cooper had asked in vain "whether it be not time for our farmers and mechanics and laborers to return to their business, and the care of their families"; now in 1786 "Two Shoes" suggested: "Let the mechanics tarry at home, and follow their different employments, as I think they will not be able to do both at once."[90] And "Censor" denounced

those narrow, contracted, self-taught politicians who are for selecting out of each class of citizens a person to represent them, whether he is to be found competent or not, and think none would serve them honestly but those of their own body. . . . How can they expect that men, such as the laborious mechanic, whose whole study and progress in life has been to secure a maintenance for himself and family . . . are calculated to frame laws for a large and commercial community?[91]

As it turned out no mechanics were elected in 1786. The Committee of Mechanics "with a Committee from a number of Merchants and other Citizens" put forward a slate of assemblymen including William Goforth. Newspaper correspondents suggested Boyd and carpenter Anthony Post.[92] But none of the three were

[88] *New York Daily Advertiser*, Apr. 1, 1786.
[89] *Ibid.*, Apr. 5, 1786.
[90] Becker, *Political Parties*, 161n.; *New York Daily Advertiser*, Apr. 14, 1786.
[91] *Ibid.*, Apr. 15, 1786.
[92] *New York Packet*, Apr. 24, 1786; *Independent Journal*, Apr. 26, 1786.

chosen, while the mechanics' erstwhile *bête noire*, Alexander Hamilton, was elected with support from "some of the Mechanics" to mount the campaign which led to the Annapolis Convention, the Constitutional Convention, and the New York ratifying convention of 1788.[93]

IV.

Becker was right, then, in his contention that mechanic radicalism began before the War for Independence and continued after it. Economically disadvantaged, socially excluded, only partially enfranchised, the mechanics sought by a variety of methods to influence the making of political and economic policy; by the mid-1780's, they were insisting on the election of men of their own "class."

But Becker was wrong in supposing that the mechanics were hostile to centralization. The distinctive feature of the political demands of the mechanics throughout the period 1774-1785 was to combine a concern for democracy with unwavering support for a policy of arming the central government with sufficient power to combat the British enemy. To this end the Committee of Mechanics would join with the city merchants after 1785 to seek more power for Congress.[94]

[93] Philip Schuyler wrote to Stephen Van Rensselaer, Apr. 20, 1786: "Colo. Hamilton will serve if elected. The Quakers, Merchants, and some of the Mechanics are for him, but part of the latter averse" (quoted in E. Wilder Spaulding, *New York in the Critical Period, 1783-1789* [New York, 1932], p. 111).

[94] [See Essay 5.]

5

A Governing Class
on The Defensive:
The Case of New York

New York Antifederalists were for the most part "new men" of plebeian origin, striving for equal access to economic opportunity, social acceptance, and political leadership.[1] But they

[1] [See Essay 2.] Since the stress in the present essay falls on the Federalists rather than the Antifederalists, I take this opportunity to state that the Antifederalist leaders in New York City as well as in the countryside were for the most part "new men." The merchants who had been active in the Sons of Liberty before the Revolution became Federalists, with three exceptions, John Lamb, Marinus Willett, and Peter Curtenius, all of whom held important offices in the Clintonian administration (Isaac Sears, Alexander McDougall and John Morin Scott all died before the ratification struggle). New York City's Antifederalist leaders, typically, were merchants who came into the city at the end of the war, traded with the West Indies rather than with Europe, and did not belong to the New York Chamber of Commerce or attend Mrs. John Jay's dinner parties.

This is one of the many aspects of the American Revolution which cries out to be compared with the corresponding facets of the great European revolu-

Reprinted, in somewhat altered form, from *Science and Society*, XXVII (1963).

were not merely self-interested: for, resenting the pervasive domination of farm and forum by men of wealth and rank, they also genuinely sought to enlarge the number of people involved in the political process.

The Federalists of New York exemplify even more dramatically the two-sided, ambiguous nature of the Revolutionary movement. Their brilliant leaders—Hamilton, Schuyler, Robert R. Livingston, Gouverneur Morris, Duane and Jay—*were* conservatives, and not merely in the revisionist sense that what they sought to conserve was liberal.[2] They took it for granted that society was a hierarchy of ranks, with a wealthy and leisured elite at its head and "the lower orders" and "the peasants" under their rule.[3] They were conservative also in the very modern sense of resisting fiercely government intrusions on free enterprise. Yet they were *also* deeply

---

tions. Thus in seventeenth century London, supporters of Parliament tended to be "merchants of middle rank" who had not held important commercial and administrative appointments under the crown, nor leading positions in the municipal government and the principal chartered companies, before 1640 (Valerie Pearl, *London and the Outbreak of the Puritan Revolution: City Government and National Politics, 1625-1643* [London, 1961], pp. 243, 245, 282-283). Similarly, county studies of the countryside show that the King's party "drew its main strength from the old ruling families," while the Parliamentary leaders were in general "of markedly lower social origin" (Christopher Hill, *Puritanism and Revolution: Studies in Interpretation of the English Revolution of the 17th Century* [London, 1958], pp. 21-23, and local studies there cited).

2 The phrase, that in the revisionist interpretation "what it [the Revolution] conserves is liberal," is borrowed from Wesley Frank Craven, "The Revolutionary Era," *The Reconstruction of American History*, ed. John Higham (New York, 1962), p. 59.

3 Such phrases will be found in, e.g., Philip Schuyler to Gouverneur Morris, Feb. 3, 1778, Gouverneur Morris Papers, Columbia University; Gouverneur Morris to Robert R. Livingston, Sept. 22, 1778, Robert R. Livingston Papers, New-York Historical Society. Schuyler, according to his army chaplain, had "never been accustomed to seeing men that are reasonably well taught and able to give a clear opinion and to state their grounds for it, who were not also persons of some wealth and rank" (quoted in George F. Scheer and Hugh F. Rankin, *Rebels and Redcoats* [New York, 1957], p. 251).

public-spirited men, critical of any tendency in each other to put private concerns before devotion to country and firmly committed to republican government.

The following pages will document and attempt to clarify these paradoxes in the politics of New York ratification. To Beard it seemed obvious, by analogy to the robber barons of his own day, that if the Founding Fathers were substantial capitalists, concerned to fashion a society in which men of wealth and good family would have a decisive voice, then their professed devotion to popular government was hypocritical, and resistance to their rule by the mass of commen men inevitable. It seemed obvious, but, as I hope to demonstrate, it was not true.

I.

Power in the State of New York before the American Revolution lodged in the hands of a small group of families whose income derived both from commerce and land. This was a ruling class, not merely in the sense that its members had similar interests, but also in the sense that they were bound together by close family ties (thus Hamilton married into the Schuylers, and Duane and Jay into the Manor Livingstons), shared a common ethos of *noblesse oblige*, and, at least in crises, tended to act together as a political unit. Beard's famous mistake (corrected in the 1935 reprinting of his *Economic Interpretation*) of supposing that the Hudson Valley landlords opposed the Constitution, sprang from his over-narrow conception of economic interest, and in particular, from his artificial distinction between "realty" and "personalty." To which group did James Duane, proprietor of Duanesburg, kin to Livingstons, and Mayor of New York in the Critical Period, belong? Obviously to both. Chancellor Robert R. Livingston declared in 1780 that "I have no personal property," as his father had lamented eighteen years earlier that "my personall Estate is no more, and we ought to take care of the Reall."[4] Alexander

---

[4] Robert R. Livingston to George Clinton, May 21, 1780, and Robert R. Livingston, Sr., to Robert R. Livingston, Mar. 1, 1762, R. R. Livingston Papers.

Hamilton, in contrast, was the principal spokesman of the nation's investors in fluid capital. Yet Livingston and Hamilton found common cause in the proposed United States Constitution and were the two principal Federalist speakers at the state ratifying convention.

What was at stake, in 1788, for both up-river landlords and metropolitan merchants, was aptly expressed in an exchange of letters between Alexander Hamilton and Robert Livingston, Jr. (the aged Lord of Livingston Manor) on the eve of the New York elections of 1785. "The situation of the state at this time is so critical," Hamilton wrote

that it is become a serious object of attention to those who are concerned for the *security of property* or the prosperity of government, to endeavour to put men in the Legislature whose principles are not of the *levelling kind* [italics in original]. . . . All men of respectability, in the city, of whatever party, who have been witnesses of the despotism and iniquity of the Legislature, are convinced, that the principal people in the community must for their own defence, unite to overset the party I have alluded to. I wish you to be persuaded Sir, that I would not take the liberty to trouble you with these remarks with a view to serving any particular turn; but, from a thorough conviction, that the safety of all those who have anything to lose calls upon them to take care that the power of government is intrusted to proper hands.

After the election, Livingston replied:

In this last election, by Compleating the necessary Junction previous to the day of Election [which] we have so often desired & Endeavourd for; by uniting the interests of the Rensselaer, Schuyler, & our family, with other Gentm. of property in the County in one Interest . . . we Carryed this last Election to a man.

"I trust," concluded the Third Lord, "we Shall always have the like Success provided we Stick Close to Each other."[5]

In this illuminating exchange, property spoke to property, pow-

[5] Alexander Hamilton to Robert Livingston, Jr., Apr. 25, 1785, and Livingston to Hamilton, June 13, 1785, *The Papers of Alexander Hamilton*, ed. Harold C. Syrett (New York, 1961–), III, 609, 615.

er to power, and the barriers separating proud great families and dividing city from country were overcome. The link between Hamilton and Livingston, as revealed by these letters, was surely basically economic: the political convictions on which they stood stemmed from a struggle for power between contending economic groups, and the power they sought meant economic security and dominion for their kind of people. Note that this is not economic interest in Beard's restricted sense of "advantages which the beneficiaries expected would accrue to themselves first" or an immediate interest in "personal possessions."[6] That is what economic interest may mean in a stable society wherein legislation centers on the allocation of a pork barrel of discrete economic advantages among competing claimants. But the Constitution was the settlement of a revolution. What was at stake for Hamilton, Livingston, and their opponents, was more than speculative windfalls in securities: it was the question, what kind of society would emerge from revolution when the dust had settled, and on which class the political center of gravity would come to rest.

In 1788, in the State of New York, it was not at all certain which class would rule. However it may have been in other states, it was not true in New York that "leadership at the close of the [Revolutionary] era belonged substantially to the same segment of the society as it did at the beginning"; nor was it the case "that the social conventions governing the employment of the colonial franchise survived the Revolution without serious impairment."[7] It was not true in Dutchess County, where landlords dropped out of politics after 1777, and not a single member of the old ruling fam-

[6] Charles A. Beard, *An Economic Interpretation of the Constitution of the United States* (New York, 1913), pp. 18, 324.

[7] Craven, "Revolutionary Era," pp. 60, 62. [The best recent discussion of democracy in the American Revolution, Jackson Main's "Government by the People: The American Revolution and the Democratization of the Legislatures," *William and Mary Quarterly*, third series, XXIII (1966), agrees that the New York legislature was substantially democratized by the Revolution (pp. 394, 399-400).]

ilics held important elective or appointive office until after 1788.[8] It was not true in New York City, where the artisans fought bitterly in 1785 and 1786 for artisans in the legislature, and sought to make elective all important municipal offices from the mayoralty down.[9] Nor was it true in New York State as a whole, governed throughout this period by a man whose "family and connections," in the words of his defeated opponent, did "not entitle him to so distinguished a predominance."[10] Philip Schuyler, who said this about George Clinton, had boasted before the election of 1777, "they may chuse who they will I will command them all."[11] It did not work out quite this way. Late in the war, Schuyler's son-in-law tactfully commented that the great man, then serving in the New York Senate, was "exposed to the mortification of seeing important measures patronised by him frequently miscarry."[12]

A strong anti-aristocratic spirit was at work among the common people of the state during the years 1777-1788, and in state politics the little group of conservative nationalists was consistently on the defensive. When, in the spring of 1784, Robert R. Livingston acquired Oliver Delancey's "large square pew" at St. Paul's church,[13] one might have thought the Revolution had been a per-

---

[8] [See Essay 2.]

[9] An example: on March 14, 1785, over 350 New York City residents petitioned the state legislature to make the municipal offices of Mayor, Recorder, Sheriff, and Coroner elective (Senate Legislative Papers, X, Box 1, New York State Library). Of ninety-nine mechanics who attended the General Society of Mechanics and Tradesmen in the years 1785-1788, twenty-five signed this petition; whereas of 122 merchants attending meetings of the Chamber of Commerce in 1784-1785, only four signed. The mechanic signers included three chairmen of the Committee of Mechanics: Dunscomb, Bicker, and Boyd.

[10] Philip Schuyler to John Jay, July 14, 1777, *Correspondence and Public Papers of John Jay*, ed. Henry P. Johnston (New York, 1890), I, 147.

[11] *Historical Memoirs from 12 July 1776 to 25 July 1778 of William Smith*, ed. William H. W. Sabine (New York, 1958), p. 151.

[12] Alexander Hamilton to Robert Morris, Aug. 13, 1782, *Papers of Hamilton*, III, 138.

[13] Thomas Tillotson to Robert R. Livingston, June 15, 1784, R. R. Livingston Papers.

sonal success for him; but the triumph was tainted by the fact that in 1785, as in 1777, the Chancellor had to withdraw from the race for Governor "on account of the prejudices against his family name."[14] Livingston himself was able to respond flexibly to the new times. Others were more impatient. On the eve of the Army-Congress plot of 1783, Morris wrote to John Jay (a passage omitted by Sparks from his version of the letter in his *Life of Morris*):

> You and I, my friend, know by Experience, that when a few Men of Sense and Spirit get together, and declare that they are the Authority, such few as are of a different Opinion may easily be convinced of their mistake by that powerful Argument the Halter.[15]

The political challenge to conservative power in New York came from aspiring new men like George Clinton, Abraham Yates, and Melancton Smith, figures who in many cases had begun their careers as stewards and surveyors for the great landed magnates whose power they now began to contest.[16] In the first election under the new state constitution, in 1777, the old Son of Liberty John Morin Scott ran for governor along with Schuyler and Clinton, "rail[ed] at an *Aristocratic Faction* which he pretends has formed and organized the new government," and blamed his failure to obtain high office on Duer, Duane, Robert R. Livingston, Philip Livingston, and Gouverneur Morris, "whom he described as a faction & tends [*sic*] to a family interest."[17] Defeated in the gubernatorial election, Scott used his Senate seat to introduce legislation for price-fixing and land confiscation. Gouverneur Morris commented on this radical program: "It was hardly possible to embitter [the] bitter Draught these Laws had prepared, yet it was effected by the man-

14 Robert R. Livingston to William Duer, June 12, 1777, R. R. Livingston Papers; Philip Schuyler to John Jay, May 30, 1785, *Papers of Jay*, III, 151.

15 Gouverneur Morris to John Jay, Jan. 1, 1783, Morris Papers.

16 Thus Clinton had been a surveyor for Beverly Robinson (James Duane Papers, N.-Y.H.S.) and John Lansing a steward for Schuyler (Philip Schuyler Papers, N.Y.P.L.).

17 William Duer to Philip Schuyler, two letters dated June 19, 1777, Schuyler Papers.

ner of enforcing them. Men of old approved Character who respected their Neighbours and were respected would not descend to
it. The Executors of these new Laws therefore were Men who like
the Laws themselves were new."[18] The Clintonian tax program,
Hamilton agreed, was put into the hands of local assessors who
used their power to punish Tories.[19]

It was only as the New York conservatives lost control of state
government to their upstart opponents, that the thought of the
conservatives turned clearly in a centralist direction. At first, they
were by no means the centralizing nationalists which they later
became. "I am resolved," Edward Rutledge wrote John Jay on the
eve of the Declaration of Independence, "to vest the Congress with
no more Power than that [which] is absolutely necessary, and to
use a familiar Expression, to keep the Staff in our own Hands."[20]
This mood lasted just so long as the conservatives retained their
confidence in controlling what Robert R. Livingston called the
"torrent" of democratic sentiment in the states. When that confidence failed, when in 1779-1780 the conservatives turned to Congress to effect their program, they turned to it as "a refuge against
majority rule."[21] Hamilton wrote in July 1781 that "it would be the
extreme of vanity in us not to be sensible, that we began this
revolution with very vague and confined notions of the practical
business of government."[22] The remark applied as much to the
future authors of *The Federalist* as to anyone else.

Among the vague and confined notions which New York conservatives had to unlearn, was their visceral opposition to govern-

[18] Fragment, n.d., Morris Papers.

[19] Alexander Hamilton to Robert Morris, [June 17, 1782] and Aug. 13,
1782, *Papers of Hamilton*, III, 93-94, 135-137.

[20] Edward Rutledge to John Jay, June 29, 1776, *Papers of Jay*, I, 67-68.

[21] E. James Ferguson, *The Power of the Purse: A History of American Public Finance, 1776-1790* (Chapel Hill, 1961), p. 337. For Livingston's changing attitude, see George Dangerfield, *Chancellor Robert R. Livingston of New
York, 1746-1813* (New York, 1960), Part II, chap. IV [and Essay 2, pp. 40-42].

[22] "The Continentalist No. I," *Papers of Hamilton*, II, 649.

ment intervention in the economy. Early in the war it was radicals, not conservatives, who favored a managed economy. Marinus Willett, for instance, wrote to John Jay in 1777 that he approved New York's embargo on the export of flour. "I am not unaware," Willett explained, "of that common argument that trade will regulate itself [but] a virtuous private trader appears to me as rare in this day as the Phoenix; trade is got into the hands of I don't know who: but am sure it is not in the hands of men of public virtue."[23] Gouverneur Morris was an outstanding exponent of the "common argument" mentioned by Willett. Morris, like Adam Smith, believed that "the Principle of self Interest is like the Power of Gravity to Fluids, which brings them to a level, merely by the Mutability of their component Parts." Writing to Livingston, Morris declared that "Restrictions of Commerce injure the State without serving the general Cause and undue Exertions of Government like the Convulsions of Delirium exhaust the Patient in unproductive Efforts." In the midst of the financial crisis of 1779, when the Continental currency dropped from a ratio of 8:1 to specie to a ratio of something like 40:1, and when (in the words of General Washington) it took a wagonload of money to buy a wagonload of provisions, Morris could write:

> Nothing therefore is requisite than that the People should be actuated by that Regard to private Interest which has been ineffectually written and preached and prayed against from the Fall of Adam to the present Hour.[24]

Gouverneur Morris' unblushing advocacy of laissez-faire was typical of the New York conservative leaders. Although they sometimes voted for price-fixing or confiscation bills for reasons of expediency, the New York conservatives unanimously condemned

[23] Marinus Willett to John Jay, Dec. 17, 1777, John Jay Papers, Columbia University.

[24] Fragment on paper currency, Feb. 1780, Morris Papers; Gouverneur Morris to Robert R. Livingston, Feb. 21, 1781, R. R. Livingston Papers; "Letters to the Inhabitants of America," n.d., Morris Papers.

them in their private correspondence.[25] Egbert Benson of Dutchess, for example, voted for price regulation although in private he declared:

A regulating scheme has not been attempted anywhere in the State except at Albany. . . . It is amazing that people should still pursue a system so evidently futile and absurd. I sincerely wish the *limitation* may be *limited* to the City of Albany. I possibly am in the opposite extreme and so far from reducing prices agreeable to this plan, I think the Embargo Act ought immediately to be repealed and our farmers indulged with an opportunity of carrying their produce to the highest market.[26]

How did these vigorous proponents of free enterprise come to adopt the mercantilist program of currency devaluation, national impost, central bank, and stronger Federal government? The catalyst seems to have been the financial crisis of 1779-1780, which persuaded even Morris of the need for a "regular Plan." This crisis was as significant in shaping the outlook of the Federalist leaders as was the depression of 1785-1786 (to be discussed presently) in fixing the sentiments of the Federalist voters. Once converted, the New York conservatives played a key role in pushing through Congress the first steps of the new nationalist program. The little group decided collectively how to distribute themselves between the state legislature and the national Congress. In Congress, James Duane was particularly conspicuous, "no

[25] See, for example, in the R. R. Livingston Papers: Morris to Livingston, May 27, 1778; John Sloss Hobart to same, November 15, 1779; Livingston to Morris, Jan. 29, April 6, Sept. 10, 1778; same to Jay, Mar. 4 and April 20, 1779; same to Schuyler, Mar. 29, 1778; and Schuyler to Livingston, Mar. 5, 1778. The general conservative opinion was expressed by Morris when he said that price regulation "gave a Woeful Impression of the new Governments by laying down a Violation of the Rights of Property as the Corner Stone on which they were to be erected" (fragment on price regulation, n.d., Morris Papers).

[26] Egbert Benson to John Jay, July 6, 1779, *Papers of Jay*, I, 213. For Benson's explanations of his votes, see Egbert Benson to John Jay, June 23, 1779, Jay Papers, and same to Robert R. Livingston, Jan. 3 and July 28, 1780, R. R. Livingston Papers.

other member," as he wrote to Livingston, "having knowledge of our money matters sufficiently comprehensive."[27] Three years later, when that "intriguing industrious body" (as his friend Morris called him)[28] had successfully lobbied through Congress the currency devaluation of March 1780, and, in February 1781, the proposal for a Federal impost and the appointment of Robert Morris as Financier, Duane referred to the latter as a plan "on which I hazarded my political Reputation."[29]

Hamilton expounded the changed conservative attitude in his "Continentalist" essays of 1781-1782.

There are some, who maintain, [he wrote] that trade will regulate itself, and is not to be benefitted by the encouragements, or restraints of government. Such persons will imagine, that there is no need of a common directing power. This is one of those wild speculative paradoxes, which have grown into credit among us, contrary to the uniform practice and sense of the most enlightened nations.

"Unless," Hamilton concluded, "we can overcome this narrow disposition and learn to estimate measures, by their general tendency, we shall never be a great or a happy people, if we remain a people at all."[30] Public banks, for example, were "like all other good things . . . subject to abuse and when abused, become pernicious. . . . But no wise statesman will reject the good from an apprehension of the ill."[31]

[27] James Duane to Robert R. Livingston, Jan. 3, 1779, R. R. Livingston Papers.

[28] Gouverneur Morris to Robert R. Livingston, Sept. 22, 1778, R. R. Livingston Papers.

[29] James Duane to George Washington, Aug. 7, 1782, Duane Papers. See also in this collection: Duane to Mrs. Duane, May 26, 1779; Schuyler to Duane, Dec. 16, 1779; Livingston to Duane, Mar. 13 and Nov. 12, 1780. For Duane's role in pushing through Congress the nationalist program, see also Edmund C. Burnett, The Continental Congress (New York, 1941), pp. 384-385, 449, 483, 485, 487, 490-492; and for the program itself, Ferguson, Power of the Purse, chap. VI and pp. 334-335.

[30] "The Continentalist No. V," Papers of Hamilton, III, 76, 82.

[31] Alexander Hamilton to Robert Morris [Apr. 30, 1781], ibid., II, 617-618.

Well before the end of the war, the Federalist leadership had evolved the program and the ideology which they would champion in 1787-1788. In the process, these powerful New Yorkers had moved beyond the circle of state affairs. By 1783 they were working intimately and continuously with other middle-state conservatives to strengthen the federal government. Thus, as New York Receiver of Taxes for Robert Morris toward the end of the war, Alexander Hamilton also served as lobbyist for Morris' plans to repeal the legal tender and punitive features of state paper-money laws. In July 1782, Hamilton and Schuyler saw through the New York legislature resolutions calling for a national convention to strengthen the Confederation (the last nationalist act of that body for half a decade); in the same month, a meeting of public creditors in Philadelphia called for stronger federal powers; in September 1782, New York answered Pennsylvania with a convention of creditors at Albany, chaired by Schuyler, which planned an abortive state convention for November.[32] The same handful of men founded the banks in New York City and Philadelphia which were rallying points for investors in the Critical Period. Hamilton's brother-in-law, John B. Church, was a leading stockholder of both institutions. New Yorker Robert R. Livingston suggested the Philadelphia Bank of North America in 1780, while in 1783 Gouverneur Morris, by then a Philadelphia resident, proposed to Alexander Hamilton a Bank of New York.[33] "A consolidated group whose interests knew no state boundaries and were truly national in their scope"[34] was taking shape. Nothing illustrated it better than a letter Robert Morris wrote to Philip

[32] See Thomas C. Cochran, *New York in the Confederation: An Economic Study* (Philadelphia, 1932), p. 137; *New York Packet*, Oct. 24, 1782.

[33] Robert R. Livingston to Philip Schuyler, June 17, 1780, Bancroft Transcripts—Schuyler, New York Public Library; Gouverneur Morris to Robert Morris, Nov. 22, 1783, Morris Papers, wherein Morris says: "I have consulted Hamilton on the Subject of the Bank who thinks the Proposition may be eligible but must consider."

[34] Beard, *Economic Interpretation*, p. 325.

Schuyler shortly after becoming Financier, early in 1781. I need, the Financier told the Patroon, one thousand barrels of flour for the new campaign; I assume your credit as a private gentleman is good for this amount; proceed accordingly, and bill me."[35] By thus harnessing the energies of private enterprise to the national need, supplies were obtained for the triumph of Yorktown.

II.

By 1783, the cause of stronger Federal government had a brilliant galaxy of leaders in New York; what the cause needed was popular support.

Twice during the war the Federalist leaders had seriously considered strengthening Congress by dictatorial means. The first occasion was the crisis of 1780. In May, Schuyler wrote to Duane that it was necessary to "lodge dictatorial powers" either in the Commander-in-Chief, or in him, together with a small committee; Schuyler went on to suggest names for the committee. In November 1780, Schuyler suggested a dictatorial central committee for New York as well. Hamilton stated in September that Congress had been too liberal in observing the letter of its instructions: "They should have considered themselves as vested with full power *to preserve the republic from harm.*" That same year Robert R. Livingston, as chairman of a committee of Congress for increasing its powers, used identical language in calling on that body to assume all necessary powers "by the authority which the nature of the trust reposed in them vests with them."[36]

Such thoughts, during the troubled eighteen months between the fall of Charleston and the surrender at Yorktown, are no proof of conspiratorial intent. Tom Paine, the voice of the Revolution,

[35] Robert Morris to Philip Schuyler, May 29, 1781, Bancroft Transcripts—Schuyler.

[36] Philip Schuyler to James Duane, May 13, 1780, and Robert R. Livingston to same, Nov. 12, 1780, Duane Papers; Alexander Hamilton to same [Sept. 3, 1780], *Papers of Hamilton*, II, 401; Dangerfield, *Chancellor Livingston*, p. 124.

quite agreed with the New York conservatives that the financial crisis of 1779-1780 called for centralized government in the hands of businessmen.[37] As late as March 1781, Robert R. Livingston wrote Philip Schuyler: "Have you devised any plan to extricate us from our present difficulties? or are we still to blunder on without object and without system?"[38] When the two principal New York conservatives expressed bewilderment, lesser men could hardly have had a surer sense of purpose.

In the spring of 1783, however, Gouverneur Morris and Hamilton, at least, were involved in conspiratorial designs much less creditable. With peace at hand, they made their desperate bid to utilize the army's demand for pay in forcing through Congress the nationalist program. Morris, as quoted earlier, spoke at this time of the persuasion of the halter, while Hamilton wrote to the reluctant Washington: "I confess could force avail I should almost wish to see it employed."[39]

This seems to be all the evidence for unrepublican intentions on the part of the New York Federalist leaders. After 1783, they settled down to search for a constituency. The Federalists found their strongest popular support among the artisans of New York City.

The genuineness of artisan support for the Constitution is beyond question. The election for delegates to the New York ratifying convention was (as in no other state) by secret ballot and open to all adult males, and the New York City Federalist margin was

[37] Paine said that when the war was carried on by emissions "the poor were of equal use in government with the rich," but that the crisis required "the wealthier part [to] throw in their aid" (to Joseph Reed, June 4, 1780, *The Complete Writings of Thomas Paine*, ed. Philip Foner [New York, 1945], II, 1186). Livingston defended the conservative proposals as asking "a momentary submission to . . . vigorous exertions of government" (quoted in Burnett, *Continental Congress*, p. 455).

[38] Robert R. Livingston to Philip Schuyler, Mar. 28, 1781, Schuyler Papers.

[39] Alexander Hamilton to George Washington, Mar. 25, 1783, *Papers of Hamilton*, III, 306.

twenty-to-one[40]: since the artisans were a good half of the city's adult male population, they must have voted overwhelmingly for ratification. Moreover, as in all the other large cities,[41] the city mechanics capped their ballots with a victory parade in which craft after craft marched under its banners.

Jackson Main has pointed up the theoretical significance of the artisans' Federalism. "The most serious of all objections to an interpretation based exclusively on an alignment along class lines," Main wrote, "is the complete absence of a division of opinion in the towns. Where there should have been the most feeling, the least existed."[42] How shall we account for the artisans' enthusiasm for a document which, according to Beard, was the reactionary and antidemocratic product of a ruling class?

The answer must go right back to John Fiske. The Federalist *leaders* knew what they wanted before 1783, but the New York City artisans, who would become Federalist *voters*, were preoccupied in 1783 and 1784 with a belligerent, class-conscious attempt to rewin a foothold in the city from which the war had exiled them seven years.[43] The depression of the mid-1780's transformed their outlook. The spring of 1785 saw a general uneasiness about trade stagnation suddenly grow acute and urgent. Then, as John Jay remarked, Federal ideas began to thrive;[44] the early sum-

---

[40] [See Linda Grant De Pauw, *The Eleventh Pillar: New York State and the Federal Constitution* (Ithaca, N.Y.; 1966), pp. 157, 167.]

[41] For the mechanics in the ratification struggle, see Jackson T. Main, *The Antifederalists: Critics of the Constitution, 1781-1788* (Chapel Hill, 1961), pp. 266-268.

[42] *Ibid.*, p. 266.

[43] [See Essay 4.]

[44] John Jay to Marquis de Lafayette, Jan. 19, 1785, Papers of Jay, III, 138. The "depression" of the mid-1780's was not a stoppage of work or a financial panic, but a condition of falling prices, shortage of money, and an adverse balance of trade, caused by the inflooding of British goods at the end of the war and the British restrictions on trade with the West Indies. Evidence for a depression in this sense is overwhelming. Merchants' complaints begin in the spring of 1783 (see e.g., John Holker to William Duer, Apr. 22, 1783, Duer Papers, N.-Y.H.S.;

mer of 1785 produced in every major American city a merchant-mechanic alliance on behalf of stronger Federal government.[45]

The objects of the merchant-mechanic committees formed in Boston, New York, Philadelphia, Baltimore and Charleston in 1785 were, first, to press for stronger Federal power to regulate trade, and second, to reinforce legislation—as in Non-Importation days—by the moral sentiment and direct action of local communities. The first concern is illustrated by a petition from "Artificers, Tradesmen and Mechanics" of New York City to the Continental Congress, early in 1785, which stated that "we sincerely hope our Representatives will coincide with the other States, in augmenting your power to every exigency of the Union."[46] The second concern is exemplified by the resolve of the Philadelphia shoemakers not to buy, sell, repair, let be repaired by an employer, or work for employers who bought, sold or repaired, imported European boots or shoes.[47]

William Constable to Edward Jones, May 29, 1783, to Gabriel Tegelaer, June 8, 1783, and to Henry Budde, June 1, 1783, Letter Book 1782-1790, Constable-Pierrepont Papers, N.Y.P.L.). Early in 1785 the volume of complaint markedly increased. Thus, the New York Chamber of Commerce memorialized the state legislature on March 3, 1785 regarding "trade [which] is daily on the decline" (Assembly Papers, Box 43, N.Y.S.L.), and the firm of Stewart and Jones asserted that "cash was never known so scarce as at present" (Stewart and Jones to William Stewart, Jan. 27, 1785, Letter Book, Aug. 14, 1784-Sept. 27, 1786, Stewart and Jones Papers, N.Y.P.L.; see also Beekman Papers, N.-Y.H.S. and Champlin Papers, N.Y.S.L.). During the three-year period March 1784-April 1787, the exports of the port of New York amounted to only £162,554, while imports were £4,826,312, more than twenty times as much (Walter Livingston, "Exports and Imports, Port of New York, 1765-1787," Box 15, R. R. Livingston Papers).

[45] See Beard, *Economic Interpretation*, p. 45. The New York City press carried full reports of the collaboration of merchants and mechanics in other cities, e.g., *New York Packet*, June 2, Aug. 22, Oct. 10, Nov. 21, 1785 and Mar. 16, 1786; *New York Journal*, May 19, June 9, Sept. 1 and 12, Oct. 13 and 27, 1785; *New York Gazetteer*, May 31, 1785; *New York Daily Advertiser*, Nov. 29, 1786.

[46] *New York Journal*, Feb. 24, 1785.

[47] *Ibid.*, Mar. 24, 1785.

Imported manufactures brought the menace of British economic power directly home to the New York City artisans. Thirty thousand hats and 97,000 pairs of shoes, for example, poured into the city during the three years 1784-1786.[48] Here again was an echo of "the ever-memorable period of the Stamp-Act": after, as before, the Revolution, the encouragement of native manufactures seemed a part of the struggle for independence. "When the minds of the people of America were really virtuous," wrote a newspaper correspondent in 1785, "at the beginning of the late contest, every man was convinced of the necessity of our encouraging manufactures, and employing our own people, that we might be truly independent."[49] The General Society of Mechanics and Tradesmen struck the same note. European imports, the Society told its Boston counterpart, "are not only highly unfavorable to every mechanical improvement, but . . . nourish a spirit of dependence which tends in some degree to defeat the purpose of our late revolution."[50]

Men of all classes rejoiced that, toward the end of the eighties, articles such as nails, oil, linens and glass were more cheaply manufactured in America than abroad. Robert Boyd, chairman of the General Society of Mechanics and Tradesmen, and Peter Curtenius, bitter Antifederalist merchant, joined with conservatives John Jay, Alexander Hamilton, Richard Varick, and Robert Troup, in promoting the all-important iron industry. By 1787, Curtenius' Air Furnace could offer iron articles ranging from tea kettles to the heavy pots and rollers used in sugar-refineries and slitting-mills, "equal to any imported from Europe, and the Price less."[51]

[48] Walter Livingston, "Exports and Imports, Port of New York, 1765-1787," R. R. Livingston Papers.

[49] *New York Packet*, Sept. 1, 1785.

[50] Letter of Nov. 18, 1788, quoted in *Annals of the General Society of Mechanics and Tradesmen of the City of New York from 1785 to 1880*, ed. Thomas Earle and Charles T. Congdon (New York, 1882), pp. 12-13.

[51] *New York Journal*, Nov. 9, 1786; Robert R. Livingston to Chevalier de la Luzerne, May 7, 1788, R. R. Livingston Papers; "Original Articles of Agreement of the associated Manufacturing Iron Company" of the City and

To the artisans, the campaign for the Constitution seemed a direct continuation of the independence struggle. It was symbolic that in Boston, a meeting of tradesmen and artisans at the old Revolutionary meeting-place, the Green Dragon tavern, chaired by Paul Revere, rousingly supported the Constitution and allegedly swayed Samuel Adams to vote for ratification. In New York, politicians of all persuasions shared with the artisans a fear that England, by dumping goods on the American market, closing the West Indies, and other harassments, could destroy *de facto* the independence it had granted *de jure*. "What most immediately and deeply impresses me," John Morin Scott had written to James Duane even before the evacuation of New York City, "is the apprehension that a Treaty of Amity and Concord may be consorted with Great Britain, which may ultimately sap and overturn the Independence of these United States." Reciprocity, Scott concluded, would not be real equality.[52] The Lord of Livingston Manor believed that unless the British allowed Americans "to trade to their West Indian Islands on the Same footing as we did formerly, to enable us to make remittances & Supply ourselves with Salt Rum Sugar molasses etc. in our own bottoms," American trade would soon dwindle "to little or nothing."[53] John Jay, now Secretary of State, agreed that the British insistence on repayment of old debts, while forbidding Americans to obtain means of payment from the West Indian trade, had placed merchants of the newly-independent nation in an intolerable vise.[54] In that same summer of 1785 when American merchants and mechanics were combining to protect themselves, John Adams, America's repre-

County of New York, Aug. 26, 1786, *Papers of Hamilton*, III, 682 (the names of the subscribers appear in the manuscript agreement which is summarized in the published *Papers*); advertisement for Peter Curtenius' Air Furnace, 1787, broadside, N.Y.P.L.

[52] John Morin Scott to James Duane, Aug. 6, 1783, Duane Papers.

[53] Robert Livingston, Jr., to James Duane, Sept. 12, 1783, Duane Papers; same to Walter Livingston, Feb. 4, 1785, R. R. Livingston Papers.

[54] John Jay to John Adams, Sept. 6, 1785, *Papers of Jay*, III, 165.

sentative in England, wrote that "the [English] *disigns of ruining, if they can our carrying Trade, and annihilating all our Navigation, and Seamen is* [*sic*] *too apparent.*" He who had fought for the Massachusetts cod in the peace negotiations of 1782 was in no yielding mood.

If the English will persevere in excluding our Ships from their West India Islands, Canada, Nova Scotia, and Newfoundland . . . we must adopt in all the States the Regulations which were once made in England. . . . I should be sorry to adopt a Monopoly. But, driven to the necessity of it, I would not do Business by the Halves. . . . We must not, my Friend, be the Bubbles of our own Liberal Sentiments. If we cannot obtain reciprocal Liberality, We must adopt reciprocal Prohibitions, Exclusions, Monopolies, and Imposts.[55]

Tom Paine, the former stay-maker, as usual caught the national feeling in a phrase when he wrote that a stronger Federal government would be "our anchor in the world of empires."[56]

New York publications were quick to transfer the old anti-Tory sentiment to the new Federalist cause. When the Chamber of Commerce appointed a committee to deal with the trade depres-

[55] John Adams to Thomas Jefferson, July 18, Aug. 7, Sept. 4, 1785, *The Adams-Jefferson Letters*, ed. L. J. Cappon (Chapel Hill, 1959), I, 43, 50-51, 61.

It is important to realize that when John Fiske spoke of America in the 1780's as "drifting toward anarchy," it was America's international weakness which came first to his mind: the first ten pages of Fiske's chapter by this name are devoted to America's foreign troubles, not to its domestic condition. Quoting these same letters of John Adams, Fiske commented: "There was an intention of humiliating the Americans, and it was commonly said that under a sufficient weight of commercial distress the states would break up their feeble union, and come straggling back, one after another, to their old allegiance"; and again: "In a certain sense, it was keeping up warfare by commercial instead of military methods, and there was danger that it might lead to a renewal of armed conflict" (John Fiske, *The Critical Period of American History*, 1783-1789 [Boston and New York, 1888], pp. 141, 142). Newly-independent colonial nations today often find themselves in identical circumstances. Perhaps it was difficult for Beard, writing between the Spanish-American and first World Wars, to imagine that America had ever been so weak.

[56] "In Answer to the Citizen of Rhode-Island on the Five Per Cent. Duty," *The Complete Writings of Thomas Paine*, II, 341.

sion, it was presented to the public as a step "to break the fetters and restraints which we have tamely suffered the British to fix on our trade."[57] A newspaper writer asked: "Is it any breach of charity to suppose, that those men who oppose the increase of the power of Congress for regulating our commerce—or who oppose laws for imposing duties on British goods—are under the influence of British principles or connections?"[58] By thus fusing the old radical anti-British sentiment with the conservative interest in a stronger Federal government, the merchants destroyed whatever hope there might have been for Antifederalism in New York City.

Throughout the pregnant summer of 1785, newspaper correspondents addressed themselves directly to the need to bury old class antagonisms and cement a merchant-mechanic alliance. Merchants and mechanics, one writer said, must sink "all old causes of difference in eternal oblivion."[59] "A Friend to the Community" expressed the same sentiment forcibly.

> The present unsettled state of our trade and commerce is truly alarming [he began], and much depends on the exertions of the merchants and mechanics among us. . . . However secure either may feel with respect to their own strength and consequence—however determined they may be to abide by the resolutions formed by their own particular class, unless the merchants and mechanics *mutually* request and obtain the assistance of each other, their attempts to subvert the machinations of our enemies will prove entirely futile and abortive. . . . Thus . . . we shall see the mechanic look with pleasure on the prosperity of the merchant, and the merchant will view with a smile of approbation the system which shall be adopted to promote the interest of the honest mechanic.[60]

Farmer, merchant, and mechanic, said another statement, had united in '76 to withstand their common foes; they must do so again.[61]

[57] *New York Journal*, May 26, 1785.
[58] "Andrew Marvel," *ibid.*, June 16, 1785.
[59] *Loc. cit.*
[60] *Ibid.*, June 2, 1785.
[61] *New York Packet*, Nov. 10, 1785.

And they did. When the New York legislature rejected a Federal impost in the spring of 1785, a committee was set up by the Chamber of Commerce to protest the legislature's action and to correspond with the counties. The committee included former merchant Sons of Liberty Isaac Sears, John Broome, Isaac Ledyard and William Malcolm, conservative businessmen William Duer and William Constable, and mechanic-manufacturer White Matlack. Believing that "no partial or limited determination upon such questions could produce substantial Effects," the committee enlarged itself to include three prominent mechanics—silversmith William Gilbert, carpenter Anthony Post, and ropemaker Thomas Ivers—together with some new faces from the old Sons of Liberty: Jacobus Van Zandt and Nathaniel Hazard. The committee proceeded to memorialize the rest of the state, requesting that their memorial be laid "before the inhabitants of the several districts in your county, and that you will unite in giving pointed instructions to your representatives."[62] In March 1786, when the Federal impost again hung in the balance in the New York legislature, a general meeting of city inhabitants unanimously approved the impost, and left copies of a petition at three taverns for signature.[63]

Well before the ratification debate of 1787-1788, the Federalists had won to their cause not only most of the old radical leaders of New York City, but much of the mechanic rank-and-file. In 1785, Hugh Hughes observed that a "coalition" had been formed between all parties in the city, although a few mechanics still hung back.[64]

[62] Minutes of the New York Chamber of Commerce, photostat, N.Y.P.L.; *New York Journal*, Apr. 7 and June 23, 1785; broadside of the Committee of Correspondence of the Chamber of Commerce of New York City, n.d., N.Y.P.L.

[63] *New York Packet*, Mar. 27, 1786.

[64] Hugh Hughes to Charles Tillinghast, Mar. 7, 1785, Lamb Papers, N.-Y. H.S. In Philadelphia, too, the onset of depression enabled the city's conservatives to win substantial mechanic support for the first time since the end of the war. In the fall elections of 1785, the "pendulum began to swing back towards conservatism." (Robert L. Brunhouse, *The Counter-Revolution in Pennsylvania, 1776-1790* [Harrisburg, 1942], p. 176.)

The city Antifederalist leaders became generals without an army. Melancton Smith was not supported by the Mechanics' Committee when he sought an Assembly seat in 1785, and was rejected again when he and David Gelston ran for the Senate in 1787.[65] On the eve of elections for the ratifying convention in 1788, Marinus Willett was said to have "become a proselyte, declaring it [the proposed Constitution] might be right—since it appears to be the sense of a vast majority"; while at the same time Hamilton observed that the city Antifederalists, fearing that New York City would secede from the state, did not advocate outright rejection of the Constitution.[66] Thus, before the famous drama at Poughkeepsie had begun, the issue was in some sense already settled. Those debates on which so much attention has been lavished were, so far as New York City is concerned, the froth cast up by a wave which had already done its work.

As the artisan population of the city, three or four thousand strong, marched down Broadway on July 23, 1788, to celebrate adoption of the Constitution by the requisite nine states, their floats and slogans testified to their enthusiasm. A "federal loaf," 10 feet long, 27 inches in breadth, and 8 inches in height, was carried by the Bakers, together with "a flag, representing the declension of trade under the old Confederation." "Americans, encourage your manufactures!" proclaimed the Skinners, Breeches Makers, and Glovers, while the Peruke Makers and Hairdressers rejoined, "May we succeed in our trade and the union protect us." The Blacksmiths chanted, "Forge me strong, finish me neat, I soon shall moor a Federal fleet," as sturdy members of the trade, riding the float, hammered away at an anchor. On they came—

[65] *New York Packet*, Apr. 25, 1785; *New York Daily Advertiser*, Apr. 20, 1787.

[66] Morgan Lewis to Margaret Beekman Livingston, May 4, 1788, R. R. Livingston Papers; Alexander Hamilton to James Madison [June 8, 1788], *Papers of Hamilton*, V, 3. Curiously, Melancton Smith was also accused in the rural press for having grown "cool" in his Antifederalism after ratification by Massachusetts (*Poughkeepsie Country Journal*, Mar. 4, 1788).

the Ship Joiners, with their motto: "This federal ship will our commerce revive, And merchants and shipwrights and joiners shall thrive"; the humble Cartmen, saying: "To every craft she gives employ, Sure Cartmen have their share of joy"; the Brush Makers, who proclaimed: "May love and unity support our trade, And keep out those who would our rights invade." And after these there came several dozen more trades, including the Cordwainers, Carpenters (the largest trade, with 392 marchers), Hatters, Cabinet Makers, Sail Makers, Gold Smiths, Tobacconists, Paper Stainers, Artificial Florists, and last but not least the Tailors, with their magnificent slogan: "And they sewed fig leaves together."[67]

III.

Thus the United States Constitution, sponsored in New York as elsewhere in the nation by patricians such as Philip Schuyler and the Livingstons, was ardently supported, in New York as elsewhere, by those "restless mechanics"[68] who regarded the patricians as their traditional enemies. Does this disprove the thesis that the Constitution was the instrument whereby a governing class on the defensive recovered its traditional power?

Not at all. To begin with, scholars on both sides of the question agree that New York's well-to-do supplied the Federalist *leadership.* "It seems clear," writes Jackson Main, "that most of the wealthy landowners and merchants, in and out of the [state ratifying] convention, were Federalists and that the Antifederalists, while drawing some of their leaders from this class, were on the whole men of lesser means."[69]

[67] The parade is described in *New York Packet*, Aug. 5, 1788. [See also De Pauw, *Eleventh Pillar*, pp. 237-240.]

[68] Robert Livingston, Jr., to James Duane, Mar. 22, 1784, Duane Papers, N.-Y.H.S.

[69] Main, *Antifederalists*, p. 242. [Linda DePauw concurs: "it cannot have been a fact that all New York Federalists were rich and well-born—there were far too many of them—but it was true that most of the rich and well-born in the state were Federalists" (De Pauw, *Eleventh Pillar*, pp. 165-166)].

The financial crisis of 1779-1780 crystallized the mercantilist, nationalist program of these Federalist leaders. The depression of 1785-1786 swung the artisan voters behind this program. Both groups felt an economic interest in the Constitution. To the Federalist leaders it offered a check on interference with property by the states. To the artisans it offered jobs and markets. But for each group, in addition, strengthening the Federal government seemed a way to promote the Revolution. In the eyes of the artisans in the mid-1780's, as in those of the well-to-do leaders of the "counter-revolutions" of 1780-1781 and 1787-1788, no contradiction existed between immediate, personal economic interests and the patriotic goal of sustaining the national economy and preserving national independence.

That ratification attracted many voters from the urban poor proves only that the Antifederalists failed to voice the aspirations of much of that humble constituency to which their rhetoric was addressed, and that, for the moment, other things were more important to the artisans than the struggle over who should rule at home. But only for the moment. The alliance between merchants and mechanics was, as Walsh says of Charleston, "not completely natural."[70] When Hamilton, once in power, catered to the needs of importing merchants rather than to mechanic demands for protection against British manufactures, the artisans deserted him.[71] As early as the fall of 1788 a spokesman for New York City's "middling or lower class of people" reopened the controversy, asserting that if this group "had any regard to their independence and liberty, parties must be formed, and a contention arise between the different classes."[72]

[70] Richard Walsh, *Charleston's Sons of Liberty: A Study of the Artisans,* 1763-1789 (Columbia, 1959), p. 136.
[71] Alfred Young, "The Mechanics and the Jeffersonians, 1789-1801," *Labor History,* V (1964).
[72] "Temon," *New York Journal,* Sept. 25, 1788.

PART TWO

Slavery

6

On Turner, Beard,
and Slavery

The significance of slavery in American history is a largely unexplored theme. Despite the recent increase of interest in such topics as abolitionism, prejudice, and the plantation as a social system, these subjects tend to be kept separated (one might almost say, segregated) from the rest of American history. We have not yet begun to view slavery as a key to the meaning of our national experience.

The thesis of this essay is that the significance of slavery in American history has been obscured partly because the twin giants of modern American historiography, Frederick Jackson Turner

Reprinted with permission of the Association for the Study of Negro Life and History, Inc., from *The Journal of Negro History*, XLVIII (1963), 235-250.

and Charles Beard, systematically minimized its importance. Believing that a sentimental memory of the Civil War was being used to veil an emerging conflict between the capitalist and the common man, these two great historians went to an opposite extreme. Turner, I shall argue, attempted to shift attention from slavery to the frontier, and in so doing tended to forget that there was a Southwestern as well as a Northwestern frontier[1] and that Simon Legree was a frontier farmer. Beard, similarly, portrayed slavery both in the era of the Revolution and at the time of the Civil War as merely a form of "agrarianism." Thereby Beard blurred the fact that the Constitution was not a victory of capitalism over slavery, but a compromise between capitalism and slavery, and accomplished the difficult feat of presenting the Civil War as a revolution, while deftly moving off-stage the abolitionist revolutionaries who made it. By minimizing the significance of slavery, Turner and Beard inevitably also minimized the significance of abolitionism, and paved the way for the revisionist view of the abolitionist as an impractical fanatic.

For both Turner and Beard, the characteristic social struggle in American history was that between the Eastern financier and the Western farmer. "We may trace the contest between the capitalist and the democratic pioneer from the earliest colonial days," Turner wrote; and Beard set this quotation at the beginning of his *Economic Origins of Jeffersonian Democracy*.[2] Both were heavily influenced by the Populist Revolt of the 1890's, and tended to use the Populist analogy in interpreting earlier American history. Thus Beard entitled the chapter of his *Rise of American Civilization* which dealt with the 1780's, "Populism and Reaction." Tur-

[1] Avery Craven has commented on Turner's tendency to assume that his native Middle West was typical: "Professor Turner's chief weaknesses lay in an uneven knowledge of the varied units which made up and contributed to American life." (Introduction to Frederick Jackson Turner, *The United States, 1830-1850: The Nation and its Sections* [New York, 1935], p. vii.)

[2] Turner used this phrase in his "Social Forces in American History" (1911), *The Frontier in American History* (New York, 1920), p. 325.

ner, likewise, said in an introduction to Orin Libby's pathbreaking
study of the vote on the United States Constitution:

the present Populistic agitation finds its stronghold in those western
and southern regions whose social and economic conditions are in
many respects strikingly like those existing in 1787 in the areas that
opposed the ratification of the Constitution.[3]

The Populist analogy led both historians to believe that throughout American history "the democratic party was the agrarian element."[4] And in their histories those aristocratic agrarians, the
slaveholders of the South, quietly drop out of sight.

The ironic result was that although Turner and Beard called for
a new history written from the standpoint of "the fourth estate,
the great mass of the people,"[5] they ended in directing attention
away from the most exploited group in our history: the Negroes.
In their indifference to the Negro, Turner and Beard were typical
of Northern liberals at the turn of the century. This attitude was
also common among historians. Turner, as will appear, followed
his University of Wisconsin colleague Ulrich Phillips' appraisal
of slavery, and Beard's views on Reconstruction were akin to those
of his fellow-Columbians, Burgess and Dunning. Yet there was
special irony in the fact that as Turner and Beard were neglecting
the Negro and exalting the frontier Populist, many real Populists
in the South were building a new, if fleeting, unity between white
and Negro tenants. Equally paradoxical was the fact that the
Negro's betrayal by the Republican Party had been engineered by

[3] Orin G. Libby, *The Geographical Distribution of the Vote of the Thirteen
States on the Federal Constitution, 1787-8* (Madison, 1894), pp. vi-vii.

[4] Charles A. Beard, *An Economic Interpretation of the Constitution of the
United States* (New York, 1913), p. 258.

[5] Turner, "The Significance of History" (1891), *The Early Writings of
Frederick Jackson Turner*, ed. Everett E. Edwards and Fulmer Mood (Madison,
1938), p. 47. See also, in the same essay, Turner's description of his own time
as "the age of socialistic inquiry" which requires historians to be concerned
with "the economic basis of society in general" (*ibid.*, pp. 51-52).

the same force which Turner and Beard denounced: capitalist finance.[6] In their neglect of the Negro, therefore, Turner and Beard reflected the viewpoint of a social group which they opposed and ignored the efforts of a group which they championed; in this aspect of their writings, they stood not with the farmer but with the financier.

I.

In "The Significance of the Frontier in American History," Turner made it quite clear that he sought to displace a view of American history which stressed the struggle over slavery, a view symbolized at that time by the writing of Hermann von Holst. "When American history comes to be rightly viewed," Turner said, "it will be seen that the slavery question is an incident."[7] Earlier, in an essay called "Problems in American History," Turner had developed this idea as follows:

In commenting upon the constitutional history of a recent American writer, Professor von Holst remarks that the work is the play of *Hamlet* with Hamlet omitted, because the slavery struggle is not brought into prominence. Future critics may say of Professor von Holst's great work on the same subject that it also is the play of *Hamlet* with the title role left out, because in his attention to slavery he has lost sight of the fundamental, dominating fact in United States history, the expansion of the United States from the Alleghenies to the Pacific.

"The struggle over slavery," Turner went on, "is a most important incident in our history, but it will be seen, as the meaning of

6 The most recent study concludes: "Far from being the exclusive work of social and intellectual forces, the sectional realignment of the last quarter of the nineteenth century was largely the product of powerful economic forces. More than any other Northern groups, merchants engaged in Southern trade and Eastern industrialists frustrated Republican attempts to stress the war issues." (Stanley P. Hirshson, *Farewell to the Bloody Shirt: Northern Republicans and the Southern Negro, 1877-1893* [Bloomington, 1962], p. 252).

7 "The Significance of the Frontier in American History" (1893), *Early Writings*, p. 213.

events unfolds, that the real lines of American development, the forces dominating our character, are to be studied in the history of westward expansion"; and in his more famous essay, Turner repeated much the same thought in much the same language.[8] For a generation since 1861, slavery had been cast as the central character of the historical drama. Now, in the belief that he expressed the new needs of a new day, Turner brought the frontier forward in its stead.

The most troublesome obstacle to Turner's frontier thesis was the Southwestern frontier with its plantation pioneers. Here the covered wagons had been followed by long lines of slaves; here, as Jefferson Davis observed in 1861, it was slaves not freemen who had made farms out of the wilderness; here the structure of power was aristocratic not egalitarian;[9] here the effect of frontier life was to coarsen and brutalize the peculiar institution, not to humanize it. Great historian that he was, Turner sensed this contradiction in his argument. His answer was that there had originally existed in the Southern uplands a democratic frontier society similar to that in the Northwest, but that the advance of slavery had overlaid and destroyed it. Very briefly mentioned in "The Significance of the Frontier" as first delivered, this important corollary was expanded at no less than three points in the text when Turner revised it for subsequent publication.[10] Again and again in later writings Turner repeated the thought that originally, before "the

[8] "Problems in American History" (1892), *ibid.*, pp. 71-72. In "The Significance of the Frontier," Turner designates the period in which slavery had "primary but far from exclusive importance" as "the period from the end of the first half of the present century to the close of the Civil War": that is, merely the fifteen years 1850-1865 (*ibid.*, p. 213).

[9] For a recent, well-documented exposition of this point, see Stanley Elkins and Eric McKitrick, "A Meaning for Turner's Frontier. Part II: The Southwest Frontier and New England," *Political Science Quarterly*, LXIX (1954), 565-588.

[10] These additions are presented in an appendix to Turner's *Early Writings*, pp. 283, 285-286, 289-290.

fall" as it were, the Southern frontier like the Northern frontier had been a place of democracy and freedom.[11]

The belief that slavery was a late-coming and transitional force in the Southern interior underlay Turner's conception of Andrew Jackson, a key to the whole of Turner's thought. For Turner, Jackson was a personification of frontier ideals of "human rights" and "democracy," and Jacksonian Democracy "was based on the good fellowship and genuine social feeling of the frontier, in which classes and inequalities of fortune played little part."[12] This view of Jackson assumed a late dating of the moment when slavery overwhelmed the original Piedmont democracy and set the stamp of the plantation on the whole of the South. It presupposed that the transition (in Thomas P. Abernethy's words) "from frontier to plantation in Tennessee" had not been consummated in 1828, when Jackson was elected to the Presidency. Throughout his life Turner vigorously defended the proposition that as late as 1830 the small farmer was the dominant social type of the Southwest, his "persistent contest against slavery" still in doubt.[13]

Turner's picture of the Southwest in Jackson's day is not convincing. Professor Abernethy has recently summed up a lifetime of research on the problem with the statement that by 1820 "the slaveowning planter was now the pioneer."[14] During Turner's lifetime,

[11] See "Problems in American History" (1904), *The Significance of Sections in American History* (New York, 1932), pp. 12-13; "Is Sectionalism in America Dying Away?" (1908), *ibid.*, pp. 293-295; "The Problem of the West" (1896), *The Frontier in American History*, pp. 216-217; "The Old West" (1908), *ibid.*, pp. 91 ff., 114 ff.; "Dominant Forces in Western Life" (1897), *ibid.*, p. 241; *The Rise of the New West, 1819-1829* (New York, 1906), pp. 52-53, 183; *The United States, 1830-1850*, pp. 18, 30-31.

[12] "Contributions of the West to American Democracy" (1903), *The Frontier*, pp. 252-254; "The West and American Ideals" (1914), *ibid.*, pp. 302-303; "Western State-Making in the Revolutionary Era" (1895-1896), *Sections*, 138; *The United States, 1830-1850*, p. 30.

[13] *The United States, 1830-1860*, p. 18; "The Old West" (1908), *The Frontier*, p. 122.

[14] Thomas Perkins Abernethy, *The South in the New Nation, 1789-1819* (Baton Rouge, 1961), p. 475.

Edward Channing suggested that Jackson was a slaveholder who represented not frontier farmers but a solid slave South. In his last book Turner, with uncharacteristic passion, was still attacking Channing's thesis. "There was no 'solid South' in 1828," Turner declared and continued:[15]

> The Mississippi Valley's psychology and politics were shaped by its pioneering experience to such an extent that it had a sectional attitude of its own. It would be impossible to understand the events of Jackson's administration if we regarded that portion of the Mississippi Valley which lies south of the Ohio River, reinforced by the slaveholding state of Missouri, as a part of a 'solid South,' dominated by slaveholding cotton planters in 1828.

Hence, Turner concluded, Andrew Jackson "was not so much a cotton planter and slaveholder as a personification of Western

---

See also Abernethy, *From Frontier to Plantation in Tennessee* (Chapel Hill, 1932), p. 208:

> Slaves had been brought out by Robertson and the earliest settlers and figured in the life of the frontier stations. . . . A traveler in 1802 reported that plantations along the Knoxville road as far east as the Cumberland crossing at Cairo were within a mile or two of each other. . . . In 1795 the slave population of Middle Tennessee was more than 20 per cent of the whole, whereas in East Tennessee it was not more than 12½ per cent.

Andrew Jackson bought a Negro girl shortly after his arrival in Tennessee in 1788 *(ibid.,* p. 123).

Everett Dick, in his *The Dixie Frontier* (New York, 1948), presents similar evidence regarding Kentucky: "The first Kentucky settlers brought with them their slaves. . . . In 1777, when a census of the inhabitants of Harrodsburg, Kentucky, was taken, ten per cent of the population was slave" (p. 87; see also p. 17).

In 1820, there were more than 350,000 slaves in the states and territories of the frontier South (Kentucky, Tennessee, Alabama, Mississippi, Louisiana, Arkansas, Missouri, and western Georgia). In none were slaves less than 10 per cent of the total population; in Mississippi and Louisiana they were more than 40 per cent. (For these statistics, see Bureau of the Census, *A Century of Population Growth* . . . [Washington, 1909], pp. 82, 133, 222). Wagon trains moving west with their slaves about 1820 are described, e.g., by Abernethy, *The Formative Period in Alabama, 1815-1828* (Montgomery, 1922), p. 26, and by Timothy Flint, *Recollections of the Last Ten Years* (Boston, 1826), p. 201.

[15] *The United States, 1830-1850*, pp. 31-32.

wishes and Western will." In the evaluation of Jackson, Turner's desire to center attention on Westward expansion met head-on with the fact of slavery which he wished to ignore. Turner was much more willing to recognize the influence on Jacksonian Democracy of the Eastern workingman[16] and the capitalist entrepreneur,[17] than he was to concede the influence of the Southern slaveholder.[18]

Turner's conception of a diversified South wore a more unpleasant aspect as he applied it to the South of his own day. The old division of the South into democratic upland and aristocratic Black Belt still revealed itself, said Turner, in primary elections "in which the negro issue is eliminated," although that division had been "obliterated in large measure in the era of civil war and reconstruction and in the later Solid South under the influence of the negro problem."[19] Is it merely hyper-sensitiveness that makes the reader today perceive in these words a wish that not only "the Negro problem" but the Negro himself could, somehow, be "eliminated" from

[16] As early as 1896, Turner followed his famous statement that American democracy "came, stark and strong and full of life, from the American forest," with the sentence: "But the triumph of this Western democracy revealed also the fact that it could rally to its aid the laboring classes of the coast, then just beginning to acquire self-consciousness and organization" ("The Problem of the West" [1896], *The Frontier*, p. 216). Turner never lost sight of the workingman; see "Social Forces in American History" (1911), *ibid.*, pp. 326-327; "The West and American Ideals" (1914), *ibid.*, p. 303; "Middle Western Pioneer Democracy" (1918), *ibid.*, pp. 347-348; *The United States, 1830-1850*, pp. 578-579.

[17] Turner discussed the conception that Jacksonian Democracy was essentially a movement of "expectant capitalists" in "Middle Western Pioneer Democracy" (1918), *The Frontier*, pp. 342-343, and in *The United States, 1830-1850*, p. 20.

[18] Compare Arthur Schlesinger, Jr.'s brilliant but essentially unsuccessful attempt to explain away the ties between Jacksonian Democracy and the slave South in his *The Age of Jackson* (Boston, 1945), e.g., pp. 407-410, 424-427, 490-493, 505-507.

[19] "Geographical Influences in American Political History" (1914), *Sections*, p. 190.

the American scene? Perhaps not; for coincidentally with the founding of the National Association for the Advancement of Colored People, Turner was writing:[20]

the negro is still the problem of the South and while he remains there will be a Southern sectionalism. If the negro were removed, it seems not unlikely that the unity of the Mississippi Valley would once more have free play.

Turner went so far as to perceive in the triumph of the red neck and Jim Crow a victory for frontier egalitarianism. "Along the Southern Atlantic and the Gulf Coast," he wrote in 1914,[21]

in spite of the preservative influence of the negro, whose presence has always called out resistance to change on the part of the whites, the forces of social and industrial transformation are at work. The old tide-water aristocracy has surrendered to the up-country democrats.

Only a man profoundly insensitive to the experience of one-fifth of his fellow-citizens could have spoken, in 1904, of "the wonderful development of the nation since the Reconstruction period," or could have called the generation 1889-1924 "these marvelous years."[22]

Tolerance toward the institution of slavery and intolerance toward the abolitionist movement are attitudes usually found together, for they support and supplement each other. So it was with Turner. As early as 1906, Turner accepted the authority of Ulrich Phillips on slavery; and almost a generation later, at the end of his life, the historian of democracy still shared Phillips' conception of "the presence of the negro" and "slavery as the mode of dealing

[20] "Is Sectionalism in America Dying Away?" (1908), *ibid.*, p. 307.

[21] "The West and American Ideals" (1914), *The Frontier*, p. 295.

[22] "Problems in American History" (1904), *Sections*, p. 19; "Since the Foundation" (1924), *ibid.*, p. 215.

with the negro" (the phrases are Turner's).[23] Most explicitly, Turner wrote:[24]

It would seem that Northern men, in their conclusion that the slave was unhappy, tended to attribute to him their own feelings and reactions to the conditions under which he lived. In general, he was sufficiently fed, with a coarse diet, adequately clothed, but poorly housed (though not to such a degree as to produce discontent in the slave's mind), and allowed opportunity for expressing the natural joyousness of the African temperament; and hardship was felt rather by individuals than by the mass of slaves.

Abolitionism, accordingly, was mentioned by Turner (on the rare occasions when he mentioned it at all) as a diversion of the energies of American reform from its proper ends. Thus he wrote in his last book of "the diversion of the reformers to the abolition issue," as earlier he had insisted that the struggle over slavery and Reconstruction was "only one of the interests" of the years 1850-1870.[25]

It would have been difficult for any historian who identified himself so completely with the advance of the white settler across the continent to avoid insensitivity toward the victims of this process. Though he departed from the emphasis on Teutonic institutions prominent in the late nineteenth century, Turner did not altogether escape the biological presuppositions of the "germ" theory. "American colonization," he wrote in the early 1890's, "is part of a great historic movement—the Aryan migrations."[26] The American Indian was for Turner an obstacle in the path: Red Cloud of the Sioux, for example, was described by Turner as one who resisted "the march of civilization."[27] Most flagrant, perhaps because Turner's hero Jackson was involved, was Turner's attitude toward

[23] *Rise of the New West*, p. xvii; *The United States, 1830-1850*, pp. 149n., 209.

[24] *Ibid.*, p. 167.

[25] *Ibid.*, p. 589; "Social Forces in American History" (1911), *The Frontier*, p. 330.

[26] Introduction to extension lectures (1891), quoted in *Early Writings*, p. 33n.

[27] "The Middle West," *The Frontier*, p. 144.

the removal of the Cherokees from Georgia. His account of the expulsion of this civilized nation, possessed of an alphabet, a newspaper, and a written constitution, began as follows: "From the beginning of the nation, the Indians on the borders of the settled area of Georgia were a menace and an obstacle to her development."[28] Turner was, in fact, very much a believer in Manifest Destiny. Thus he wrote:[29]

De Tocqueville exclaimed, with reason, in 1833: "This gradual and continuous progress of the European race toward the Rocky Mountains has the solemnity of a providential event. It is like a deluge of men, rising unabatedly, and driven daily onward by the hand of God."

Such blindness was not the whole of Frederick Jackson Turner's vision. But it restricted Turner's range as a historian. It confined his sympathies to those of his countrymen who were also white, and cut him off from the new viewpoints toward American history suggested by the experience of "the fugitive slave, and the Mexican prisoner on parole, and the Indian come to plead the wrongs of his race."[30]

II.

Charles Beard did not share the quasi-racist attitude toward the Negro expressed by the older, more provincial Turner. He did view the Negro's role in American history as altogether passive: thus he characterized the attitude of slaves during the Civil War as a blend of contentment, affection for their owners, inertia, and helplessness.[31] But Beard's essential disservice to the effort to grasp what American slavery means for American his-

[28] See the combined excerpts from Turner's writings on the Cherokee removal in *The Removal of the Cherokee Nation*, ed. Louis Filler and Allen Guttmann (Boston, 1962), pp. 102-105.

[29] "The Middle West," *The Frontier*, p. 153.

[30] The quoted phrase is, of course, from Henry David Thoreau's *Essay on Civil Disobedience*.

[31] Charles and Mary Beard, *The Rise of American Civilization* (New York, 1927), II, 116. At the same point Beard says of the slaves before the Civil War: "At any rate they had made no striking development in intelligence."

tory lay in his view of slavery as an economic system. Beard's approach to slavery, whether in the era of the American Revolution or in the period of the Civil War, was characterized above all by a tendency to regard slavery as merely a form of "agrarianism." In analyzing the social conflicts of both these American revolutions, Beard was inclined to lump together three very different groups: frontier subsistence farmers, Northern commercial farmers, and Southern plantation-owners.

One of the confusions resulting from Beard's use of the term "agrarianism" was a blurring of the distinction between subsistence and commercial farmers. Orin G. Libby had labored to make this distinction in his work on the ratification of the Constitution, concluding that farmers who lived near cities or near navigable rivers were for the most part Federalists. Beard's insistence on the conflict of capitalism and agrarianism (or as he put it in *An Economic Interpretation of the Constitution*, "personalty" and "realty") left little place for the commercial farmer, whose importance had recently to be re-emphasized by Jackson Main.[32] In the era of the Civil War, too, many farmers, far from opposing capitalism, "saw their futures linked" with industrial and commercial development.[33]

More fundamental was Beard's failure to distinguish the freehold farmer with his 200 acres from the slaveholding planter. The *locus classicus* for Beard's attitude is his analysis of the Civil War in *The Rise of American Civilization*. Describing the irrepressible conflict as one between Northern capitalism and Southern agrarianism, Beard argued that "the institution of slavery was not the fundamental issue" on the ground that no major political party, including the Republican Party of 1860, put the abolition of slavery

[32] Jackson T. Main, *The Antifederalists: Critics of the Constitution, 1781-1788* (Chapel Hill, 1961), pp. 270-274.

[33] Eugene D. Genovese, "The Significance of the Slave Plantation for Southern Economic Development," *Journal of Southern History*, XXVIII (1962), 427.

in its platform.[34] This was strange reasoning for a historian whose stock-in-trade was to discern the economic motives which underlay men's declared intentions. And why did Beard take at face value the planks on tariffs, railroads, and homesteads in the platform of the Republican Party, but disregard the equally explicit statements of Alexander Stephens and Jefferson Davis that slavery was the cornerstone of the Confederacy?

What is at issue here is not economic interpretation as such. Obviously an economic interpretation is possible which stresses slavery, rather than minimizing it. As Thomas Pressly observes,[35] no less an economic interpreter than Karl Marx poured scorn on the belief that the tariff caused the war; Marx, unlike Beard, regarded the abolitionists as heroes, and considered the war's central issue to be the survival of democracy (albeit "bourgeois democracy") in America and all over the world.[36] Thus Beard did not propose an analysis which followed inevitably from an emphasis on economics. Beard's theory of the Civil War, like Turner's theory of the frontier, was distinctive not so much because it was economic, as because it attacked a previously-prevailing theory based on slavery.

If for Beard the Civil War was a bloodbath inspired by sordid motives, Reconstruction was an equally self-interested attempt by Northern capitalists to ensure the fruits of victory. Don Fehrenbacher comments that "by disparaging the outcome of the war and the motives of Radical Republicanism, the Beard thesis tended to merge with the Dunning interpretation of Reconstruction."[37] Particularly noteworthy is Beard's remark about Negro suffrage in the

[34] Beard, *Rise of American Civilization*, II, 40.

[35] Thomas J. Pressly, *Americans Interpret Their Civil War* (Princeton, 1954), p. 216.

[36] See Karl Marx and Friedrich Engels, *The Civil War in the United States* (New York, 1937), pp. 13, 58-59, 202-206, 255, 258, 279.

[37] Don E. Fehrenbacher, "Disunion and Reunion," *The Reconstruction of American History*, ed. John Higham (New York, 1962), p. 110.

Reconstruction period, that it "was tried with results which, to a large degree, would have been ludicrous if they had not been pitiable."[38] Beard's shallow and essentially uninterested attitude toward the adventure of Black Reconstruction is another illustration of the point made earlier, that to minimize the significance of slavery is to miss the meaning of the struggle against slavery, too.

Less obvious is the fact that Beard also neglected the impact of slavery in his most famous historical analysis, *An Economic Interpretation of the Constitution of the United States.* Here Beard's self-alienation from the abolitionist tradition cost him dearly, for he neglected entirely the abolitionist critique of the Constitution as a covenant with death and an agreement with hell because of its compromise with slavery. Beard noted the clauses of the Constitution protecting slavery; but slavery as an independent force in the shaping and ratification of the document escaped him, because it could not be fitted into the conflict of capitalism and agrarianism which, in this connection as in others, he considered quintessential.

Precise in so much else, Beard's famous book is strangely vague and confused in its handling of slavery. Was property in slaves "personalty" or "realty"? Beard wavered. In the chapter on "The Economic Interests of the Members of the Convention," Beard listed fifteen members of the Convention who owned "personalty in slaves."[39] But in the earlier chapter on "A Survey of Economic Interests in 1787," Beard classed "the slaveholders of the south" as "real property holders," and did not include slaveholding among the various "groups of personal property interests."[40]

This ambiguity in the economic analysis of slavery led to confusion in Beard's treatment of the politics of the slaveholders in the ratification struggle. Indeed, it would be more accurate to say that Beard nowhere squarely confronted the question of whether the Southern slaveholders were Federalists or Antifederalists. In survey-

---

[38] *American Government and Politics* (New York, 1910), p. 86.
[39] *Economic Interpretation*, p. 151.
[40] *Ibid.*, pp. 29-30.

ing the ratification process in the several states, Beard built on
Libby's conclusion that voters favoring the Constitution were concentrated near the coast. Libby's map should have made clear
to Beard what has since been demonstrated in detail, that the great
slaveholders were for the most part Federalist,[41] but when two
years later he committed himself on the matter in the *Economic
Origins of Jeffersonian Democracy* Beard came down on the wrong
side.

Critics of Beard's work on the Constitution have made inadequate use of the *Economic Origins*, at the end of which Beard
summarized the conclusions of both his books on the foundation
of our national government. In this summary, Beard began by presenting the familiar capitalist-agrarian dualism.[42]

> It is established upon a statistical basis that the Constitution of the
> United States was the product of a conflict between capitalistic and
> agrarian interests. The support for the adoption of the Constitution
> came principally from the cities and regions where the commercial,
> financial, manufacturing, and speculative interests were concentrated
> and the bulk of the opposition came from the small farming and debtor
> classes, particularly those back from the sea board.

From this opening statement Beard went on in subsequent paragraphs to reiterate his view that the core of both the Antifederalists
of 1788 and the Jeffersonian Republicans of 1800 was made up of
"backwoods agrarians" and "farmers." But then came a new
thought, evidently the fruit of grappling with the role of Jefferson:
the idea of "the agrarian masses led by an aristocracy of slave-own-

---

[41] See Main, *Antifederalists*, pp. 219n., 232, 245. It is possible that Beard
picked up the idea that Southern slaveholders largely opposed the Constitution
from Federalist polemics of the 1790's. Thus Fisher Ames wrote to George
Richards Minot, Nov. 30, 1791, that "the men of weight in the four southern
States (Charleston city excepted) were more generally *antis*" (*Works of Fisher
Ames* . . ., ed. Seth Ames [Boston, 1854], I, 103.)

[42] *Economic Origins of Jeffersonian Democracy* (New York, 1915), pp.
464-465.

ing planters."[43] At this point Beard finally brought into the structure of his analysis the slaveholding planters of the South.

Beard analyzed the relations of frontier farmers to plantation owners at one other place in the *Economic Origins*. Turner, we recall, had set these two groups in fiercest opposition, and Beard himself conceded that antagonism between them was "natural." But, Beard went on, "in a conflict with capitalism, the agrarians rallied around that agrarian class which had the cultural equipment for dominant direction," and so, by "a curious freak of fortune," the most aristocratic group in the nation became the spokesman for frontier democracy.[44] This was a suggestive formulation. It helped to explain how slaveowning Andrew Jackson had become a spokesman for the hill farmers of Tennessee. But it did *not* explain why the Southern slaveholders, enemies of Hamiltonian Federalism in 1800, had worked with the Federalists to make the Constitution in 1787. Beard wrongly supposed that the clash of 1800 was a continuation of the alignment of 1787, whereas in fact the party battles of the 1790's represented a breaking-up of the coalition which drafted and promoted the Constitution.

Adequately to explain the forces behind the Constitution, Beard would have had to jettison his fundamental dichotomy of "personalty" and "realty," and to recognize that men of wealth, rural as well as urban, had joined to make a stronger national government. This would have been just as "economic" an interpretation as the interpretation Beard proposed.[45] But Beard like Turner was wedded

[43] *Economic Origins*, pp. 466-467.

[44] *Ibid.*, pp. 398-399. Schlesinger repeats this formulation in his *Age of Jackson*, p. 20: "Only in the planting South did agriculture possess concentrated holdings, alert leadership and a compulsion to run the state. To the Southern planters thus fell the main responsibility of opposing the Hamiltonian tendencies in the government." Beard himself quotes Richard Hildreth, *History of the United States of America* (1856 edition), IV, 348-350.

[45] E. James Ferguson, for example, interprets the Constitution from an economic standpoint but sharply disavows Beard's dichotomy of "personalty" and "realty" ("The Forces Behind the Constitution," *William and Mary Quarterly*, third series, XIX [1962], 436).

to a particular economic interpretation which aligned all agrarians, rich or poor, freehold-farming or plantation-owning, against capitalism. And so, Beard failed to see that the Constitution was a compromise between capitalists and slaveholders, the product as much of James Madison and the South Carolina Pinckneys as of Hamilton, Gouverneur Morris and James Wilson.

Two scraps of evidence suggest that Beard was uneasy with his resolution of the role of slavery in early American politics, and might have modified his thinking. In a footnote to his *Economic Origins*, Beard promised that "a fuller review of the political economy of the Republicans after the inaugural of Jefferson will be given in a forthcoming volume on agrarianism and slavocracy."[46] Twenty years later, in a preface to the second edition of *An Economic Interpretation*, Beard demonstrated his flexibility by acknowledging that the great landlords of the Hudson valley, whom in 1913-1915 he classified as Antifederalists, had in fact supported the Constitution. But a similar confrontation with the politics of the plantation-owners never took place. Two years after the publication of his book on Jeffersonian Democracy, Beard resigned from Columbia University on the issue of free speech and never returned to original research on the early national period.

III.

In summary, it is clear that Turner and Beard sought to turn the attention of historians away from slavery toward the struggle of "capitalism" with "agrarianism." Much was gained thereby; but any sharply-defined insight must throw some things into shadow as it illuminates others, and the effect of the neglect of slavery by Turner and Beard has been to postpone the day when slavery will be recognized as one of the two or three distinctive themes of the American experience. When that day comes, it will seem grotesque that historians of the 1950's proposed "equality" as the concept which best enclosed the meaning of American his-

[46] *Economic Origins*, p. 440n.

tory, or found the uniqueness of the American story in the absence of feudalism, while forgetting the presence of slavery.

It is past time for American historians to expose themselves to the presence of slavery, to the full force and the pain of it. Only then can they begin to understand the meaning for all American history of the great and terrible reality which the Founding Fathers of this country did not hesitate to call its original sin.

7

The Abolitionist Critique
of the United States
Constitution

"The Constitution of the United States.—What is it? Who made it? For whom and for what was it made?" So Frederick Douglass wrote in his paper *The North Star* in 1849.[1]

It was natural for abolitionists to ask these questions. Their efforts to uproot the peculiar institution were continually frustrated by clauses of the United States Constitution: by Article I, Section 2, which gave the South disproportionate strength in the House of Representatives by adding three-fifths of the slaves to the number of white persons in apportioning Congressmen to the several states; by Article I, Section 8, which gave Congress the power to suppress insurrections; by Article I, Section 9, which postponed prohibition

---

[1] "The Constitution and Slavery," *The North Star*, March 16, 1849, from *The Life and Writings of Frederick Douglass*, ed. Philip Foner (New York, 1950), I, 362.

Reprinted from *The Antislavery Vanguard: New Essays on the Abolitionists*, ed. Martin Duberman (Princeton, 1965), 209-239.

of the slave trade until twenty years after the Constitution's adoption; by Article IV, Section 2, which provided for the return of fugitive slaves. Little wonder, then, that John Stuart Mill could say that "abolitionists, in America, mean those who do not keep within the Constitution."[2]

Like the Progressives in a subsequent generation, abolitionists sought to undermine the Constitution's authority. When in 1840 James Madison's notes on the proceedings of the Constitutional Convention were published, abolitionists seized on them to show in detail what they had long suspected: that the revered Constitution was a sordid sectional compromise, in Garrison's words "a covenant with death and an agreement with hell."

On this as on all other policy questions there were a variety of abolitionist views, not a single party line. Abolitionists who believed in political action were naturally reluctant to condemn the Constitution root and branch. Political abolitionists tended to stress the document's preamble, with its promise to "establish Justice . . . promote the general Welfare, and secure the Blessings of Liberty to ourselves and our Posterity," and to explain away the enabling clauses previously cited. Richard Hildreth, for example, argued that the fugitive slave clause was intended to refer only to apprentices and indentured servants; and on the eve of the Civil War Douglass asserted that the three-fifths clause "leans to freedom."[3]

It was the Garrisonian wing of the movement, therefore, which produced the most rigorous critique of the United States Constitution. These men saw the Constitution as a patchwork of incompatible parts. It was, said Wendell Phillips, "a wall hastily built, in hard times, of round boulders"; it was an artificial, not a natural

[2] John Stuart Mill, *Dissertations and Discussions: Political, Philosophical, and Historical* (New York, 1882), I, 11.

[3] Richard Hildreth, *Despotism in America: An Inquiry into the Nature, Results, and Legal Basis of the Slave-Holding System in the United States* (Boston, 1854), pp. 235-239; Douglass, "The Constitution of the United States: Is it Pro-Slavery or Anti-Slavery?", March 26, 1860, *Life and Writings*, II, 472.

growth; it was "a 'hodge-podge,' . . . a general mess, a bowl of punch, of all the institutions of the nation."[4] Douglass, while still a Garrisonian, contended that no man could consistently take an oath to uphold the Constitution, for the Constitution was contradictory. "Liberty and Slavery—opposite as Heaven and Hell—are both in the Constitution; and the oath to support the latter," Douglass wrote,

is an oath to perform that which God has made impossible. The man that swears to support it vows allegiance to two masters—so opposite, that fidelity to the one is, necessarily, treachery to the other. If we adopt the preamble, with Liberty and Justice, we must repudiate the enacting clauses, with Kidnapping and Slaveholding. . . .

Garrison and Calhoun, Douglass continued, both saw the real nature of the Constitution. "Garrison sees in the Constitution precisely what John C. Calhoun sees there—a compromise with Slavery—a bargain between the North and the South; the former to free his soul from the guilt of slaveholding, repudiates the bond; and the latter, seeing the weakness of mere parchment guarantees, . . . seeks a dissociation of the Union as his only means of safety."[5]

The analysis of the Constitution by abolitionist publicists was given more scholarly form in such works as Richard Hildreth's *History of the United States of America* (Vol. III, 1849), George Ticknor Curtis' *History of the . . . Constitution of the United States* (Vol. II, 1858), Horace Greeley's *The American Conflict* (1864), and Henry Wilson's *Rise and Fall of the Slave Power in America* (1872). Like Beard, the abolitionist historians believed that the American Revolution was betrayed by what Horace Greeley called a "counterrevolution."[6] But they saw the Revolution betrayed by

[4] Wendell Phillips, "Disunion," January 20, 1861; "Progress," February 17, 1861; "The State of the Country," January 21 and May 11, 1863 (*Speeches, Lectures and Letters* [Boston, 1863], pp. 351, 375, 537).

[5] *The North Star,* April 5, 1850, *Life and Writings,* II, 118.

[6] Horace Greeley, *The American Conflict: A History of the Great Rebellion . . .* (Hartford, 1864), I, 53.

its compromise with slavery rather than by its compromise with capitalism. These scholars established the tradition according to which the Constitutional Convention experienced two great crises: one in late June and early July concerning the basis of representation in Congress; the other, in mid-August, arising from the questions of slave importation and the power of the Federal government over commerce. In this canon the settlement of the two great crises was accomplished by two (or, if one counted separately the agreement about representation in the House and the agreement about representation in the Senate, three) great compromises. The first compromise, of course, was that which gave the states equal representation in the Senate and apportioned representation in the House on the basis of a "Federal ratio" adding three-fifths of the slaves to the white population; the second compromise permitted the importation of slaves until 1808 while making it possible for Congress to pass laws regulating commerce by a simple majority. This way of looking at the Constitutional Convention was concisely summarized by James Schouler in his *History of the United States of America under the Constitution,* which appeared during the last two decades of the nineteenth century.[7]

In 1903, in a paper delivered before the American Historical Association, Max Farrand undertook to correct this traditional account. "It can not be too strongly emphasized," Farrand argued, "that in 1787 the slavery question was not the important question, we might say it was not the moral question that it was in 1850." Stressing the fact that Madison's notes on the Convention had been published in 1840 in the midst of controversy over slavery, Farrand remarked that "it is not surprising that the historical writers of that time, in treating of the formation of the Constitution,

[7] For early enumeration of the compromises, see Richard Hildreth, *The History of the United States of America* (New York, 1849), III, 520; George Ticknor Curtis, "The Constitution of the United States, and its History," *Narrative and Critical History of America,* ed. Justin Winsor (Boston and New York, 1888), VII, 238-239, 243-244; James Schouler, *History of the United States of America, under the Constitution,* I (New York, 1880), 41-42.

should overemphasize the slavery questions in the Convention."
In this paper, and more fully ten years later in his *Framing of the
Constitution of the United States*, Farrand attacked the view that
the important compromises at the Convention were compromises
over slavery. The three-fifths ratio, he said, had been devised in
1783 and accepted by eleven states before the Convention met:
thus it was not really a Convention compromise. The bargain over
slave importation and commercial laws was a compromise of the
Convention, but less important than a number of others, such as
those concerning the admission of new states and the mode of
electing the President.[8]

Farrand's revision of the abolitionist critique found a ready response in an America which was accepting the new Jim Crow laws
and beginning to rewrite the history of Reconstruction. Frederick
Jackson Turner anticipated Farrand when, in the 1890's, he insisted
that the frontier rather than slavery was the major theme of the
American experience.[9] Beard, iconoclast though he was, gave slavery and slaveholders a most shadowy role in his analysis of the Constitution: he was uncertain whether slaves were "personalty" or
"realty"; he nowhere commits himself as to whether Southern slaveholders, as a group, were for or against the Constitution; he ignores
almost entirely the profound sectional antagonisms evident in the
debates of the Convention and of the state ratifying conventions.
Thus Beard in his 1913 classic built on Farrand's analysis.[10] In
1923, Robert Livingston Schuyler repeated the gist of Farrand's
conclusions in his *Constitution of the United States*.[11] In 1935,
Andrew C. McLaughlin concurred, writing: "In later years the
Constitution was spoken of as if it were a compact or agreement

[8] Max Farrand, "Compromises of the Constitution," *Annual Report of the
American Historical Association for the Year 1903* (Washington, D.C.; 1904), I,
73-84.

[9] [See Essay 6, Part I.]

[10] [See Essay 6, Part II.]

[11] Robert Livingston Schuyler, *The Constitution of the United States* (New
York, 1923), p. 100.

between the slave states and the free. Nothing can be more false to the fact."[12] As emphasis on slavery had dominated treatment of the Constitution from 1840 to 1900, so a neglect of slavery's role prevailed from the turn of the century to World War II.

More recently, a return toward the abolitionist critique has been evident. Even before the war Charles Warren had suggested, as a consideration "which historians have failed to emphasize," that sectional hostility explains much of the Antifederalist resistance to the Constitution.[13] And the anti-Beardian historians of the 1950's, while insisting that the Constitution was more democratic than Beard supposed, have also (rather inconsistently) brought the question of slavery back into the foreground of debate. One summary of the new revisionism states that "the really fundamental conflict in American society at the time . . . [was] the division between slave and free states, between North and South."[14] The floor would thus seem to be open for a detailed reconsideration of the abolitionist contention that, in the words of Gouverneur Morris at the Convention, "Domestic slavery is the most prominent feature in the aristocratic countenance of the . . . Constitution."[15]

I.

According to the abolitionist critique, slavery helped to shape the Constitution because slavery was the basis of conflict between North and South, and compromising that conflict was the main work of the Constitutional Convention.[16]

[12] Andrew C. McLaughlin, A Constitutional History of the United States (New York, 1935), p. 190.

[13] Charles Warren, The Making of the Constitution (Boston, 1928), pp. 23-30, 755-758.

[14] Robert E. Brown, Reinterpretation of the Formation of the American Constitution (Boston, 1963), p. 48.

[15] The Records of the Federal Convention of 1787, ed. Max Farrand (New Haven, London; 1911), II, 222.

[16] My emphasis on sectional conflict in the Revolutionary period follows John R. Alden's The First South (Baton Rouge, La.; 1961). The corollary contention that slavery was not dying in 1787 is strongly supported by Robert

Both in the nineteenth and twentieth centuries, one line of argument against the significance of slavery in the genesis of the Constitution has stressed the fact that the words "slave" and "slavery" do not appear in the Constitution, and contended that, to quote Farrand, "there was comparatively little said on the subject [of slavery] in the convention."[17] This might be called the argument from silence.

But we *know* why the Founders did not use the words "slave" and "slavery" in the Constitution. Paterson of New Jersey stated in the Convention that when, in 1783, the Continental Congress changed its eighth Article of Confederation so that slaves would henceforth be included in apportioning taxation among the States, the Congress "had been ashamed to use the term 'Slaves' & had substituted a description." Iredell, in the North Carolina ratifying convention, said similarly that the fugitive slave clause of the proposed Constitution did not use the word "slave" because of the "particular scruples" of the "northern delegates"; and in 1798 Dayton of New Jersey, who had been a member of the Convention, told the House of Representatives that the purpose was to avoid any "stain" on the new government.[18] If for Northern delegates the motive was shame, for Southern members of the Convention it was prudence. Madison wrote to Lafayette in 1830, referring to emancipation: "I scarcely express myself too strongly in saying, that any allusion in the Convention to the subject you have so much at heart would have been a spark to a mass of gunpowder."[19] Madi-

---

McColley's *Slavery and Jeffersonian Virginia* (Urbana, 1964), and by Melvin Drimmer in "Was Slavery Dying Before the Cotton Gin?", a paper read before the American Historical Association, December 1964.

[17] Max Farrand, *The Framing of the Constitution of the United States* (New Haven, London; 1911), p. 110.

[18] *Records of the Convention*, I, 561 (Paterson), III, 377 (Dayton); *The Debates in the Several State Conventions, on the Adoption of the Federal Constitution*, ed. Jonathan Elliot, second edition (Washington, D.C.; 1836), IV, 182 (Iredell).

[19] James Madison to General LaFayette, February 1, 1830, *Letters and Other Writings of James Madison* (Philadelphia, 1865), IV, 60.

son's metaphor hardly suggests that the subject of slavery was of secondary importance to the Convention.

Farrand's own magnificent edition of the Convention records amply refutes his contention that the subject of slavery was little discussed. The South Carolinians in particular were often on their feet demanding security for what one of them called "this species of property."[20] And yet the role of slavery in the Convention went much further than this. For we have it on Madison's authority that it was "pretty well understood" that the "institution of slavery & its consequences formed the line of discrimination" between the contending groups of States in the Convention.[21] Slavery, that is to say, was recognized as the basis of sectionalism; and it is not a difficult task to show that sectional conflict between North and South was the major tension in the Convention.

According to Franklin, debate in the Convention proceeded peaceably ("with great coolness & temper") until, on June 11, the rule of suffrage in the national legislature was discussed.[22] Farrand would have us believe that the three-fifths ratio which resulted was not a compromise in the Convention, that it had been recommended by Congress in 1783 and adopted by eleven states before the Convention met, and was part of the original New Jersey Plan.[23] Farrand's statement is misleading, however, for all the above remarks refer to counting three-fifths of the slaves *in apportioning taxation*. What was at issue in Convention was the *extension of this ratio to representation*: what George Ticknor Curtis called "the naked question whether the slaves should be included as persons, and in the proportion of three fifths, in the census for

[20] *Records of the Convention*, III, 254. See also *ibid.*, I, 534, 542, 594, 605; II, 95, 364, 371-373; III, 135, 378.

[21] *Ibid.*, II, 10.

[22] *Ibid.*, I, 197. The question had been postponed on May 30 and again on June 9.

[23] Farrand, *Framing of the Constitution*, pp. 107-108. For the New Jersey Plan, see *Records of the Convention*, I, 242-245.

the future apportionment of representatives among the States."[24] The two applications were very different. As Luther Martin told the Maryland legislature, taxing slaves discouraged slavery, while giving them political representation encouraged it.[25] Thus tempers rose in the Convention from the moment that Rutledge and Butler of South Carolina asserted that representation in the House should be according to quotas of contribution; years later Rufus King observed that the three-fifths clause "was, at the time, believed to be a great [concession] and has proved to have been the greatest which was made to secure the adoption of the constitution."[26]

On June 25 there occurred the first perfectly sectional vote of the Convention, the five States from Maryland to Georgia voting to postpone consideration of the election of the Senate until the three-fifths clause regarding elections for the House had been settled. On June 29, Madison made the first of many statements as to the sectional nature of the issue:

> If there was real danger, I would give the smaller states the defensive weapons.—But there is none from that quarter. The great danger to our general government *is the great southern and northern interests of the continent, being opposed to each other. Look to the votes in congress, and most of them stand divided by the geography of the country, not according to the size of the states.* (Italics in original.)[27]

The next day Madison reiterated that "the States were divided into different interests not by their difference of size, but by other circumstances; the most material of which resulted partly from cli-

[24] *History of the . . . Constitution of the United States* (New York, 1858), II, 153.

[25] *Records of the Convention*, III, 197.

[26] Speech in the Senate, March 1819, *ibid.*, III, 428-430. While Farrand presents the compromise regarding representation in the Senate as more important than the adoption of the three-fifths rule for elections to the House, a South Carolina delegate said that "the rule of Representation in the 1st. branch was the true condition of that in the 2d. branch" (*ibid.*, II, 263).

[27] *Ibid.*, I, 476.

mate, but principally from the effects of their having or not having slaves."[28] Farrand comments on these observations that "Madison was one of the very few men who seemed to appreciate the real division of interests in this country."[29] Yet Madison's emphasis on sectional conflict at the Convention was echoed by Pinckney on July 2, by King on July 10, by Mason on July 11, and, with reluctance, by Gouverneur Morris on July 13; and when on July 14 Madison once more asserted that slavery, not size, formed the line of discrimination between the States, as previously remarked he said that this was "pretty well understood" by the Convention.[30] Slavery was thus the basis of the great Convention crisis, when, as Gouverneur Morris later said, the fate of America was suspended by a hair.

But this crisis, and the crisis which followed over the import of slaves,[31] cannot be understood from the records of the Convention alone. The great Convention compromises involving slavery were attempts to reconcile disputes which had been boiling up for years in the Continental Congress.

II.

Sectional conflict, like the ghost in *Hamlet*, was there from the beginning. When in September 1774 at the first Continental Congress Patrick Henry made his famous declaration "I am not a Virginian, but an American," the point he was making was that Virginia would not insist on counting slaves in apportion-

[28] *Ibid.*, I, 486.

[29] *Framing of the Constitution*, p. 110. This statement is a little difficult to reconcile with Farrand's general position that slavery was not an important issue in 1787.

[30] *Records of the Convention*, I, 510, 566, 578, 586, 604.

[31] As to the magnitude of the crisis over slave importation, George Bancroft concluded that had it not been compromised Georgia, South Carolina, North Carolina and Virginia would have formed a Southern confederacy (*History of the Formation of the Constitution of the United States of America* [New York, 1882], II, 157).

ing representation; Henry's next sentence was: "Slaves are to be thrown out of the Question, and if the freemen can be represented according to their Numbers I am satisfyed."[32] The next speaker, Lynch of South Carolina, protested, and the question was left unsettled. Thus early did South Carolinian intransigence overbear Virginian liberalism.

Again in July 1776, the month of the Declaration of Independence, the problem of slave representation was brought before Congress in the debate over the proposed Articles of Confederation. The Dickinson draft of the Articles produced three controversies, strikingly similar to the three great compromises of the subsequent Constitutional Convention: "The equal representation of all the states in Congress aroused the antagonism of the larger states. The apportionment of common expenses according to total population aroused the bitter opposition of the states with large slave populations. The grant to Congress of broad powers over Western lands and boundaries was resisted stubbornly by the states whose charters gave them large claims to the West."[33] In the remainder of its existence the Continental Congress succeeded in solving only the last of these controversies, the question of Western lands, and accordingly emphasis has tended to fall on it in histories of the Confederation. But the other two problems were just as hotly debated, in much the same language as in 1787; and on these questions, as Channing observes, there was a "different alignment in Congress" than on the matter of Western lands: a sectional alignment.[34]

The eleventh article of the Dickinson draft stated that money contributions from the states should be "in Proportion to the Number of Inhabitants of every Age, Sex and Quality, except Indians

[32] *Diary and Autobiography of John Adams*, ed. Lyman H. Butterfield (Cambridge, Mass.; 1961), II, 125.

[33] Merrill Jensen, *The Articles of Confederation: An Interpretation of the Social-Constitutional History of the American Revolution, 1774-1781* (Madison, 1940), pp. 138-139.

[34] Edward Channing, *A History of the United States* (New York, 1912), III, 451.

not paying Taxes." On July 30, 1776, Samuel Chase of Maryland (later a prominent Antifederalist) moved the insertion of the word "white," arguing that "if Negroes are taken into the Computation of Numbers to ascertain Wealth, they ought to be in settling the Representation"; Gouverneur Morris would use this same formula in July 1787 to resolve the deadlock over representation in the House.[35] In the debate which followed, the changes were rung upon several themes of the Constitutional Convention. Wilson of Pennsylvania said that to exempt slaves from taxation would encourage slaveholding; in response to the observation that if slaves were counted, Northern sheep should also be counted, Benjamin Franklin remarked that "sheep will never make any Insurrections"; Rutledge of South Carolina anticipated the August 1787 debate on navigation laws by warning that "the Eastern Colonies will become the Carriers for the Southern. They will obtain Wealth for which they will not be taxed"; and his colleague Lynch again threw down a South Carolina ultimatum: "If it is debated, whether their Slaves are their Property, there is an end of the Confederation."[36]

The war had scarcely ended when the sectional debate resumed. We tend to think of Thomas Jefferson as a national statesman, and of the controversy over whether new states would be slave or free as something subsequent to 1820. How striking, then, to find Jefferson writing from Congress to Governor Benjamin Harrison of Virginia in November 1783 about the Northwest Territory: "If a state be first laid off on the [Great] lakes it will add a vote to the

[35] Adams, *Diary and Autobiography*, II, 245.

[36] *Ibid.*, II, 246. As early as 1776 one South Carolina delegate voiced fear that Congress would become too powerful, as early as 1778 another demanded that important business be approved by eleven states (Edward Rutledge and William Henry Drayton, quoted in John R. Alden, *The South in the Revolution, 1763-1789* [Baton Rouge, La.; 1957], pp. 216, 219). We know from Jefferson's notes on the debates of July-August 1776 that Chase's motion, described in the text, was defeated 7-5 on August 1, 1776 by a strictly sectional vote (*The Papers of Thomas Jefferson*, ed. Julian P. Boyd [Princeton, 1950–], I, 323).

Northern scale, if on the Ohio it will add one to the South-ern."[37] This concern would never be out of the minds of Southern politicians until the Civil War. Jefferson did, of course, attempt to exclude slavery from the Territories. But on the ninth anniversary of Lexington and Concord, Congress, on motion of Spaight of North Carolina, seconded by Read of South Carolina, struck this provision from Jefferson's draft proposals.[38]

A principal issue between North and South in these first years of the Critical Period was financial. Southern resistance to Northern financial manipulations did not wait until the 1790's: it began, if one must choose a date, when Delaware, Maryland, Virginia, and both the Carolinas voted against the devaluation plan of March 18, 1780, with every Northern state except divided New Hampshire voting Aye.[39] After the war the issue became still more intense. The Revolutionary campaigns in the South took place largely in the last three years of the war "when neither Congress nor the states," in the words of E. James Ferguson, "had effective money and the troops were supported by impressments." The result was that of the three major categories of public debt—Quartermaster and Com-missary certificates issued to civilians; loan certificates; and final settlement certificates issued to the Continental army—the South held only 16 per cent.[40] The public debt of the South was a state

---

[37] Thomas Jefferson to the Governor of Virginia (Benjamin Harrison), November 11, 1783, *Letters of the Members of the Continental Congress*, ed. Edmund C. Burnett (Washington, D. C.; 1921–1936), VII, 374. Nearly a century ago Hermann von Holst remarked on "the erroneous view . . . that the mischievous political division of the country by a geographical line dates back only to the Missouri compromise" (*The Constitutional and Political History of the United States* [Chicago, 1876], I, 86-87), but that view still prevails today.

[38] Bancroft makes the point about the date in his *Formation of the Con-stitution*, I, 157.

[39] *Journals of the Continental Congress, 1774-1789*, ed. Gaillard Hunt *et al.* (Washington, D.C.; 1904-1937), XVI, 267.

[40] E. James Ferguson, *The Power of the Purse: A History of American Public Finance, 1776-1790* (Chapel Hill, 1961), pp. 181-183.

debt, while the various kinds of Federal debt were held by Northerners: as Spaight of North Carolina put it, "the Eastern [i.e., Northern] States . . . have got Continental Securities for all monies loaned, services done or articles impressed, while to the southward, it has been made a State debt."[41] Hence when Congress sought to tax all the states to repay the Federal debt, the South protested; and when Congress further provided that Northern states could meet their Congressional requisitions with securities, so that only the South need pay coin, the South was furious. Madison told Edmund Randolph in 1783 that unless the public accounts were speedily adjusted and discharged "a dissolution of the Union will be inevitable." "The pious New-Englanders," Read of South Carolina wrote in April 1785, "think tis time to carry their long projected Scheme into Execution and make the southern states bear the burthen of furnishing all the actual money."[42]

Sectional considerations underlay many an action of the early 1780's where they might not, at first glance, seem evident. Jefferson's appointment as United States representative in France is an example. Jefferson had been appointed to the commission to negotiate a peace, as had Laurens of South Carolina; but Jefferson did not go and Laurens was captured by the British en route to Europe, so that three Northerners—John Jay, John Adams, and Benjamin Franklin—carried the burden of the peace talks. The treaty completed, the same three men stayed on in Europe to represent Amer-

[41] Richard Dobbs Spaight to the Governor of North Carolina (Alexander Martin), April 30, 1784, *Letters of Continental Congress*, VII, 509.

[42] James Madison to Edmund Randolph, February 25, 1783, *The Papers of James Madison*, ed. Henry D. Gilpin (Washington, D.C.; 1840),I, 512; Jacob Read to Charles Thomson, April 26, 1785, *Letters of Continental Congress*, VIII, 105. See also: Ephraim Paine to Robert R. Livingston, May 24, 1784, *ibid.*, VII, 534-535; John Francis Mercer to the Executive Council of Virginia, April 10, 1784, *ibid.*, VII, 491; William Grayson to James Madison, September 16, 1785, *ibid.*, VIII, 217; James McHenry to John Hall [September 28? 1785], *ibid.*, VIII, 223; Richard Henry Lee to James Monroe, October 17, 1785, *ibid.*, VIII, 238-239; Nathan Dane to Jacob Wales, January 31, 1786, *ibid.*, VIII, 296-297.

ican interests there, and it was this that aroused Southern concern. James Monroe expressed it in March 1784, writing to Governor Harrison. Monroe pointed out that Virginia owed British merchants £2,800,000 in debts, which according to the peace treaty must now be paid. "It is important to the southern States to whom the negotiation of these treaties are committed; for except the fishery and the fur-trade (the latter of w'h Mr. Jeff'n thinks . . . may be turn'd down the Potow'k). the southern States, are as States, almost alone interested in it."[43] In May, with Jefferson's appointment achieved, the Virginia delegates in Congress wrote the governor: "It was an object with us, in order to render the Commission as agreable as possible to the Southern States to have Mr. Jefferson placed in the room of Mr. Jay." The previous arrangement, the Virginians went on, involved "obvious inequality in the Representation of these States in Europe"; had it continued, it would have presented "an insurmountable obstacle" to giving the commission such great powers.[44]

Here in microcosm was the problem of the South until its victory at the 1787 Convention: recognizing the need for stronger Federal powers, it feared to create them until it was assured that the South could control their use.

III.

Even as early as the 1780's the South felt itself to be a conscious minority. This was evident, for example, in the comment of Virginia delegates as to the location of the national capital. "The votes in Congress as they stand at present," wrote the delegates from the Old Dominion, "are unfavorable to a Southern situation and untill the admission of Western States into the Union, we apprehend it will be found impracticable to retain that Body

[43] James Monroe to the Governor of Virginia (Benjamin Harrison), March 26, 1784, *ibid.*, VII, 478.
[44] The Virginia delegates to the Governor of Virginia (Benjamin Harrison), May 13, 1784, *ibid.*, VII, 525.

[Congress], any length of time, Southward of the middle States."[45] In the fall of 1786, when the clash over shutting the Mississippi to American commerce was at its height, Timothy Bloodworth of North Carolina remarked that "it is wel known that the ballance of Power is now in the Eastern States, and they appear determined to keep it in that Direction."[46] This was why such Southerners as Richard Henry Lee, later the nation's leading Antifederalist pamphleteer, were already opposing stronger Federal powers in 1785. "It seems to me clear, beyond doubt," Lee wrote to Madison, "that the giving Congress a power to Legislate over the Trade of the Union would be dangerous in the extreme to the 5 Southern or Staple States, whose want of ships and seamen would expose their freightage and their produce to a most pernicious and destructive Monopoly."[47] This was a strong argument, which would be heard throughout the South till 1861; it was this fear which in all probability caused George Mason and Edmund Randolph of Virginia to refuse to sign the Constitution in 1787.[48] Recognizing the force of Lee's argument, Madison wrote to Jefferson in the summer and fall of 1785 that commercial distress was causing a call for stronger powers in Congress throughout the North, but that the South was divided. Lee was "an inflexible adversary, Grayson [William Grayson, another Virginia Antifederalist in 1788] unfriendly." Animosity against Great Britain would push the South toward commercial regulation, but the high price of tobacco would work against it. "S. Carolina I am told is deliberating on the distresses of her commerce and will probably concur in some general plan; with a pro-

[45] The Virginia delegates to the Governor of Virginia (Benjamin Harrison), May 13, 1784, ibid., VII, 524.

[46] Timothy Bloodworth to the Governor of North Carolina (Richard Caswell), September 29, 1786, ibid., VIII, 474.

[47] Richard Henry Lee to James Madison, August 11, 1785, ibid., VIII, 181.

[48] See Edmund Randolph to the Speaker of the Virginia House of Delegates, October 10, 1787; George Mason's "Account of certain Proceedings in Convention"; and on Mason's motives, James Madison to Thomas Jefferson, October 24, 1787 and The Landholder [Oliver Ellsworth], VI (Records of the Convention, III, 127, 136, 164-165, 367).

viso, no doubt against any restraint from importing slaves, of which they have received from Africa since the peace about twelve thousand." Madison concluded by telling his comrade in France that he trembled to think what would happen should the South not join the other states in strengthening Congress.[49]

Others beside Madison trembled at this thought: the possibility of disunion was openly and seriously discussed in the 1780's, particularly by those who knew of the fiercely sectional debates in Congress.[50] And if disunion was only the speculation of a few in 1785, the great controversy over the Mississippi in 1786 shook many more from their complacence.

The Mississippi question of the 1780's was a part of the larger question of the destiny of the West which, ultimately, would be the immediate cause of the Civil War. Farrand is less than accurate in his attempt to disengage the question of the admission of new states at the Constitutional Convention from sectional strife. For if there is a single key to the politics of Congress and the Convention in the Critical Period, it is that the South expected the West to be slave rather than free and to tilt the balance of power southward, while in Bancroft's words "an ineradicable dread of the coming power of the Southwest lurked in New England, especially in Massachusetts."[51] That group in Congress recognized as "the Southern Interest (1786), "the southern party" (1787) or "the

[49] James Madison to Thomas Jefferson, August 20 and October 3, 1785, *The Writings of James Madison*, ed. Gaillard Hunt (New York, 1900–1910), II, 160-165, 178-183. The price of tobacco fell precipitously during the following year and Virginia's desire for a stronger federal government correspondingly grew.

[50] See Richard Dobbs Spaight to the Governor of North Carolina (Alexander Martin), October 16, 1784; Rufus King to John Adams, November 2, 1785; Nathan Dane to Edward Pullen, January 8, 1786; Theodore Sedgwick to Caleb Strong, August 6, 1786; Timothy Bloodworth to the Governor of North Carolina (Richard Caswell), September 4, 1786 (*Letters of Continental Congress*, VII, 602-603; VIII, 247, 282, 415-416, 462). See also James Monroe to the Governor of Virginia (Patrick Henry), August 12, 1786 and to James Madison, September 3, 1786 (*ibid.*, VIII, 424-425, 461-462).

[51] *Formation of the Constitution*, II, 80.

Southern Delegation" (1788)[52] fought throughout the 1780's to
forestall the admission of Vermont until at least one Southern
state could be added simultaneously, to hasten the development of
the West, and to remove all obstacles to its speedy organization
into the largest possible number of new states.[53] It was here that
the Mississippi question entered. What was feared if America permitted Spain to close New Orleans to American commerce was not
only a separation of the Western states, but a slackening of the
southwestward migration which Southerners counted on to assure
their long-run predominance in the Union.

"The southern states," wrote the French minister to his superior
in Europe,

are not in earnest when they assert that without the navigation of the
Mississippi the inhabitants of the interior will seek an outlet by way of
the lakes, and will throw themselves into the arms of England. . . .
The true motive of this vigorous opposition is to be found in the great
preponderance of the northern states, eager to incline the balance toward their side; the southern neglect no opportunity of increasing the
population and importance of the western territory, and of drawing
thither by degrees the inhabitants of New England. . . . These new
territories will gradually form themselves into separate governments;

[52] James Manning to Nathan Miller, May 19, 1786. *Letters of Continental
Congress*, VIII, 364; Otto to Vergennes, February 10, 1787, quoted in Ban-
croft, *Formation of the Constitution*, II, 410; James Madison to Edmund
Randolph, August 11, 1788, *Letters of Continental Congress*, VIII, 778.

[53] As early as May 1, 1782, Madison wrote in his "Observations Relating
to the Influence of Vermont, and the Territorial Claims, on the Politics of
Congress," that the Vermont question excited in the Southern states "an
habitual jealousy of a predominance of Eastern interest." (*Papers of Madison*,
I, 123). On June 8, 1784, Hugh Williamson of North Carolina wrote James
Duane that if Vermont were to be independent he wanted to see "at least
two Southern States formed at the same Time" (*Letters of Continental Congress*, VII, 547); and at the very moment when the Constitution was being
ratified by state conventions, the expiring Congress squabbled bitterly over
pairing the admissions of Vermont and Kentucky (*ibid.*, VIII, 708, 714, 724,
733, 741, 757). See the Virginia delegates to the Governor of Virginia (Edmund Randolph), November 3, 1787, for comment on the South's desire
to admit the Western states rapidly (*ibid.*, VIII, 672-673).

they will have their representatives in congress, and will augment greatly the mass of the southern states.[54]

Otto is abundantly confirmed by the debates of the Virginia ratifying convention,[55] and still more by Monroe's correspondence of late 1786. On August 12, 1786, Monroe wrote from Congress to Patrick Henry:

> P.S. The object in the occlusion of the Mississippi on the part of these people so far as it is extended to the interest of their States (for those of a private kind gave birth to it): is to break up so far as this will do it, the settlements on the western waters, prevent any in future, and thereby keep the States southward as they now are—or if settlements will take place, that they shall be on such principles as to make it the interest of the people to separate from the Confederacy, so as effectually to exclude any new State from it. To throw the weight of population eastward and keep it there. . . .

Like many another Southerner in the next seventy-five years, Monroe ended by saying that, if it came to separation, it was essential that Pennsylvania join the South.[56] So forceful was the effect of his letter on Henry, Madison wrote Washington in December, that Henry, who had hitherto advocated a stronger Union, began to draw back. By 1788 he, like Lee, Grayson, and Monroe, would be an Antifederalist.

The effect of the Mississippi squabble was that the long efforts to vest Congress with power over commerce were threatened with failure at the very brink of success. As delegates made their way to the Annapolis Convention in the fall of 1786, Bloodworth of North Carolina wrote that because of debate on the Mississippi "all

[54] Otto to Vergennes, September 10, 1786, quoted in Bancroft, *Formation of the Constitution*, II, 392.

[55] *Debates in the State Conventions*, III, especially the debates of June 13-14, during which, for example, Grayson stated: "This contest of the Mississippi involves this great national contest: That is, whether one part of the continent shall govern the other" (*ibid.*, III, 343).

[56] James Monroe to the Governor of Virginia (Patrick Henry), August 12, 1786, *Letters of Continental Congress*, VIII, 424-425.

other Business seem to be out of View at present." "Should the measure proposed be pursued," Grayson told the Congress, "the S. States would never grant those powers which were acknowledged to be essential to the existence of the Union."[57] When Foreign Secretary Jay had instructions authorizing him to give up American insistence on using the Mississippi river adopted by a simple Congressional majority of seven states it stirred in many Southern breasts the fear of being outvoted. Even before the Mississippi question came before Congress, Southerners like Monroe had insisted that, if Congress were to regulate commerce, commercial laws should require the assent of nine or even eleven states.[58] Jay's unfairness (as Southerners saw it) in using a simple majority to push through a measure fundamentally injurious to the South greatly intensified this apprehension. When the Constitutional Convention met, the so-called Pinckney Plan would suggest a two-thirds Congressional majority for commercial laws, and both the Virginia ratifying convention (which voted to ratify by a small majority) and the North Carolina convention (which rejected ratification) would recommend the same amendment.[59]

In the midst of the Mississippi controversy, men hopeful for stronger government saw little chance of victory. Madison wrote Jefferson in August 1786 that he almost despaired of strengthening Congress through the Annapolis Convention or any other;[60] in September, Otto wrote to Vergennes: "It is to be feared that this discussion will cause a great coolness between the two parties, and may be the germ of a future separation of the southern states."[61]

[57] Timothy Bloodworth to the Governor of North Carolina (Richard Caswell), September 4, 1786, *ibid.,* VIII, 462; Charles Thomson, Minutes of Proceedings, August 18, 1786, *ibid.,* VIII, 438.

[58] See James Monroe to James Madison, July 26, 1785, *ibid.,* VIII, 172.

[59] For the Pinckney Plan, see *Records of the Convention,* III, 604-609; for the amendments proposed in the Virginia and North Carolina ratifying conventions, *Debates in the State Conventions,* III, 595 and IV, 241.

[60] James Madison to Thomas Jefferson, August 12, 1786, *Writings of Madison,* II, 262.

[61] Otto to Vergennes, September 10, 1786, quoted in Bancroft, *Formation of the Constitution,* II, 391.

IV.

Why then did the South consent to the Constitutional Convention? If the South felt itself on the defensive in the 1780's, and particularly so in the summer and fall of 1786, why did its delegates agree to strengthen Federal powers in 1787? If a two-thirds majority for commercial laws seemed essential to Southerners in August of one year, why did they surrender it in August of the next? Were Madison and Washington, as they steadfastly worked to strengthen the national government, traitors to the interests of their section, or was there some view of the future which nationalist Southerners then entertained which enabled them to be good Southerners and good Federalists at the same time?

It is Madison, once more, who provides the clue. He saw that if the South were to agree in strengthening Congress, the plan which gave each state one vote would have to be changed in favor of the South. And in letters to Jefferson, to Randolph, and to Washington in the spring of 1787 he foretold in a sentence the essential plot of the Convention drama. The basis of representation would be changed to allow representation by numbers as well as by states, because a change was "recommended to the Eastern States by the actual superiority of their populousness, and to the Southern by their expected superiority."[62]

So it fell out. Over and over again members of the Convention stated, as of something on which all agreed, that "as soon as the Southern & Western population should predominate, which must happen in a few years,"[63] the South would be compensated for any advantages wrung from it by the North in the meantime. "He must be short sighted indeed," declared King on July 12,

who does not foresee that whenever the Southern States shall be more numerous than the Northern, they can & will hold a language that will

---

[62] James Madison to Thomas Jefferson, March 19[18], 1787, *Writings of Madison*, II, 327; also same to Edmund Randolph, April 8, 1787 and to George Washington, April 16, 1787 (*ibid.*, pp. 340, 345).

[63] These were the words of George Mason on July 11 (*Records of the Convention*, I, 586); see also, e.g., Madison that same day (*ibid.*, I, 585-586).

awe them [the Northern States] into justice. If they threaten to separate now in case injury shall be done them, will their threats be less
urgent or effectual, when force shall back their demands.[64]

"It has been said," Gouverneur Morris added, "that N.C. [,] S.C.
and Georgia only will in a little time have a majority of the people
of America. They must in that case include the great interior
Country, and every thing was to be apprehended from their getting
the power into their hands."[65]

This false expectation explains why Georgia and the Carolinas
who should by present population have been "small" states, considered themselves "large" states at the Convention.[66] This expectation
clarifies, it seems to me, why the South gave way in its demand
that commercial laws require a two-thirds majority; for would not
time and the flow of migration soon provide such a majority without written stipulation? Later, at the Virginia ratifying convention,
no one questioned that (as Grayson put it) "God and nature have
intended . . . that the weight of population should be on this side
of the continent."[67] Antifederalists reasoned from this assumption
that Virginia should wait until a Southern majority in Congress
made it safe to transfer power from the states to the national government. Federalist Wilson Nicholas reasoned from the identical
premise to a contrary conclusion. "The influence of New England,
and the other northern states is dreaded," Nicholas said,

there are apprehensions of their combining against us. Not to advert to
the improbability and illiberality of this idea it must be supposed, that
our population, will in a short period, exceed theirs, as their country
is well settled, and we have very extensive, uncultivated tracts. We
shall soon out-number them in as great a degree as they do us at this
time: therefore this government, which I trust will last to the remotest
ages, will be very shortly in our favor.[68]

[64] *Ibid.*, I, 595-596.
[65] *Ibid.*, I, 604-605.
[66] [See Essay 8, p. 204]
[67] Speech of June 14, *Debates in the State Conventions*, III, 343.
[68] Speech of June 6, *ibid.*, III, 121-122.

Nicholas' argument did not convince George Mason. Nicholas showed, stated Mason, "that though the northern states had a most decided majority against us, yet the increase of population among us would in the course of years change it in our favor. A very sound argument indeed, that we should cheerfully burn ourselves to death in hopes of a joyful and happy resurrection."[69]

The irony, of course, was that the expectation was completely erroneous. The expected Southern majority in the House never materialized, and the Senate, not the House, became the bulwark of the South. In 1790, the population of the South had been growing more rapidly than the North's population for several decades, and was within 200,000 of the population north of the Potomac. True to the general expectation in 1787, the Southwest filled up more rapidly than the area north of the Ohio River. In 1820, Ohio, Indiana, Illinois, and Michigan contained a population of almost 800,000, but Missouri, Kentucky, Tennessee, Alabama, Mississippi, Louisiana, and Arkansas held over 1,300,000 persons. Nevertheless, in the original thirteen states the Northern population pulled so far ahead of the Southern that by 1820 the white population of Northern states and territories was almost twice that of Southern states and territories. Thus the South never obtained the Congressional majority which statesmen of both sections had anticipated at the time of the Constitutional Convention.

When the dream of a Southern majority in Congress and the nation collapsed, there fell together with it the vision of a Southern commercial empire, drawing the produce of the West down the Potomac and the James to "a Philadelphia or a Baltimore" on the Virginia coast.[70] It was not, as it so often seems, an accident that the Convention of 1787 grew from the Annapolis Convention, or that Virginians were the prime movers in calling both. Throughout the 1780's Madison, Jefferson, Monroe, and to an almost fanatical

[69] Speech of June 11, *ibid.*, III, 260-261.
[70] James Madison to James Monroe, June 21, 1785, *Writings of Madison*, II, 148.

degree, Washington, were intent on strengthening the commercial ties between Virginia and the West. As early as 1784, Jefferson suggested to Madison cooperation with Maryland in opening communication to the West, and during that year and the next both Washington and Monroe toured the Western country with their grand plan in mind.[71] Jefferson and Monroe pushed a Potomac location for the national capital partly with the hope that it would "cement us to our Western friends when they shall be formed into separate states" and help Virginia to beat out Pennsylvania and New York in the race for Western trade.[72] Virginia had given up its claims to Western land, but its leaders hoped for a commercial dominion just as satisfactory: as Jefferson put it, "almost a monopoly of the Western and Indian trade."[73] "But smooth the road once," wrote the enraptured Washington, "and make easy the way for them, and then see what an influx of articles will be poured upon us; how amazingly our exports will be encreased by them, and how amply we shall be compensated for any trouble and expence we may encounter to effect it."[74] The West, then, would not only give the South political predominance but also, as Madison wrote Jefferson, "double the value of half the lands within the Commonwealth, . . . extend its commerce, link with its interests those of the Western States, and lessen the emmigration of its Citizens."[75] This was the castle-in-the-air which Virginians pictured

[71] See Bancroft, *Formation of the Constitution*, I, 151-152, and Book 2, chap. 3. Bancroft seems to have had a better grasp of this phenomenon, as well as of the false Southern expectations about population growth (*ibid.*, II, 87), than any subsequent student.

[72] Thomas Jefferson to George Rogers Clark, December 4, 1783, *Letters of Continental Congress*, VII, 378; also James Monroe to the Governor of Virginia (Benjamin Harrison), June 11, 1784, *ibid.*, VII, 550.

[73] Thomas Jefferson to James Madison, February 20, 1784, *Papers of Jefferson*, VI, 548.

[74] George Washington to the Governor of Virginia (Benjamin Harrison), October 10, 1784, *The Writings of George Washington*, ed. John C. Fitzpatrick (Washington, D. C.; 1938), XXVII, 476.

[75] James Madison to Thomas Jefferson, January 9, 1785, *Writings of Madison*, II, 109.

as they worked to bring about the Constitutional Convention, this was the plan for economic development so abruptly and traumatically shattered by Secretary of the Treasury Alexander Hamilton.

In the Spring and Summer of 1788, however, as the South with the North moved to ratify the Constitution, few foresaw the clouds on the horizon. The Constitutional Convention, with a Southern majority (in Bancroft's words) "from its organization to its dissolution,"[76] seemed to have wrought well for the South. Madison alone, from his vantage-point in Congress, fretted about that body's continued preoccupation with sectional issues. After wrangling all Spring about the admission of Kentucky, Congress turned to that old favorite, the location of the capital. "It is truly mortifying," Madison wrote to Washington, to see such "a display of locality," of "local and state considerations," at the very "outset of the new Government." The behavior of Congress would give "countenance to some of the most popular arguments which have been inculcated by the southern antifederalists," and "be regarded as at once a proof of the preponderancy of the Eastern strength." "I foresee contentions," he wrote the next Spring, "first between federal and anti-federal parties, and then between northern and southern parties."[77] Before long he would be leading the opposition.

V.

Even this sampling of the printed sources suggests that sectional conflict based (to quote Madison once more) on "the institution of slavery and its consequences" was a potent force in the shaping of the Constitution. The conclusion seems inescapable that any interpretation of the Convention which stresses realty and

[76] Bancroft, *Formation of the Constitution*, II, 75. The South had a majority in the Convention because Rhode Island did not send a delegation, the New Hampshire delegation came late, and the New York delegation left early.

[77] James Madison to George Washington, August 24, 1788 and September 14, 1788, *Letters of Continental Congress*, VIII, 786, 795-796; letter by Madison (otherwise unidentified), March 6, 1789, quoted in Bancroft, *Formation of the Constitution*, II, 358.

personalty, large states and small states, or monarchy and democracy, but leaves slavery out, is an inadequate interpretation.

Scholarly effort to bring slavery back into the story of the Revolutionary and Early National periods might do worse than begin with those much-maligned exponents of the abolitionist critique, Horace Greeley and Henry Wilson. They, like Beard, believed that a counterrevolution took place, but they saw as its victim the slave rather than the white artisan or farmer. Moreover, they viewed the counterrevolution not as a sudden *coup d'état* in the years 1787-1788, but as a long-drawn-out process which drew strength from the fatal concessions (as Wilson called them) of the Convention, but required such events as the cotton gin and the Louisiana Purchase for its completion.

Crude though they may be, these early abolitionist historians have the power to show us familiar events in a new light. They knew that Adams would have been President in 1800 had the three-fifths clause not existed, and they understood why the Hartford Convention made the abrogation of that clause the first plank of its platform. They viewed the accession of Jefferson as a triumph for slavery; in their accounts the Louisiana Purchase figures not as a diplomatic triumph or an instance of loose Constitutional construction, but as an event by which slavery acquired "a vast extension of its power and influence."[78] They were fully aware of the part which Southern fear of a San Domingo in Cuba played in the genesis of the Monroe Doctrine, and in the American reaction to the Panama Congress.[79] No doubt all these insights are half-truths, but they are half-truths which have been neglected in this century and deserve to be reincorporated into the mainstream of scholarly interpretation.

If it be granted that sectional conflict based on slavery was real and intense long before 1820, our final evaluation of the abolitionist critique of the United States Constitution will still depend on

<hr/>

[78] Greeley, *American Conflict*, I, 57.
[79] See especially Henry Wilson, *History of the Rise and Fall of the Slave Power in America* (Boston, 1872), I, 115-117.

how we answer the question, *Could* the Revolution have abolished slavery?

It came very close. During the Revolutionary War the importation of slaves ceased. In 1779 the Continental Congress agreed unanimously to arm 3,000 slaves in South Carolina and Georgia, with freedom as a reward. In 1784 Congress failed by one vote to prohibit slavery in the Western territories.[80] These facts support von Holst in his remark that "but one more impulse was needed."[81] Jeffrey Brackett, writing in 1889, suggested the sense of lost possibilities that was felt when the South Carolina and Georgia legislatures refused to adopt the plan to enlist slaves of the Deep South against the British:

It was on hearing of the failure of this plan that Washington wrote, that that spirit of freedom which had so strongly marked the beginning of the war, had subsided. It is private not public interest, he added, which influences the generality of mankind.[82]

Many abolitionists, concerned to identify their cause with the charisma of the Founding Fathers, contended that at the time of the Convention all public men expected slavery to die a natural death. This was far from the case. As Hildreth observed a century ago, the delegates from Georgia and South Carolina did not expect slavery to end: "S. Carolina & Georgia," Madison reported to Jefferson, "were inflexible on the point of slaves."[83] Nor is it safe

[80] The 1779 and 1784 episodes are described by Alden, *South in the Revolution*, pp. 225-226, 345-346.

[81] *Constitutional and Political History*, I, 31.

[82] Jeffrey R. Brackett, "The Status of the Slave, 1775-1789," *Essays In The Constitutional History Of The United States In The Formative Period, 1775-1789*, ed. J. Franklin Jameson (Boston and New York, 1889), p. 311. The letter paraphrased was written to Lt. Col. John Laurens, July 10, 1782, and will be found in Washington's *Writings*, XXIV, 421.

[83] Hildreth, *Despotism in America*, p. 304; James Madison to Thomas Jefferson, October 24, 1787, *Records of the Convention*, III, 135. For confirming evidence as to the inflexible attitude of South Carolina and Georgia, see, *ibid.*, I, 534, 542, 594, 605; II, 95, 364, 371-373; III, 135, 378. The Deep South attitude was one reason a Bill of Rights was omitted from the Constitution (*ibid.*, II, 137 and III, 256).

to assume that the Upper South looked forward to emancipation. If so, why did every Southern delegation oppose Jefferson's 1784 proposal to prohibit slavery in the West? And if the South was rigid, the North gave way almost without protest. Farrand misses the tragedy of the situation when he says that the majority "regarded slavery as an accepted institution, as a part of the established order."[84] It would be more accurate to say that almost without exception the Fathers felt that slavery was wrong and almost without exception they failed to act decisively to end it.

Among the obvious reasons for the Revolution's failure to cope with slavery were an inability to imagine a genuinely multi-racial society, and an over-scrupulous regard for private property.

Even the most liberal of the Founding Fathers were unable to imagine a society in which whites and Negroes would live together as fellow-citizens. Honor and intellectual consistency drove them to favor abolition; personal distaste, to fear it. Jefferson said just this when he wrote: "Nothing is more certainly written in the book of fate, than that these people are to be free; nor is it less certain that the two races, equally free, cannot live in the same government."[85] These were also the sentiments of Northerners like Otis, Franklin, and John Quincy Adams. Otis condemned slavery in the abstract, but also prided himself that North America was settled "not as the common people of *England* foolishly imagine, with a compound mongrel mixture of *English, Indian* and *Negro,* but with freeborn *British white* subjects."[86] On the eve of his career as an abolition-

[84] *The Fathers of the Constitution: A Chronicle of the Establishment of the Union* (New Haven, Toronto, London; 1921), p. 130.

[85] *The Writings of Thomas Jefferson,* ed. Andrew A. Lipscomb, I (Washington, 1904), 72-73.

[86] The quoted phrases are from *The Rights of the British Colonies Asserted and Proved* (Boston, 1764), p. 24; the same pamphlet which also says: "The Colonists are by the law of nature free born, as indeed all men are, white or black. . . . Does it follow that tis right to enslave a man because he is black? Will short curl'd hair like wool, instead of christian hair, as tis called by those, whose hearts are as hard as the nether millstone, help the argument?" (*ibid.,* p. 29).

ist, John Quincy Adams praised Andrew Jackson for destroying the "motley tribe of black, white, and red combatants," the "parti-colored forces" of the "negro-Indian banditti" in Florida.[87] As for Franklin, the future president of the Pennsylvania Abolition Society wrote in 1751:

> . . . the Number of purely white People in the World is proportionably very small. All Africa is black or tawny. Asia chiefly tawny. America (exclusive of the new Comers) wholly so. And in Europe, the Spaniards, Italians, French, Russians and Swedes, are generally of what we call a swarthy Complexion; as are the Germans also, the Saxons only excepted, who with the English, make the principal Body of White People on the Face of the Earth. I could wish their Numbers were increased. And while we are, as I may call it, *Scouring* our Planet, by clearing America of Woods, and so making this Side of our Globe reflect a brighter Light to the Eyes of Inhabitants in Mars or Venus, why should we in the Sight of Superior Beings, darken its People? why increase the Sons of Africa, by Planting them in America, where we have so fair an Opportunity, by excluding all Blacks and Tawneys, of increasing the lovely White and Red?[88]

A second reason why the Fathers turned aside from an attack on slavery was their commitment to private property. Gouverneur Morris was the Convention's most outspoken opponent of slavery, the South Carolina delegates were its frankest defenders; but their

[87] John Quincy Adams to George William Erving, Nov. 28, 1818, *Writings of John Quincy Adams*, ed. Worthington Chauncey Ford (New York, 1916), VI, 477, 488. Adams characterized the struggle of General Jackson's antagonists as "all in the name of South American liberty, of the rights of runaway negroes, and the wrongs of savage murderers" (*ibid.*, p. 496).

[88] "Observations Concerning the Increase of Mankind" (1751), *Papers of Benjamin Franklin*, ed. Leonard W. Labaree (New Haven, 1959—), IV, 234. Contrast Bolívar: "The blood of our citizens is varied: let it be mixed for the sake of unity" (*Selected Writings of Bolívar*, ed. Harold A. Bierck, Jr. [New York, 1951], I, 191); and again, to Miranda: "Neither we nor the generation following us will see the glory of the republic which we are founding. There will be a new caste composed of an amalgamation of all races, which will produce a homogeneous people" (Victor Andres Belaunde, *Bolívar and the Political Thought of the Spanish American Revolution* [Baltimore, 1938], p. 166.

identical assumptions about the place of property in society drove them to similar conclusions. Thus, in the Convention debates of July 5 and 6, Morris declared that "life and liberty were generally said to be of more value, than property," but that "an accurate view of the matter would nevertheless prove that property was the main object of Society."[89] This was a view which the South Carolinians could only echo. What it came down to was, as Charles Cotesworth Pinckney put it, that "property in slaves should not be exposed to danger under a Govt. instituted for the protection of property."[90] And so, while Morris stated on July 11 that if compelled to do injustice to human nature or the southern states, he must do it to the latter, that same evening he worked out the formula proportoning representation to direct taxation which proved a "bridge" to the three-fifths compromise; and in August it was he who proposed what he termed a "bargain" between North and South over slave importation.[91]

As late as 1833, Madison could write that the good faith of the North was "sufficiently guarantied by the interest they have, as merchants, as Ship owners, and as manufacturers, in preserving a Union with the slaveholding states."[92] But apart from interest, the belief that private property was the indispensable foundation for personal freedom made it more difficult for Northerners to confront the fact of slavery squarely.

A third, more subtle reason for the failure of nerve of the Founding Fathers when confronting slavery, was precisely that economic realism which Beard so much admired. Harrington's "balance" warred uneasily in their minds with Locke's law "writ in the hearts of mankind." They knew only too well that "power follows prop-

[89] *Records of the Convention*, I, 533.

[90] *Ibid.*, I, 594.

[91] The "bridge" (July 24), *ibid.*, II, 106; the "bargain" (August 22), *ibid.*, II, 374.

[92] James Madison to Henry Clay, June, 1833, *Writings of Madison*, IX, 517.

erty": when statecraft was defined as the mutual adjustment of existing economic interests, uprooting so substantial a reality as slavery was much to ask. Lee Benson says aptly that Madison presented "an essentially fatalistic theory of politics."[93] Having observed at the Convention how the existence or non-existence of slavery shaped men's politics, Madison became in 1790-1792 a victim of that very process. There was a greater irony. In contending for discrimination between original and subsequent holders of Federal securities he found himself pleading for a justice based not on the letter of the law but on the promptings of the heart: the very logic abolitionists would use to defy the Constitution Madison had helped to form, and to destroy the peculiar institution by which, not just in the last analysis but also in his analysis, Madison's own politics were shaped.

Unable to summon the moral imagination required to transcend race prejudice, unwilling to contemplate social experiment which impinged on private property, too ready to rationalize their failure by a theory of economic determination, the Fathers, unhappily, ambivalently, confusedly, passed by on the other side. Their much-praised deistic coolness of temper could not help them here. The abolitionists were right in seeing the American Revolution as a revolution betrayed.

[93] Lee Benson, *Turner and Beard: American Historical Writing Reconsidered* (Glencoe, 1960), p. 102.

8

The Compromise of 1787

On July 12, 1787, the Constitutional Convention, meeting in Philadelphia, adopted the three-fifths compromise regarding apportionment of the House of Representatives. On July 13 the Continental Congress, meeting in New York City, adopted the Northwest Ordinance. The three-fifths compromise sanctioned slavery more decidedly than any previous action at a national level.[1] The Ordinance, on the other hand, was in Ulrich Phillips' words "the first and last antislavery achievement by the central govern-

---

[1] This essay takes issue with Professor Max Farrand's belief that the three-fifths compromise was of secondary importance at the Convention, and that the question of the West was separate from the sectional conflict between North and South (Max Farrand, *The Framing of the Constitution of the United States* [New Haven, London; 1913], pp. 107-111). [My reasons for questioning Farrand's approach are presented more fully in Essay 7.]

Reprinted with permission from the *Political Science Quarterly*, LXXXI (1966), 225-250.

ment in the period."[2] The Ordinance has become a symbol of the Revolution's liberalism, while the compromise, if not a covenant with death and an agreement with hell, is at least a dramatic instance of its pragmatic conservatism. Why did Congress and Convention act so differently? The answer to this question, could it be found, would surely throw much light upon the troubled relation between the Founding Fathers and the peculiar institution.

Apart from the coincidence of dates, two circumstances make this problem still more intriguing. One is that the Continental Congress, at the time it adopted the Ordinance, was controlled by the South. Its temporary president was a Southerner (William Grayson of Virginia); three of the committee of five which drafted the Ordinance were Southerners (Richard Henry Lee and Edward Carrington of Virginia, John Kean of South Carolina); and a Congress with a Southern majority adopted the Ordinance with a single dissenting vote (by a Northerner, Abraham Yates of New York). Why these Southern delegates voted to ban slavery in the Northwest puzzled Nathan Dane of Massachusetts at the time,[3] and has remained a puzzle to historians. Thus B. A. Hinsdale commented that an antislavery clause "had been rejected by Southern men when Mr. Jefferson first brought it forward, and now five of the eight States present are Southern States and eleven of the eighteen men Southern men, and it prevails."[4] Southern support for the

[2] Ulrich B. Phillips, *American Negro Slavery* (New York, London; 1918), p. 128.

[3] Dane to Rufus King, July 16, 1787, *Letters of the Members of the Continental Congress,* ed. Edmund C. Burnett (Washington, D. C.; 1921-1936), VIII, 622.

[4] B. A. Hinsdale, *The Old Northwest: The Beginnings of Our Colonial System* (New York, 1899), p. 266. John M. Merriam said, similarly, in "The Legislative History of The Ordinance of 1787," *Proceedings of the American Antiquarian Society,* new series (Worcester, 1889), V, 336: "The most surprising facts in connection with this article are that it hung fire so long when it would seem that its best friends were interested in it; that Dane and King especially were ready on May 10th to vote for an ordinance which omitted it, and that when proposed in Congress as an amendment to a matured plan, it

Ordinance must puzzle us still more when we set it side-by-side with the determined defense of slavery at the Convention by Deep South delegates such as William Davie of North Carolina and the entire South Carolina group: Pierce Butler, the Pinckneys, and John Rutledge.[5]

A second, less familiar circumstance which thickens the mystery surrounding these events of mid-July is that a number of men were members of both Congress and Convention, and communication between the two bodies was apparently frequent and full. Members of Congress in 1787 who were also named delegates to the Convention were Gorham and King of Massachusetts, Johnson of Connecticut, Blount of North Carolina, Few and Pierce of Georgia, and James Madison of Virginia, who went directly from

---

was so readily adopted." Perhaps the fullest set of questions was posed by William F. Poole, *The Ordinance of 1787, And Dr. Manasseh Cutler As An Agent In Its Formation* (Cambridge, Mass.; 1876), p. 19: "Why were three Southern members, all new men, and constituting a majority of the committee, put in charge of drafting an antislavery ordinance for a Northern territory, which had been defeated by the entire vote of the South three years before? If antislavery principles were so popular with Southern members, why did not Mr. Dane insert an antislavery clause in the ordinance which was to have taken its third reading on the 10th day of May? As Mr. Johnson of Connecticut was the chairman of that committee, and three out of five of its members were Northern men, why did not the committee make it an antislavery ordinance? Whence did so much light dawn so suddenly upon the mind of Mr. Dane, when associated with a majority of Southern members on another committee? What is the explanation of the entire unanimity of feeling and action on the slavery question, then exhibited for the first and last time, in the whole history of our national legislation?" Poole answered his own questions by saying that Southerners doubtless were thinking of the public revenue the Northwest lands would bring (*ibid.*, p. 27). Francis S. Philbrick in the monumental introduction to *The Laws Of Illinois Territory, 1809-1818* (Springfield, Ill.; 1950), p. clxxxvin., stresses that by creating a buffer against British and Indian aggression, the Northwest Territory would promote settlements in the Southwest. No wholly satisfactory explanation has yet been suggested.

[5] See Davie and C. C. Pinckney on July 12, Butler on July 13, C. C. Pinckney on July 23, C. Pinckney, C. C. Pinckney, and Rutledge on Aug. 22, *The Records of the Federal Convention of 1787*, ed. Max Farrand (New Haven, London; 1911), I, 593-594, 605; II, 95, 371-373.

New York to Philadelphia in early May. A number of men traveled back and forth between the two cities while the Convention was in session. William Pierce returned to New York, where he remained from June 14 to June 18, just after discussion of the rule of representation had begun in Philadelphia, and according to Nathan Dane spoke freely of sectional conflicts at the Convention.[6] Blount and his fellow North Carolinian, Benjamin Hawkins, visited Philadelphia from June 19 to July 2, returning to Congress when work on the Northwest Ordinance began. At the same time Pierce again came back from Philadelphia to New York along with his fellow Georgian, Few, like himself a member of both bodies.[7] Others, who, although not members of both groups, very likely carried news from one to the other, included Gouverneur Morris, a Convention delegate who returned to Philadelphia July 2 after a lengthy New York sojourn, and Richard Henry Lee, a member of Congress who took his seat on July 9 after a week in Philadelphia en route.[8] The full text of the Ordinance was, of course, available in Philadelphia soon after it was passed; however, its essential provisions may have been known to some members of the Convention as early as July 11 or 12.[9]

According to his secretary, Edward Coles, Madison years later suggested that there had been a bargain or compromise between

[6] Dane to Rufus King, June 19, 1787, *Letters of Continental Congress*, VIII, 611.

[7] William Blount to John Gray Blount, June 15, 21, 1787, *ibid.*, VIII, 610, 613; Blount to the Governor of North Carolina (Richard Caswell), July 10, 1787, *ibid.*, VIII, 618; Richard Dobbs Spaight to John Gray Blount, July 3, 1787, *The John Gray Blount Papers*, ed. Alice Barnwell Keith (Raleigh, 1952), I, 315; *Records of Federal Convention*, III, 587, 589.

[8] Lee to Thomas Lee Shippen, July 22, 1787, *Letters of Continental Congress*, VIII, 627, 613n.

[9] Dane sent a copy of the Northwest Ordinance to King on July 16 (*Letters of Continental Congress*, VIII, 621). Madison sent a copy to Col. James Madison on July 28 (*Letters and Other Writings of James Madison* [Philadelphia, 1865], I, 335). According to Poole, *Ordinance of 1787*, 28n., the Ordinance was first publicly printed in the *Pennsylvania Herald*, July 25, 1787.

the sections involving both the Ordinance and the Constitution. He said, so Coles stated in the eighteen-fifties:

Many individuals were members of both bodies, and thus were enabled to know what was passing in each—both sitting with closed doors and in secret sessions. The distracting question of slavery was agitating and retarding the labors of both, and led to conferences and intercommunications of the members, which resulted in a compromise by which the northern or anti-slavery portion of the country agreed to incorporate, into the Ordinance and Constitution, the provision to restore fugitive slaves; and this mutual and concurrent action was the cause of the similarity of the provision contained in both, and had its influence, in creating the great unanimity by which the Ordinance passed, and also in making the Constitution the more acceptable to the slave holders.[10]

Coles, speaking shortly after the passage of the Fugitive Slave Act of 1850, may well have exaggerated the importance of that aspect of the compromise of 1787. But it is difficult to imagine that he misremembered the broad idea that communication and compromise had occurred between Congress and Convention, or that Madison, a member of both bodies, was misinformed.

If other direct testimony exists supporting Madison's account it has not come to my attention. Nevertheless, I believe it is possible to make a tentative reconstruction of Southern motives for accepting the Northwest Ordinance, and of the impact of the Ordinance on the work of the Constitutional Convention.

I.

"The clause respecting slavery was agreed to by the Southern members for the purpose of preventing tobacco and indigo from being made on the N. W. side of the Ohio as well as

---

[10] Coles' statement begins: "This brings to my recollection what I was told by Mr. Madison, and which I do not remember ever to have seen in print" (Edward Coles, *History of The Ordinance Of 1787* [Philadelphia, 1856], pp. 28-29). A similar theory is presented by Peter Force (*Life, Journals and Correspondence of Rev. Manasseh Cutler, L.L.D.* [Cincinnati, 1888], II, Appendix D, 419).

for sev'l other political reasons." So William Grayson wrote to James Monroe on August 8, 1787.[11] What were the "sev'l other political reasons"? Why did the Southern majority of the Continental Congress unanimously vote for the Northwest Ordinance, despite its antislavery clause?

One answer is as simple as it is surprising: the South expected that the states formed from the Northwest Territory would vote with the South in the sectional conflict then raging in Congress. Late in 1783, when congressional acceptance of Virginia's cession was finally in sight, Thomas Jefferson had written the governor of Virginia: "If a state be first laid off on the [Great] lakes it will add a vote to the Northern scale, if on the Ohio it will add one to the Southern."[12] Jefferson had proposed, and Congress had essentially accepted, a plan to divide the Territory into ten states, some near the lakes and others near the Ohio River. The Ordinance of 1787 provided instead that there be three states running from the river to the lakes, the present Ohio, Indiana, and Illinois. The result was that *both* North and South could hope for their allegiance. Dane of Massachusetts wrote to Rufus King on July 16 that the easternmost state of the three would "no doubt" be settled chiefly from the East, "and there is, I think, full an equal chance of its adopting Eastern politics."[13] A month later he was more confident. Writing again to King on August 12, Dane said:

Much will depend on the directions given to the first settlements in my opinion, and as the Eastern states for the sake of doing away the temporary governments, etc. established in 1784, and for establishing some order in that Country, gave up as much as could be reasonably expected, I think it will be just and proper in them to establish as far as they can consistently, Eastern politics in it, especially in the state adjoining Pennsylvania.[14]

[11] *Letters of Continental Congress*, VIII, 632.
[12] Jefferson to the Governor of Virginia (Benjamin Harrison), Nov. 11, 1783, *Letters of Continental Congress*, VII, 374.
[13] *Ibid.*, VIII, 622.
[14] *Ibid.*, VIII, 636. One might say that the Northwest was an eighteenth-

But the Southern States, too, hoped and expected to dominate the Northwest. On November 3, 1787, the Virginia delegates in Congress wrote to Governor Edmund Randolph:

Indeed, if it is thought Material to the interest of the Southern States, that their Scale be Strengthened by an accession in this quarter, that object will be better secured by the New, than the old plan, because upon the former there may be an early admission of a State [since the states under the new plan would be larger], but upon the latter such an event must be long, or perhaps forever, postponed.[15]

If it was not because they would be slaveholding, it was also not because they were "agrarian" that the South looked forward to the admission of states from the Northwest Territory. Vermont was agrarian, but throughout the seventeen-eighties the South opposed the admission of Vermont because of what Madison called "an habitual jealousy of a predominance of Eastern interest."[16] Clearly the South believed that, unlike Vermont, the Northwest would be settled mainly by Southerners, by an outcropping of the great tide of migrants then flowing over the mountains into Kentucky and Tennessee. Conversely, Rufus King was relying on a predominance of Easterners in the area to produce the "Eastern politics" for which he hoped. Only the event could prove which section's expectations were correct, and so in July 1787 they could join almost unanimously in promoting the Territory's speedy settlement and organization.

What were the other "political reasons" to which Grayson referred? Richard Hildreth, writing in 1849, supposed that the Southern states were "reconciled" to the Ordinance "by the idea, afterward acted upon, of securing the continuation of slavery in the territory south of the Ohio, under future terms of cession."[17] As

---

century Kansas, in that each section knew its political destiny would be determined by the geographical origins of its settlers.

[15] *Ibid.*, VIII, 672-673.

[16] [See Essay 7, p. 170.]

[17] Richard Hildreth, *The History of the United States of America* (New York, 1849), III, 528-529.

we have seen, the South did not need to be reconciled to the Ordinance: it welcomed it in the belief that, even without slaveholding, the Northwest would support the South in national politics. But it is perfectly possible that Hildreth correctly identifies a second motive. For he stresses what many subsequent historians have forgotten, that as late as May 1787 Congress was on the verge of passing an ordinance for the West "the provisions of which extended to the whole western district, both that ceded [the Northwest] and that of which the cession was anticipated [the Southwest]."[18] The ordinance reported on April 26, 1787, was an ordinance "for the government of the western territory."[19] It was read twice but its third and final reading scheduled for May 10 was postponed, and on July 11, "the Committee . . . to whom was referred the report of a committee touching *the temporary government of the western territory* reported an Ordinance for *the government of the territory of the United States North West of the river Ohio*, which was read a first time."[20] [Italics mine.] Thus just at the moment the Convention adopted the three-fifths compromise, Congress for the first time drew an explicit East-West line through the Western territories by legislating for the Northwest alone. What if anything was implied as to the status of slavery south of that line in the region that became the Southwest Territory?

So far as I am aware, at no Southern ratifying convention was any fear expressed that the antislavery portion of the Northwest Ordinance would be applied south of the Ohio River. Southerners presumably knew that North Carolina's cession of the area later called Tennessee read in part: "Provided always, That no regula-

[18] *Ibid.*, III, 527.

[19] *Journals of the Continental Congress, 1774-1789* (Washington, D. C.; 1904-1937), XXXI, 669; XXXII, 242, 281. Actually, the title of the plan as reported on September 19, 1786, and April 26, 1787, was "a plan of a temporary government for such districts, or new states, as shall be laid out by the United States." The print ordered on May 9, when the ordinance was read for a second time, shortened this to the phrase given in the text.

[20] *Ibid*, XXXII, 313.

tions made or to be made by Congress shall tend to emancipate slaves, otherwise than shall be directed by the Assembly or legislature of such State or States."[21] Other evidence supports the supposition that in legislating against slavery in the Northwest Congress tacitly legislated for it in the Southwest. South Carolinians at the Constitutional Convention were notoriously apprehensive about their slave property, but on August 9, 1787, the South Carolina legislature, undeterred by the Northwest Ordinance, completed the cession of its Western lands.[22] Richard Henry Lee, who in 1784 voted against Jefferson's proposal to ban slavery throughout the West, was mentioned by both Dane and Cutler as a particularly warm supporter of the 1787 Ordinance which banned it only North of the Ohio.

The Northwest Ordinance legislated against slavery in that part of the West where it did not exist and left it alone in the Southwest where it already was. This was generally recognized. "The Western people are already calling out for slaves for their new lands," George Mason told the Constitutional Convention in August.[23] And forty-seven years later Nathan Dane made a revealing statement in a letter to Daniel Webster:

. . . in the years 1784, '85, '86, and '87, the Eastern members in the Old Congress really thought they were preparing the North-Western Territory principally for New England settlers, and to them the third and sixth articles of compact more especially had reference; therefore, when North Carolina ceded her western territory, and requested this

[21] *The State Records of North Carolina,* ed. Walter Clark (Goldsboro, North Carolina; 1905), XXIV, 563. Essentially the same clause was included in the North Carolina cession of December 22, 1789; the act of Congress accepting this first Southwestern cession of April 2, 1790; and the Ordinance for the Southwestern Territory of May 26, 1790 (*The Territorial Papers of the United States,* ed. Clarence E. Carter [Washington, D. C.; 1936], IV, 7, 16, 18).

[22] Neither the South Carolina cession nor the Georgia cession of February 1, 1788, mentioned slavery (*Journal of Continental Congress,* XXXIII, 475-477; XXXIV, 320-326).

[23] *Records of Federal Convention,* II, 370.

Ordinance to be extended to it, except the *slave* article, that exception had my full assent, because slavery had taken root in it, and it was then probable it would be settled principally by slaveowners.[24]

Thus, while from the standpoint of the North the Ordinance appeared an antislavery triumph, to the South it may have seemed the end of the national government's attempt to prohibit slavery South of the Ohio.

A third political reason which may have induced Southern congressmen to support the Northwest Ordinance is suggested by a letter of Benjamin Hawkins of North Carolina. Writing to the governor of North Carolina on July 10, Hawkins said that he and William Blount had returned to Congress from the Convention in the

hope of being able to procure some aid from the Union towards the protection of our Western Citizens, and of securing and preserving our right to the free and common use of the navigation of the Mississippi. . . . the latter which is very interesting to the Western citizens of the Southern States . . . has at length, from a variety of circumstances unnecessary as well perhaps as improper to relate been put in a better situation than heretofore.[25]

The question of the navigation of the Mississippi was the most serious sectional issue to come before the Continental Congress.[26] It took on new intensity in 1786 when John Jay, secretary for foreign affairs, secured congressional approval to sacrifice the right to the navigation in negotiations with Spain. The South feared, as William Grayson told the Virginia ratifying convention, that "if the Mississippi was yielded to Spain, the migration to the western country would be stopped, and the northern states would, not only retain their inhabitants, but preserve their superiority and influence

[24] Nathan Dane to Daniel Webster, March 26, 1830, in *The Part Taken By Essex County In The Organization And Settlement Of The Northwest Territory* (Salem, Mass.; 1889), p. 40.

[25] *Letters of Continental Congress*, VIII, 619.

[26] [See Essay 7.]

over that of the southern."[27] The effort of Northern Congressmen to close the Mississippi had the same sectional character as the attempt by Northern members of Congress and Convention to limit the political representation of new states.

The bitter Mississippi controversy of 1786 became "much entangled" with the problem of evolving a government for the West.[28] On May 10, 1786, a five-man congressional committee with a Southern majority recommended that the number of states to be formed from the Virginia cession be reduced to not less than two nor more than five, but that, as in the plan of 1784, each state should enter the Union when its population was equal to that of the smallest of the original thirteen.[29] This, as the Virginia delegates observed in 1787, was a change which would accelerate the admission of new states. On July 7 Congress unanimously recommended to the states that they revise their acts of cession so that three to five states be formed from the Northwest. But now Northern congressmen began to press to raise the population requirement for admission to one-thirteenth of the total population of the original thirteen states at the last census prior to the request for admission.[30] *This* change would have slowed down the admission of the new states. Indeed, had it been applied it would have delayed the admission of Ohio, Indiana, Illinois, Michigan, and Wisconsin an average of thirty-eight years, with Wisconsin excluded from

[27] Speech of June 12, 1788, *The Debates in the Several State Conventions,* ed. Jonathan Elliot (second edition; Washington, D. C.; 1836), III, 281.

[28] Edmund C. Burnett, *The Continental Congress* (New York, 1941), p. 653; *ibid.,* pp. 651-653, describes the sequence of events discussed in the following paragraph.

[29] *Journals of Continental Congress,* XXX, 251-255; James Monroe to Thomas Jefferson, May 11, 1786, *Letters of Continental Congress,* VIII, 359-360.

[30] *Journals of Continental Congress,* XXX, 390-394; James Monroe to Thomas Jefferson, July 16, 1786, *Letters of Continental Congress,* VIII, 403-404.

statehood until after 1900.[31] On July 19 a personnel change gave the committee a Northern majority, and on September 19 the committee reported a revised ordinance including both the "Northern" population formula for admission to statehood and a new condition, equally offensive to the South, which provided for admission if "the consent of so many States in Congress is first obtained as may at that time be competent to such admission."[32]

Meantime the North was using its congressional majority to change Jay's instructions regarding his negotiations with Spain about Mississippi navigation. And on September 1, 1786, a procedural rule was approved which blocked reconsideration of Jay's instructions unless the same number of states were present (twelve) that had voted them in August.[33]

During the winter Congressman Madison noted that the idea of separate confederacies had for the first time reached the newspapers;[34] and in April, learning that Jay had drawn up a draft treaty with Gardoqui in which the Mississippi navigation was given up, Madison launched a frontal attack. On April 18 he moved that negotiations be transferred to Jefferson in Madrid, a step, he confided to his journal, "which if it should answer no other purpose would at least gain time." In inconclusive debate on the motion on April 23, Gorham (soon to leave for the Convention) stated that he thought the Mississippi *should* be closed to American commerce.

[31] George Bancroft, *History of the Formation of the Constitution of the United States of America* (third edition; New York, 1882), II, 104.

[32] *Journals of Continental Congress*, XXX, 418n., XXXI, 669-673. Philbrick comments (*Laws of Illinois Territory*, cclxxvi-cclxxvii) that this proviso violated the terms of the Virginia cession just as did the clause of the Constitution giving Congress discretionary power over the admission of new states.

[33] *Journals of Continental Congress*, XXX, 323, and XXXI, 469-484; *Letters of Continental Congress*, VIII, 427-430, 438-442, 449-450. For the rule of Sept. 1, 1786, *Journals of Continental Congress*, XXXI, 620-621.

[34] "Notes of Debates In The Continental Congress," entry for Feb. 21, 1787, *Journals of Continental Congress*, XXXIII, 724.

On April 25, grasping the nettle, Madison moved to repeal the rule of September 1786. Rufus King (another member of both Congress and Convention) led the opposition which forced a postponement. Nevertheless Madison thought it a victory, writing in his journal:

It was considered on the whole that the project of shutting the Mississippi was at an end; a point deemed of great importance in reference to the approaching Convention for introducing a change in the federal Government, and to the objection to an increase of its powers foreseen from the jealously [sic] which had been excited by that project.[35]

On May 2 he left for Philadelphia.

The issue of Western government and Mississippi navigation arose once more before Congress lost its quorum in mid-May. On May 9, Congress gave the ordinance for the "western territory" its second reading, but also recorded the receipt of a memorial from Samuel Parsons and his associates which led to the postponement of the third reading ordered for May 10. On May 9 Congress received another letter from Jay requesting "express Instructions on the Points in Difference between the United States and the Crown of Spain." On the tenth Pierce and Few of Georgia (both Convention delegates) carried the motion of April 25 repealing the order of September 1786, and on May 11 a committee on new instructions was appointed with a Southern majority.[36]

Therefore, when Congress regained its quorum July 4 the trend of congressional action was favorable to the South with respect to the Mississippi issue, unfavorable in regard to the admission of Western states. Since both strands of policy directly affected Southern prospects for becoming a majority in Congress, the overall position of the South in the Union was very much in doubt.

The first business of the reactivated Congress was to hear a report

[35] *Ibid.*, XXXII, 210, 216-220; XXXIII, 734-739.

[36] *Journals of Continental Congress*, XXXII, 274-283, 292n. The members of the committee were Kearny (Delaware), Hawkins (North Carolina), Grayson (Virginia), Few (Georgia), and Pettit (Pennsylvania).

from the committee on instructions to Jay which affirmed, predictably, that it was an "indispensable obligation to preserve the right of the United States to their territorial bounds and the free Navigation of the Mississippi from its source to the Ocean . . . ."[37] One Northerner at least was not ready to concede defeat. The next day Nathan Dane wrote to Rufus King, now at the Convention in Philadelphia: "What is best for us to do about procuring an attendance of the Eastern States and to renew the subject of the S[panish] Treaty?"[38] But the stand-off achieved by Madison in April was in fact left undisturbed. "The Mississippi is where you left it; *i.e.* nothing has been done," Grayson wrote to Monroe on August 8. "I . . . think we are safe for the present."[39] The Mississippi question "has been dormant a considerable time," Madison wrote to Washington in October, "and seems likely to remain so."[40] In September 1788 Congress referred the matter to the new government with a declaration of opinion that free navigation was a clear and essential right and should be supported, thus belatedly confirming the committee report of July 4, 1787.

Dane himself joined in a more substantial concession to Southern views on Western government. The first full draft of the Northwest Ordinance, in Dane's handwriting, included a provision to admit new states when their population reached sixty thousand and completely dropped the stipulation as to the consent of a competent number of states in Congress.[41] Francis Philbrick comments: "There is no evidence on the subject, but the matter was so bit-

---

[37] *Ibid.*, XXXII, 299-300.

[38] Dane to King, July 5, 1787, *Letters of Continental Congress*, VIII, 617.

[39] *Ibid.*, VIII, 632-633.

[40] James Madison to George Washington, Oct. 28, 1787, *The Writings of James Madison*, ed. Gaillard Hunt (New York, 1900-1910), V, 43.

[41] The text reads (*Journals of Continental Congress*, XXXII, 342): "and whenever any of the said States shall have sixty thousand free Inhabitants therein, such State shall be admitted by its Delegates into the Congress of the United States, on an equal footing with the original States, in all respects whatever."

terly contested as to justify suspicion that some understanding preceded Dane's proposal of the new formula."[42]

To sum up this portion of the discussion: The foregoing pages sketch three lines of reasoning which may have led Southerners to support the Northwest Ordinance, despite its antislavery proviso. The Northwest, even without slavery, was expected to support Southern policies in Congress; the Ordinance may have been construed as a tacit endorsement of slavery in the Southwest; and the negotiations that led to the Ordinance appear to have involved an agreement to speed the admission of new states from the Northwest by lowering the population required for admission. Taken together with the continued stalemate on the issue of Mississippi navigation, the Ordinance could well have seemed a Southern victory to the Southern congressional majority.

Two qualifications need emphasis. First, in speaking of "Southerners" or "Southern attitudes" I mean to suggest only that sectional conflict was already so intense that Southern politicians as a group were conscious of defending commonly-recognized sectional interests.[43] There is no intention of obscuring the difference between Grayson and Lee on the issue of slavery, or between Lee and Blount in regard to Southwestern expansion.[44] Second, thus far I have deliberately ignored Madison's suggestion of cooperation between Congress and Convention, and approached the Northwest Ordinance as the product of sectional compromise within Congress. Whether or not the Ordinance was consciously intended

[42] *Laws of Illinois Territory*, cclxxix.

[43] See John R. Alden, *The First South* (Baton Rouge, La.; 1961), *passim.*

[44] A history of these events might be written from the standpoint of land speculation. Lee and his family, as well as Washington, were longtime investors in Ohio Valley lands; uncharacteristically for Southerners, both Lee and Washington opposed immediate opening of Mississippi navigation. Blount was a leading speculator in Southwestern lands and during the summer of 1787 wrote letters to the New York press from an imaginary Westerner demanding the opening of the Mississippi. Grayson held stock in the Indiana Company, as did James Wilson, who defended Westward expansion at the Convention.

to resolve problems in the Convention, it may have had that effect. We now turn to examine just what those problems were.

II.

The coalition which secured the three-fifths compromise at the Convention was not a combination of "large states." It comprised the states of the South aided now by one Northern state, now by another. The key votes were on July 11, when the three-fifths rule was defeated six-four; on July 12, when it was adopted; on July 13, when it was extended to prospective Western states; and on July 14, when by a five-four vote a motion to limit representatives from the West to a number no greater than that from the original thirteen states, was beaten. The sectional pattern is obscured because South Carolina voted against the three-fifths rule in an effort to have Negroes counted equally with whites. If South Carolina is placed in the "aye" column, one finds Virginia and the states South of it forming a solid South throughout these crucial votes.[45]

[45] On July 11, Massachusetts, Pennsylvania, New Jersey, Maryland, Delaware, South Carolina, voted against the three-fifths ratio, Virginia, North Carolina, Georgia, and Connecticut voted for it. On July 12, Connecticut, Pennsylvania, Maryland, Virginia, North Carolina, and Georgia voted for it, with New Jersey and Delaware opposed, and Massachusetts and South Carolina divided. On July 13, Congress was voted "authority to regulate the number of representatives" in new states on the basis of the three-fifths ratio by a 9-0 vote with Delaware divided. On July 14, Gerry, seconded by King, moved "that in order to secure the liberties of the States already confederated, the number of Representatives in the 1st. branch of the States which shall hereafter be established, shall never exceed in number, the Representatives from such of the States as shall accede to this confederation." Massachusetts, Connecticut, Delaware, and Maryland voted for this motion, Virginia, North Carolina, South Carolina, Georgia, and New Jersey opposed, with Pennsylvania divided. (*Records of Federal Convention*, I, 588, 597, 606; II, 3). It should be noted that New Jersey's delegates to Congress had been instructed to oppose closure of the Mississippi, and voted accordingly in the spring of 1787.

The struggle, as Gouverneur Morris observed, was one "between the two ends of the Union."[46] Madison was still more explicit. On June 29 he stated:

If there was real danger, I would give the smaller states the defensive weapons.—But there is none from that quarter. The great danger to our general government *is the great southern and northern interests of the continent, being opposed to each other. Look to the votes in congress, and most of them stand divided by the geography of the country, not according to the size of the states.*[47]

The next day Madison reiterated "that the States were divided into different interests not by their difference of size, but by other circumstances; the most material of which resulted partly from climate, but principally from the effects of their having or not having slaves."[48] By July 14 Madison could say that it was "pretty well understood" that the "institution of slavery & its consequences formed the line of discrimination" between the contending groups of states at the Convention.[49]

At first Madison's mention of the sectional issue was apparently intended to soften the conflict between large and small states rather than to bring forward the problems between North and South. But these problems became inescapable when the committee reports of July 5 and 9 brought the Convention to grips with allotment of representation to the West and to the slave. King said in the ensuing discussion that he "was fully convinced that the question concerning a difference of interests did not lie where it had hitherto been discussed, between the great & small States; but between the Southern & Eastern."[50]

---

[46] Speech of July 13, *Records of Federal Convention*, I, 604. Morris went on to say that in the sectional struggle the Middle States ought to "join their Eastern brethren."

[47] *Ibid.*, I, 476.

[48] *Ibid.*, I, 486.

[49] *Ibid.*, II, 10.

[50] Speech of July 10, *ibid.*, I, 566.

The three-fifths rule had been accepted by a nine-two vote on June 11, but it now became once more problematical, because it was connected with Western expansion. For the South, inclusion of slaves in the basis of apportionment for the House, and the admission of Western states represented equally with the old, were alternative means of strengthening its power in Congress. This was because it was generally asssumed that the South when strengthened by the West would become the most populous part of the country.[51] But the generally accepted premise that the weight of numbers was shifting from North to South gave both sections an interest in discarding the existing arrangement which gave each state one vote in Congress. Writing to Jefferson, Randolph, and Washington before the Convention met, Madison correctly predicted that proportional representation would be "recommended to the Eastern States by the actual superiority of their populousness, and to the Southern by their expected superiority."[52] This was the basis of compromise at the Convention.

It was a compromise excruciatingly difficult to formulate in detail. What was needed, as Mason said on July 11, was a system which accorded the North its present right to predominate but was so framed that when the Southern states grew larger, power would pass to them.[53] But Deep South delegates feared that the North might use even a temporary majority to force emancipation. Thus Butler of South Carolina stated: "The security the Southn. States want is that their negroes may not be taken from them which some gentlemen within or without doors, have a very good mind to do."[54] Northerners, in their turn, feared that the South and West

[51] [See Essay 7, pp. 173-174.]

[52] Madison to Thomas Jefferson, March 19 [18], 1787, *Writings of Madison*, II, 327; also same to Edmund Randolph, April 8, 1787, and to George Washington, April 16, 1787, *ibid.*, II, 340, 345.

[53] *Records of Federal Convention*, I, 578, 586. Mason and other Southerners were insisting that a periodic census be mandatory.

[54] Speech of July 13, *ibid.*, I, 605.

would employ their eventual majority to oppress commerce and thrust America into needless wars. "He must be short sighted indeed," King said,

who does not foresee that whenever the Southern States shall be more numerous than the Northern, they can & will hold a language that will awe them [the Northern states] into justice. If they threaten to separate now in case injury shall be done them, will their threats be less urgent or effectual, when force shall back their demands.[64]

Ironically, the South expected to dominate the House of Representatives while the North looked for its security to the Senate. Gouverneur Morris asserted on July 13 that he saw "the Southn. Gentleman will not be satisfied unless they see the way open to their gaining a majority in the public Councils." This would oblige him "to vote for ye. vicious principle of equality in the 2d. branch in order to provide some defense for the N. States agst. it."[56] Madison, speaking for the South, was equally alarmed at the idea of equal representation in the Senate because of "the perpetuity it would give to the preponderance of the Northn. agst. the Southn." states. "Should a proprtl. representation take place it was true, the N. side would still outnumber the other: but not in the same degree, at this time; and every day would tend towards an equilibrium."[57]

This tangle of anxieties was complicated further by the ordinance for government of the West which had been passed by the Continental Congress in 1784. King reminded the Convention on July 6 that Congress had "impoliticly laid it [the west] out into ten States," and covenanted with the settlers to permit any Western state to enter the Union as soon as the number of its inhabitants equalled the population of the smallest of the original thirteen.

[55] Speech of July 12, *ibid.*, I, 595-596.

[56] *Ibid.*, I, 604.

[57] Speech of July 14, *ibid.*, II, 9-10.

Since little Delaware had only thirty-five thousand inhabitants, King concluded, a large number of Western states representing very few people might soon be admitted.[58] The Senate could hardly provide a fortress for Northern interests if in the near future it were overwhelmed with twenty new senators from the West.

Thus by early July the conflict of large and small states had been partially transformed into a conflict of North and South. Georgia, the third smallest state in the Union, and South Carolina, smaller than New York or Connecticut, voted as "large" states because they expected to grow and because they expected the section of which they were a part to grow.[59] Massachusetts and Pennsylvania, the large Northern states, voted as large states when discussion centered on the balance of power in the existing confederacy; but when Western representation came on the floor, what Bancroft called New England's "ineradicable dread of the coming power of the South-west" tended to draw them toward the "small" state position.[60] Section as well as size was involved in the great Con-

[58] *Ibid.*, I, 541.

[59] In a speech of June 30, Bedford observed that Georgia, South Carolina, and North Carolina behaved as large states, along with Massachusetts and Pennsylvania, because the Southern states (with the exception of Maryland) expected to grow (*Records of Federal Convention*, I, 491). On July 2, C. Pinckney referred to Massachusetts, Pennsylvania, Virginia, North Carolina, South Carolina, and Georgia as "the large States" (*ibid.*, I, 510), they (with the exception of Georgia, which divided) having just voted against an equality of suffrage in the Senate. Luther Martin, in his *Genuine Information*, stated that Georgia voted as a large state because it had an area larger than Great Britain and thirty times the size of Connecticut, and expected in time a population proportionate to its size (*ibid.*, III, 187).

[60] Bancroft's dictum (*Formation of the Constitution*, II, 80) was illustrated when on July 5 Gouverneur Morris of Pennsylvania urged the small states to accept proportional representation but also favored "irrevocably" giving the Atlantic states more votes than new states of the West. Madison on the eleventh rightly accused him of adjusting his principles to the "points of the compass." It was Morris' plan of July 5 which two Massachusetts men moved on the fourteenth and for which Massachusetts voted, with Pennsylvania dividing (*Records of Federal Convention*, I, 533-534, 584; II, 3; see also note 45, above).

vention crisis which led Franklin to suggest prayer and Washington (as Freeman says) to express despair in a tone he had hardly used since the worst days of the war.[61]

III.

What resolved the crisis? Farrand, attempting to account for the change in the tone of the Convention after July 10, was driven to invoke the fact that the weather became cooler.[62] Bancroft, characterizing the passage of the Northwest Ordinance by a Congress racked with sectional strife, concluded that "every man that had a share in it seemed to be led by an invisible hand to do just what was wanted of him."[63] Madison's comment to Coles invites us to search for more adequate explanations by viewing as parts of one whole the events of mid-July in both New York and Philadelphia. Coles's recollection of Madison's memory of events a generation before their conversation[64] can hardly be relied on in detail. What it provides is a fresh point of departure.

The most obvious relationship between the Ordinance and the Constitution is that their fugitive slave clauses are almost identical and their clauses on the sanctity of contracts very similar.[65] There can be little question that the Convention, which worded these clauses of the Constitution in August, had the Ordinance of July in mind.

There were other ways in which the documents, without duplicating each other, were clearly supplementary. Thus the Ordinance

[61] Douglas S. Freeman, *George Washington, a Biography* (New York, 1948-1957), VI, 100.

[62] ". . . on the night of the twelfth it turned cool" (Farrand, *Framing of the Constitution*, p. 104).

[63] *Formation of the Constitution*, II, 98.

[64] One assumes that the conversation took place when Coles was Madison's secretary, 1809-1815 (E. B. Washburne, *Sketch of Edward Coles, Second Governor of Illinois* [Chicago, 1882], pp. 18-19).

[65] Northwest Ordinance, Articles 2 and 6; United States Constitution, Article I, Section 10 and Article IV, Section 2.

said nothing about retaining the right to the Mississippi navigation, although a clause providing that waterways leading into the
Mississippi and St. Lawrence shall "be common highways, and be
forever free," may have been seen as a precedent.[66] But a requirement that treaties be approved by two-thirds of the Senate was in-
serted in the Constitution "for the express purpose of preventing a
majority of the Senate . . . from giving up the Mississippi."[67] Again,
the Constitution was vague about the admission of new states. The
Randolph Plan said that admission should be "with the consent of
a number of voices in the National legislature less than the whole";
the Committee of Detail reported that the admission of new states
should require the consent of two-thirds of the members present
in each branch of the legislature; and at the insistence of Gouverneur Morris, Article IV, Section 3 merely stated that "New States
may be admitted by the Congress into this Union."[68] On the other
hand, Article I, Section 2 made it clear that the three-fifths rule
for the House would apply to "the several States which may be
included within this Union," the agreement voted by the Convention on July 13.[69] Southerners reading this clause in conjunction
with the provision of the Ordinance that "whenever any of the
said States shall have sixty thousand free Inhabitants therein, such
State shall be admitted . . . on an equal footing with the original

[66] A resolution to this effect had been moved by Grayson, seconded by
King, and passed by Congress on May 12, 1786 (*Journals of Continental Congress*, XXX, 263).

[67] Hugh Williamson to James Madison, June 2, 1788, *Letters of Continental Congress*, VIII, 746.

[68] *Records of Federal Convention*, I, 22; II, 188.

[69] Rufus King told the Senate at the time of the Missouri Compromise that
the three-fifths rule was merely "a settlement between the original thirteen
states," inapplicable to new ones (*ibid.*, III, 430). The Convention resolution
of July 13 clearly implies that the "may be included" of Article I, Section 2
was meant to refer to new as well as old states. The Committee of Detail
put it: "The members of the House of Representatives shall be chosen . . .
by the people of the several States comprehended within this Union" (*ibid.*,
II, 178).

States, in all respects whatever," might well feel that they had gained their points about *both* slave representation and the equal representation of new Western states.

All this is consistent with Madison's idea of a connection in the drafting of Ordinance and Constitution. One is, therefore, led to inquire whether consultation between Congress and Convention preceded the drafting of the Northwest Ordinance on July 9-11; whether the nature of the Ordinance was such as to ease the sectional tension then troubling the Convention; and whether the essential features of the Ordinance were reported to members of the Convention in time to influence its voting on July 12-14. Since the answer to all three questions is probably, Yes, I think one can justifiably present the hypothesis that there occurred in July 1787 a sectional compromise involving Congress and Convention, Ordinance and Constitution, essentially similar to those of 1820 and 1850. The business of a hypothesis, I take it, is to present a structure of logic which accounts for the available facts, and is susceptible to proof or disproof. Evidence proving or disproving the hypothesis of a Compromise of 1787 may come to light, or have (unknown to me) already come to light, in any of some dozens of manuscript collections. The hypothesis is brought forward in the hope that such evidence will be forthcoming.

Were there "conferences and inter-communications" (to use the words Coles attributed to Madison) between Congress and Convention in early July? When the Convention adjourned for three days on July 2 to allow a committee of all the states to seek a compromise, four congressmen, three of them members of the Convention, left for New York City. It was this journey of Blount and Hawkins of North Carolina, Pierce and Few of Georgia, that enabled Congress to achieve a quorum for the first time in almost two months.[70] (The accession of the two Southern states also gave the South a majority in Congress.) Richard Henry Lee, who

[70] See notes 6-8 above.

arrived on July 7 and took his seat on July 9, was therefore the fifth prominent Southerner to travel from Philadelphia to New York in less than a week. Hamilton, who left the Convention June 29, was in New York City by July 3.[71] On July 5 Manasseh Cutler arrived from Massachusetts. When one recalls that Pierce, on his earlier return from the convention (June 14-18), had spoken freely of "the plans of the Southern, Eastern, or Middle States,"[72] it seems a reasonable conclusion that "conference and inter-communication" occurred.

Was the nature of the Ordinance relevant to the crisis at Philadelphia? If we can assume (as contended earlier) that the prohibition of slavery in the Northwest was not threatening to the South, then the antislavery fugitive-slave clause of the Ordinance may have reassured men like Davie and Butler, just then expressing the first apprehensions about slave property on the floor of the Convention.[73] This was the element in the putative compromise stressed in Coles's recollection. But we have Dane's testimony that the antislavery proviso was added to the Ordinance at the last moment.[74] And Deep South statements of alarm at the Convention continued unabated until the compromise on the slave trade at the end of August.[75]

[71] On July 3 Hamilton wrote to George Washington from New York City: "I own to you Sir that I am seriously and deeply distressed at the aspect of the Councils which prevailed when I left Philadelphia" (*The Papers of Alexander Hamilton*, ed., Harold C. Syrett [New York, 1961—], IV, 224).

[72] See note 6, above.

[73] See note 5, above.

[74] Dane to King, July 16, 1787, *Letters of Continental Congress*, VIII, 622. Dane says he omitted an antislavery clause from the draft reported to Congress on July 11 since only Massachusetts of the New England states was present, but that "finding the House favorably disposed" he moved its inclusion, and it was "agreed to without opposition." The draft reported on July 11 did not contain the antislavery clause (*Journals of Continental Congress*, XXXII, 314-320).

[75] Another essay might be written about the compromise of late August. On August 29 Georgia, South Carolina, and North Carolina supported

More significant, surely, were the provisions of the Ordinance concerning the admission of new states. After the Ordinance passed, Dane wrote to King (as already quoted) that "the Eastern states for the sake of doing away the temporary governments, etc. established in 1784, and for establishing some order in that Country, gave up as much as could be reasonably expected." What did the North give up? It gave up its plan to require a large population for admission to statehood, and to make admission depend on the consent of a competent number of states in Congress. The Northwest Ordinance even added that "so far as it can be consistent with the general interest of the Confederacy, such admission shall be allowed at an earlier period, and when there may be a less number of free Inhabitants in the State than sixty thousand." Philbrick, the most detailed commentator on the Ordinance, judged this to be so drastic a change in the ordinance almost passed in May that it raised a "suspicion that some understanding" was involved. If the North rather than the South made the major concession in the drafting of the Ordinance, one could make better sense of Grayson's statement to the Virginia ratifying convention that the Ordinance "passed in a lucky moment," leaving Massachusetts "extremely uneasy about it."[76]

But the admission provisions of the Ordinance spoke to the needs of North as well as South. On the one hand, given the Southern assumption that the states of the Northwest (even if non-slaveholding) would strengthen the South in Congress, the provisions for easy and early admission to statehood held out hope to the South of swiftly increasing its forces in the House of Representatives. On the other hand, however, the Ordinance wrote into

---

Gouverneur Morris' motion to strike from the Constitution the idea that new states should be admitted on terms of equality with the old (*Records of Federal Convention*, II, 454). The three Deep South states had just been gratified on the issues of slave importation (which, of course, would add to their political as well as economic strength) and fugitive slaves.

[76] Speech of June 13, *Debates in the State Conventions*, III, 331.

law what had only been approved in principle the year before: that the Northwest would consist of three to five states rather than of ten. Thus it forestalled the prospect, threatening to the North, of losing control of the Senate. This would explain Dane's statement to King that he thought the population requirement for admission too small, "but, having divided the whole Territory into three States, this number appears to me to be less important."[77]

If (as George Mason put it) what the Convention needed was a plan that recognized the present dominance of the North while providing for eventual transition to a Southern majority, a plan, too, which safeguarded the present minority needs of the South and the future minority needs of the North, the Ordinance supplied a *deus ex machina* uncannily appropriate. The beauty of its admission requirements was that they appeared at the time to promote the South's interests in the House while protecting the North's interests in the Senate. Some necessary ambiguity remained. North as well as South hoped for the political allegiance of at least some of the Northwest states. The clause on slavery could be presented to Southern ratifying conventions as a guarantee of property and to Northern ratifying conventions as a bar to the creation of new slave states.[78] In place of a West vaguely attractive or dangerous, the Ordinance made available a West just sufficiently specific that each section could read in it the fulfillment of its political dreams.

Still, could the essential features of the Ordinance have become known in Philadelphia in time to affect the voting of July 12-14? The answer is, Yes. Whatever the catalyst was at the Convention, it was not yet apparent on July 10, when Washington wrote to Hamilton that matters were if anything worse than at the end of

[77] Dane to King, July 16, 1787, *Letters of Continental Congress*, VIII, 622.

[78] Thus James Wilson told the Pennsylvania ratifying convention, December 3, 1787, that "the *new* states which are to be formed, will be under *the control* of congress in this particular; and slaves will never be introduced amongst them" (*Debates in the State Conventions*, II, 423).

June.[79] That same afternoon, after returning to the appropriate congressional committee a draft of the Ordinance with several amendments, Manasseh Cutler left New York for Philadelphia. Arriving on the twelfth, he spent the evening at the Indian Queen tavern with delegates from the South and Massachusetts—Strong, Gerry, Gorham, Madison, Mason, Martin, Williamson, Rutledge, one of the Pinckneys—together with "Mr. Hamilton of New York," and other, unnamed persons. The morning of the fourteenth he spent with Strong, Martin, Mason, Williamson, Madison, Rutledge, and "Mr. Hamilton, all members of the Convention," before returning to New York City.[80] What better messenger could have been wished than the promoter of the Northwest Ordinance?

Cutler's references make clear that Hamilton was also in Philadelphia. He was not yet there on July 10, Cutler saw him on the twelfth and fourteenth, he did not represent New York at the Convention, and he was back in New York City by the twentieth.[81] The purpose of this brief and unofficial visit is unknown. Conceivably, Hamilton left New York late enough to learn the outlines of the Ordinance and arrived in Philadelphia early enough to influence the voting of the twelfth.[82] Hamilton's good friend Gouver-

[79] Washington to Hamilton, July 10, 1787, *Papers of Hamilton*, IV, 225: "I *almost* dispair. . . . I am sorry you went away. I wish you were back." At the end of July 11 the Convention "found itself without having advanced a single step" since July 5 (Farrand, *Framing of the Constitution*, p. 103).

[80] *Life of Cutler*, I, 242-272.

[81] Washington's letter cited in note 79 shows that at the time on July 10 when Washington wrote, Hamilton was not in Philadelphia, at least to Washington's knowledge. On July 14 King apologized for referring to New York at the Convention "in the absence of its representatives"; on July 16 Randolph speculated as to how "New York if present" would vote (*Records of Federal Convention*, II, 7, 78; Yates and Lansing, the other New York delegates, left July 10). On July 20 Hamilton wrote a letter to Nathaniel Mitchell from New York City (*Papers of Hamilton*, IV, 226).

[82] He might then not only have influenced Massachusetts, Pennsylvania, Maryland, and South Carolina in altering their votes on the three-fifths rule

neur Morris closed the Convention session of July 11 on a note of intransigence and opened the next morning's session with a proposal to "bridge" the sectional conflict.[83] But at this point one moves from the realm of legitimate speculation to that of uncontrolled fantasy.

If the Northwest Ordinance did in fact influence the compromises of the Constitution, how bitter a pill for its subsequently Antifederalist sponsors, Grayson, Lee, and Melancton Smith! And that would not be the only irony. It would mean that the South, backing the Ordinance on the doubly-mistaken assumption that its security lay in the House of Representatives and that the states of the Northwest would give it strength there, had produced a charter of freedom for the Negro; but also, that this charter made possible the Constitution, which gave slavery new sanctions.

Finally, why did Congress and Convention act so differently? The evidence suggests that the motives which moved men in making Ordinance and Constitution were essentially the same. The drafters at Philadelphia were troubled about slavery as were the legislators in New York. But in Congress, Southerners who sought

---

(see note 45, above), but also have arranged a meeting with Cutler for the twelfth. It does seem odd that at one of the tensest points in the Convention, a quarter of its membership accidentally (as Cutler's journal suggests) happened to be together and willingly idled away an evening with the visitor. See Irving Brant, *James Madison: Father of the Constitution*, 1787-1800 (Indianapolis, New York; 1950), pp. 98-99, who asks, What brought Madison and Pinckney to the Indian Queen? and suggests that they may have been preparing large state strategy for a last attempt to block equal suffrage in the Senate. But would they have talked to Cutler about this? My suggestion requires only that *he* talked to *them*.

[83] Morris said on the eleventh that he "could never agree to give such encouragement to the slave trade as would be given by allowing them a representation for their negroes" (*Records of Federal Convention*, I, 588). The next day, while still asserting that "he verily belived the people of Pena. will never agree to a representation of Negroes," he proposed that taxation and representation be proportional, with the object, Madison said, "to lessen the eagerness on one side, & the opposition on the other" to the three-fifths rule (*ibid.*, I, 591-593; II, 106 and *note*).

to guarantee slave property and to make possible a stronger Southern voice in Congress saw Northwest settlement, even without slavery, as a means to these ends. At the Convention, sanctions for slavery (the three-fifths clause and the slave trade clause) seemed necessary to bring about the same results: protection against emancipation and a Southern majority in the House. In each case the North made the compromises the South demanded, but in Congress, because of the South's mistaken assumptions about the future of the Northwest, an antislavery clause could be included. The fugitive slave clause adopted unanimously by both bodies shows, if not that there was a sectional compromise between Congress and Convention, at least that the makers of both Ordinance and Constitution were ready to compromise the concept that all men are equal. This was the fundamental compromise of 1787.

PART THREE

The Economic Origins of
Jeffersonian Historiography

9

**Abraham Yates's History
of the Movement for
the United States Constitution**

"At least as far back as 1871," Richard B. Morris
has observed, "Henry B. Dawson focused attention on the masses
in the Revolution and suggested the thesis of counterrevolution
and conspiracy" in interpreting the United States Constitution.[1]
In fact, an unpublished history of the movement for the Constitution made the same charge almost a century earlier. About a year
after ratification and 125 years before Charles Beard's *An Economic Interpretation of the Constitution of the United States*
(New York, 1913), Abraham Yates (1724-1796) of New York asserted in his manuscript narrative that the Federalists had "turned
a *Convention* into a *Conspiracy*, and under the Epithet *Federal*
have destroyed the Confederation." The authors of the Federalist

[1] Richard B. Morris, "Class Struggle and the American Revolution," *William and Mary Quarterly*, third series, XIX (1962), 20.

Reprinted from the William and Mary Quarterly, third series, **XX**
(1963), 223-245.

conspiracy were, according to Yates, the "aristocrats." This was an Antifederalist cliché: three-fourths of the more important Antifederalist tracts portrayed the Constitution as aristocratic.[2] Only Yates, however, combined the charge of conspiracy and the charge of aristocracy in the form of history. Every essential step in the movement for the United States Constitution as conceived by Charles Beard and Merrill Jensen will be found, dated and footnoted, in this pamphlet of 1789.

Important in the historiography of the Constitution, Yates's manuscript is equally significant for the insight it provides into the Antifederalist mind. By presenting the familiar epithets in the unconventional medium of narrative history, the manuscript throws fresh light on a movement which combined crass self-interest with a genuine concern to defend what Yates called "the *vertue* of the People."

When Abraham Yates spoke of the people, he meant people like himself: neither very rich nor very poor, but the "middle sort [which] like common sense generally hold the balance between the two extremes."[3] Like George Clinton and Melancton Smith, the other principal leaders of New York Antifederalism, Yates was one of those rising "new men" who jostled the great landed families for leadership of the Revolution in New York.[4]

Yates's Antifederalism stemmed above all from the resentment of a man of plebeian origins toward the disdainful manor lords of the Hudson Valley. The Yateses were a middle-class fam-

[2] Jackson T. Main, *The Antifederalists: Critics of the Constitution, 1781-1788* (Chapel Hill, 1961), p. 132n.

[3] "Speeches to Delegates in Congress, 1786," Abraham Yates Papers, New York Public Library, New York City. For a similar statement by another New York Antifederalist leader, see "Amendments proposed to the new Constitution of Government," Melancton Smith Papers, New York State Library, Albany, N. Y.: "all men having sufficient Evidence of permanent common Interest with, and Attachment to the Community, ought to have the Right of Suffrage."

[4] [See Essays 2 and 5.]

ily long established in Albany, New York.[5] Before the Revolution, Abraham Yates practiced law, mended shoes, and played a political role only at the city (member of the Albany common council, various terms 1754-1773) and county (sheriff of Albany County, 1754-1759) level. The Revolution shot him into state-wide prominence. He was chairman of the Committee of the City and County of Albany; chairman of the committee of the Provincial Convention which drafted New York's Revolutionary constitution in 1777; a state Senator under the new government; and New York Loan Officer for the Continental Congress. When (as conservatives complained) "Men of Substance and Importance" dropped out of New York politics,[6] men like Yates took their places. The greatest aristocrat of aristocratic Albany County, Philip Schuyler, remarked on Yates's new prominence: "Abraham Yates, I mean the Honorable Abraham Yates Esq. one of the Senate of this State, a member of the Council of Appointment—one of the Committee of the City and County of Albany, Recorder of the City of Albany—and Postmaster General, late Cobler of Laws and Old Shoes, is to be put in Nomination for Lieut. Governor."[7] Alexander Hamilton's opinion of Yates was equally scornful, and Thomas Tillotson, brother-in-law of Robert R. Livingston, referred to the Albany up-

[5] For biographical detail, consult Carol Spiegelberg, "Abraham Yates" (Master's thesis, Columbia University, 1960). [See now also Linda Grant DePauw, *The Eleventh Pillar: New York State and the Federal Constitution* (Ithaca, N. Y.; 1966), pp. 28-31]

[6] Egbert Benson to John Jay, June 23, 1779, Jay Papers, Columbia University.

[7] Philip Schuyler to Gouverneur Morris, Feb. 3, 1778, Gouverneur Morris Papers, Columbia University. During the ratification controversy, "A Lover of Truth and Decency" defended Yates from the charge that he had once been a shoemaker. The very fact that Yates had risen "from a mechanical profession" to "the highest honors in his country," declared this correspondent, was the strongest proof of his inherent worth: to attack Yates was to "trample upon the honest and free mechanics of this country, and to render them contemptible." *New York Journal*, Mar. 18, 1788, quoted by Clarence E. Miner, *The Ratification of the Federal Constitution by the State of New York* (New York, 1921), pp. 87-88.

start as an "old booby."[8] The tone of these comments tells more
about Yates's politics than could any amount of information about
his holdings of personalty or realty.

After the war, Yates divided his time between politicking in the
New York Senate and the Continental Congress, and propaganda.
In his legislative role, Yates managed Governor George Clinton's
program in the New York Senate. During the ratification debate he
fretted in New York City as a state delegate to the Continental
Congress, corresponding with the Antifederalist leaders at the
Poughkeepsie convention, and shipping them fifty copies of one of
his "Sydney" essays for distribution to the Antifederalist delegates.[9]
The latter exemplified Yates's second role as "the most active and
able Anti-Federalist pamphleteer of the post-war period" in the
state.[10] His published essays, under the pseudonyms "Sydney" and
"Rough Hewer," first appeared in the New York press in 1783 and

[8] Alexander Hamilton to Robert Morris, Aug. 13, 1782, in *The Papers of
Alexander Hamilton*, ed. Harold C. Syrett (New York, 1961—), III, 139;
Thomas Tillotson to Robert R. Livingston, May 1784, Robert R. Livingston
Papers, New-York Historical Society, New York City.

[9] See Abraham Yates to Abraham G. Lansing, May 28 and June 15, 1788,
and Lansing to Yates, June 22, 1788, Abraham Yates Papers. The essay in
question was probably that which appeared in the *New-York Journal, and the
Daily Patriotic Register*, June 13, 1788.

Although Yates was an extreme Antifederalist, he was not a consistent radical in state politics. For example, he opposed the confiscation of Loyalist lands
in 1779. On the other hand, a draft of the state constitution of 1777, in the
Abraham Yates Papers and for the most part in Yates's handwriting, called for
the secret ballot in all elections and an Assembly vote for all tax-paying freeholders. During the Critical Period, Yates voted with up-state Clintonians in
supporting paper money as legal tender for all obligations (vote of Mar. 29,
1786, *Journal of the Senate of the State of New-York at their first Meeting of
the Ninth Session* [New York, 1786]), and he antagonized many former Sons
of Liberty by opposing legislative relief for merchants sued by British creditors
("Copy of Petition [of merchants indebted to England]," 1785, N.Y.S.L.,
endorsed "N.B. This petition was strenuously opposed in the Joint Committee by A.Y. the Chairman a Senator from Albany"; see in confirmation,
"Mercator," *New York Daily Advertiser*, Apr. 22, 1786). After the dust of the
ratification contest had subsided, Clinton rewarded Yates for his many services
by appointing him mayor of Albany.

[10] Thomas C. Cochran, *New York in the Confederation: An Economic*

continued irregularly until the debate over Jay's Treaty. In addition, Yates turned out a variety of curious manuscripts in the same historical-polemical style as the present narrative, never published or used by historians. Taken together, these published and unpublished writings probably constitute the largest corpus produced by any Antifederalist in the nation.

Yates's attitude toward national questions had its roots in New York experience. In his view, an aristocratic conspiracy to put down the common man had existed from the origins of the colony. In several unpublished manuscripts on New York history, Yates attacks the usurpations of the Albany patroons. In another, he asserts that "this Colony of New York at least as far back as memory will carry us, has been divided into violent parties now known by the epithets of Whig and Tory [,] Republican or aristocratic."[11] In resisting the Constitution, these New York Antifederalists felt they were opposing (in George Dangerfield's words) "a resurgence in state and national form of that privileged government which New York had experienced as a colony."[12]

Yates finished his manuscript history in June 1789, as Congress was beginning to debate amendments to the United States Con-

---

Study (Philadelphia, 1932), p. 19. A collection of Yates's early anti-nationalist essays was published as *Political Papers, Addressed to the Advocates for a Congressional Revenue, in the State of New-York* (New York, 1786). His only other published book was apparently a vindication of his work as Loan Officer for the Continental Congress, entitled *Resolutions and extracts from the Journal of the honorable Congress, relative to the Continental Loan-Offices in the several states; and certain letters, passed between Robert Morris, Esq., superintendent of finance—the Board of Treasury of the United States and Abraham Yates, Jun., Esq., late Commissioner of the Continental Loan-Office of the State of New York* (Albany, 1786).

11 "Historical account of the colony of Rensselaerswyck," "Notes on early history of Albany," "Notes on Early History of New York, etc.," Abraham Yates Papers.

12 George Dangerfield, *Chancellor Robert R. Livingston of New York, 1746-1813* (New York, 1960), p. 228.

There was another, less creditable way in which Yates's New York experience shaped his Antifederalism. When Robert Morris became Financier, he bypassed the state Loan Officers (Yates held this position in New York) and

stitution.[13] When in September 1789 Congress recommended twelve amendments to the states, the note of Old Testament lamentation on which Yates concluded his work became (for most of the old Antifederalists) inappropriate. Congress's action, so unexpected from Yates's bitter and suspicious viewpoint, probably made him decide not to publish his manuscript.

The Bill of Rights, however, did not contain the kind of amendment which Yates most desired. He termed the proposed amendments "trivial and unimportant."[14] Yates felt that they sought only to protect the liberty of the individual, neglecting the more fundamental task of changing the structure of the new government. Like Lee, Grayson, and Henry of Virginia, like Burke and Tucker of South Carolina, Yates responded to the first ten amendments with hostility and chagrin.[15]

What the amendments lacked, as Yates saw the matter, was also lacking in the Constitution: some tangible restraint on the dangers of centralized power. Yates adhered to the decentralist tradition in

---

created the new post of state Receiver of Taxes. Yates applied for the position, but lost it to Alexander Hamilton. In the same letter in which Yates confessed himself "very much hurt" about losing the appointment, he spoke for the first time of the danger of nationalist centralization: "the Financier had too much power already" (Abraham Yates to James Duane and Ezra L'Hommedieu, Oct. 19, 1782, Abraham Yates Papers; another copy in James Duane Papers, N.-Y.H.S.). The coincidence was not lost on contemporaries; see "Adolphus," *New York Daily Advertiser*, Apr. 19, 1786.

[13] The manuscript can be dated by Yates's references to laws passed or under consideration; see notes 62 and 63 below. As the manuscript indicates, Yates had at first hoped the Constitution would be amended by a second constitutional convention. By early 1789, New York Antifederalists concluded that it was a hopeless strategy (see Melancton Smith to Gilbert Livingston, Jan. 1, 1789, Zephaniah Platt Papers, N.Y.S.L.). For the second convention movement, see Robert A. Rutland, *The Birth of the Bill of Rights, 1776-1791* (Chapel Hill, 1955), pp. 180-181, 188-191, 198-199.

[14] "Rough Hewer" transcripts, Mar. 15, Mar. 22, 1790, Abraham Yates Papers.

[15] See Rutland, *Birth of the Bill of Rights*, pp. 194-195, 204-205, 209, 213-217. At the New York ratifying convention, Antifederalists presented many amendments designed to change the structure of the government as well as to protect individual liberties. Thus Melancton Smith moved to prohibit gov-

Anglo-American political philosophy which was grounded, as Jackson Main has said, on a "mistrust of power."[16] Instancing the cabal of seventeenth-century England, the experience of his own Dutch forebears, and a host of Biblical parallels, and salting this historical stew by copious reference to Montesquieu, Burgh, Hume, Franklin, Adams, DeMably, Raynal, "Junius," and other classics of the day, Yates argued that the Constitution was only one more melancholy example of aristocracy's effort "to get the Power out of the Hands of the People."

As suggested earlier, the manuscript anticipates remarkably the Beard-Jensen version of the decade 1778-1788. Beginning with the French alliance, Yates discusses the appointment of Robert Morris as Financier; the impost struggle; the Army-Congress plot of early 1783; the connection between the party battles in Congress and those in the individual states; the centralization of Congressional administration; Morris's use of his administrative machine to promote legislation which he favored; the Federalist appeal to former Tories; the movement to have Continental obligations repaid at face value; the role of Shays' Rebellion; the supposed usurpation of the members of the Constitutional Convention, who (as Yates saw it) "paid no more regard to their orders and credentials than Caesar when he passed the Rubicon"; and the manipulation of the ratification process by the Federalists. Surely it was something of an achievement that, writing in the midst of these events with the aid of few documents beyond the journals of the Continental Congress, Yates approximated so nearly the current textbook picture of one of the most exhaustively scrutinized episodes in American history.

Limited as his sources were, Yates used them with a good eye for detail. Despite its obvious partisanship and highly colored in-

---

ernment-chartered monopolies, and others sought to increase the size of the House of Representatives, divide Congressional districts, protect the states' rights to supervise Congressional elections, etc. (McKesson Papers, N.-Y.H.S.)

[16] Main, *The Antifederalists*, p. 9.

vective, the narrative sticks close to documents. Yates is at his best in ironically contrasting the text of the Boston Port Bill with the words of a law passed by Congress in 1789 to punish nonratifying Rhode Island, or in tearing apart the verbal pretexts with which Congress had appropriated money to put down Shays' Rebellion. Effective, also, are Yates's habit of detailed comparison between the American Revolution and the revolutions of Europe, and his juxtaposition of historical happenings and the aphorisms of political philosophy.

Where the manuscript goes wrong is in interpretation. The fault is not simply a matter of tone and style. More fundamentally, Yates shows an unsophisticated—almost a theological—sense of how history takes place. His story is a tale of sinister conspiracy springing from a lust for power. In this Yates anticipated the more superficial side of Beard, who exhibited a similar cast of thought when he called the Founding Fathers "a small and active group of men immediately interested through their personal possessions in the outcome of their labors," and discussed the Convention from the standpoint of the "advantages which the beneficiaries expected would accrue to themselves first."[17]

To some extent, Yates's conspiratorial interpretation was the consequence of the paucity of his sources. Unlike the modern scholar, he did not have access to the personal papers of the leading Federalists. "What was their view in the beginning," he comments, "or [how] far it was Intended to be carried Must be Collected from facts that Afterwards have happened." This was a dangerous assumption, for it led Yates to impute an unchanging conspiratorial design to the nationalist movement from its very beginnings. Consequently, his history is most successful in its description of events where conspiracy was, in fact, at work. Thus Yates's brief notice of the effort of some Congressmen early in 1783 to use the discontent of the army as a lever to centralize the government, needs little essential correction.

[17] Charles A. Beard, *An Economic Interpretation of the Constitution of the United States* (New York, 1913), pp. 18, 324.

Yet more sophisticated interpretations of the downfall of republics were available to Yates. Many political leaders in both the Federalist and Antifederalist camps accepted an economic interpretation of history which held that a republican government could exist only when property was equally divided and the "manners of the people" were virtuous, and that the development of commerce inevitably caused luxury, corruption, and finally, the fall of republican institutions. Yates must have been aware of this theory, for in his own crabbed way he read as widely as Madison or Adams. But he eschewed such sophistication for the easier *ad hominem* approach: for Yates, if the manners of the people were corrupted, someone had to be to blame. Carl Becker's summary of the political thought of Samuel Adams applies perfectly to the ideology of Yates. "Samuel Adams," Becker wrote, "who had perhaps not heard of even one of the many materialistic interpretations of history, thought of the past as chiefly instructive in connection with certain great epochal conflicts between Liberty and Tyranny—a political Manicheanism, in which the principle of Liberty was embodied in the virtuous many and the principle of Tyranny in the wicked few."[18]

While Yates and Beard produced similar narratives of the movement for the Constitution, the animus of their histories was very different. Beard emphasized the economic motive. To Yates, in contrast, a lust for power seemed at the root of evil, with economic self-interest only supplementary. One thing, however, Yates had in common with the Populist-Progressive writers who followed in his footsteps in interpreting the Constitution: a sense of social distance from the men of power of their respective Americas.

Yates did not prepare the following manuscript for the printer, and the reader must be prepared to struggle with rambling sentences and illogical sequences quite different from the published essays of "Rough Hewer."

The manuscript was found in a folder marked "Essays on Var-

18 Carl L. Becker, *The Eve of the Revolution: A Chronicle of the Breach with England* (Toronto and London, 1918, 1921), p. 163.

ious Political Subjects" in Box 4 of the Abraham Yates Papers at the New York Public Library. It consists of sixteen sheets of six by seven inch notebook paper, somewhat worn at the edges so that a few words are missing from the text. These have been supplied in brackets. In addition I have made such absolutely necessary and minimum changes in punctuation as seemed required to ensure readability. Footnotes have been verified, and expanded within brackets for the convenience of the reader. Finally, I have added topical heads, in italics, to clarify the structure of the argument.

THE YATES MANUSCRIPT

It will appear unaccountable, but on the principle of Junius that from the Condition of the People [torn] the Corruption of their Rulers,[19] that in less than [ten?] years the People should fall from the Rich and happy Station of Human *Vertue* and *unanimity* and be debased to such a state of *Corruption* [and] *Confusion*; and that too when it appears to [have been] planned and set to work at first by so few in number. It is a matter of Doubt whether in 1779 the number in any one state (that has been active) has exceeded that of the Cabal in England at the beginning of this and Close of the last Century.

The French Alliance Ensures American Victory, and a
Few Conspirators Begin to Work for Aristocracy in the
States, and Centralization in Congress

But their councils were not less artfull and Dangerous. Having been frustrated in Introducing Aristocratic Principles in the Constitutions of the Respective states, by the *vertue* of the People and

[19] Junius 29 [*Junius* (London, 1772), I, xxix: "Is it not notorious that the vast revenues, extorted from the labour and industry of your subjects, and given You to do honour to yourself and to the nation, are dissipated in corrupting their representatives?"]

their *apprehension* about the Event of the Controversy; and Released of the latter by the News of the Treaty with France;[20] [they] now Began to prepare to counteract the former, according to a Common Maxim among Tyrants "that no free government was ever dissolved or overcome before the Manners of the People were corrupted,"[21] by securing adherents among the Rulers in the several states. [These] availed themselves in their maneuvers of the distresses of the Inhabitants occasioned by a most cruel predatory war that was carried on in the country. The most artfull means were used to propagate among the People that the Confederacy was defective, that too Much power remained in the hands of the People and the several state Legislatures and that Congress was not vested with powers sufficient for their peace or protection.

It was not long before they [had] a considerable Party in Congress (sometimes a majority) and among the *Rulers*[22] in the several

[20] [See Edmund C. Burnett on the effect of the French alliance: "The winter and spring of 1778 was probably the gloomiest period of the war. Could Congress have known that on February 6 a treaty of alliance had been signed with France, the mood of that assembly would have been altogether different. On May 2, at a moment when despair had all but taken possession of Congress and the whole country, the treaty arrived. It was like a reprieve from the gallows. But what about the Confederation, members at once began to ask one another. . . . The Confederation must be hastened to a consummation." ("New York in the Continental Congress," *History of the State of New York*, ed. Alexander C. Flick, III [New York, 1933], 305-306.)]

[21] Franklin 17 [Benjamin Franklin, *Political, Miscellaneous, and Philosophical Pieces* . . . (London, 1779), p. 17: "It is a common maxim among the advocates of liberty, that no free government was ever dissolved, or overcome, before the manners of its subjects were corrupted."]

[22] 2 Robertsons America [torn]: "The system of securing a foreign usurpation (says Robertson) under [torn] of authority derived from the natural Rulers of a Country; the device [torn] employing the magistrates, and forms already established [torn] instruments to introduce a New Dominion, of which we are [torn] a sublime Refinement in policy peculiar to the present age [torn] Invensions of a more early period" [William Robertson, *The History of America* (London, 1777), II, 65: "The system of screening a foreign usurpation, under the sanction of authority derived from the natural rulers of a country, the device of employing the magistrates and forms already established as in-

states, both in their Legislative and Judicial Capacities. The Rich,
who De Mably says Never will be Satisfyed with Common Fare,[23]
also played into their hands, to whom were added those in the
words of Congress "who like the British Nabobs of the East were
corrupting the manners of a Whole Nation and building vast
fortunes on the destruction of the Liberties of the western
world."[24] The Tories who under the former [government] went
under the name of High Prerogative Men and joined the Whigs
against Britain now came out under the [name] of federal Men
[and] cooperated with them in its propagation.

The Conspirators Consider Alternative Strategies

What was their view in the beginning or [how] far it was Intended to be carried Must be Collected from facts that Afterwards
have happened; as it was said of the Cabal that though from the
first their "Dark Councils gave anxiety to all men of Reflection
they were not thoroughly known but by the Event."[25]

Various Schemes appear to have been Suggested by these agita-
tors for a Change of government to get the Power out of the Hands
of the People. The difficulty attending them (the apprehension
that the New England States would not Submit as the People

---

struments to introduce a new dominion, of which we are apt to boast as sublime refinements in policy peculiar to the present age." The passage refers to
Cortes's treatment of Montezuma.]

[23] [Abbe (Gabriel Bonnot) de Mably, *Remarks Concerning the Government and the Laws of the United States of America* . . . (London, 1784), p.
214: "the opulent . . . are inclined to think that every article of enjoyment be-
longs to them, because they possess riches which can secure to them a general
obedience."]

[24] 3 Journals 589 [*Journals of Congress. Containing the Proceedings from
September 5, 1774 to [November 3, 1788]* (Philadelphia, 1777-1788), III,
589; hereafter cited as *Journals of Congress*.]

[25] 7 Hume 471 [David Hume, *The History of England* (Dublin, 1780),
VII, 461: "The dark counsels of the Cabal, though from the first they gave
anxiety to all men of reflection, were not thoroughly known but by the event."]

there were Republicans in their make) was explained [thus]:[26] that aristocratic[27] influence might be made to work there with as much Care as in any state in the Union. Nor was there a stronger evidence in any state, [of] certain families [being] more singularized and their Children preferred to public offices for being of Certain families, than in some New England states.

Some were of opinion that Congress like the Decemvri among the Romans ought without any other ceremony to assume the powers of government and make use of the army to enforce it. Others preferred the doing of it more circuitously by getting Congress invested with the appointment of some principal officers in Each state, an Impost, a Pole Tax, a Land Tax, an Excise upon all spirituous Liquors, all to be collected by officers in the appointment of and under the Laws of Congress.[28]

While this was in agitation the oaths of fidelity and of office, and the Rotation of the Members of Congress, were daily Reprobated in conversation, and as these oaths [and] the Rotation had not yet been put in Operation It had the effect that they were not insisted on. It was said that the inexpediency of the oaths and the Rotation was evident, If we consider thus: that the dishonest would not mind them and the Honest would do their duty without being sworn; and [that] by the Rotation we had put it out of our power to continue perhaps a man the most experienced and usefull in Congress, while no more was necessary to secure, on the one

[26] 1 Adams 111:112 [John Adams, *A Defence of the Constitutions of Government of the United States of America* (Philadelphia, 1787), I, p. 111: "Go into every village in New-England, and you will find that the office of justice of the peace, and even the place of representative, which has ever depended only on the freeest election of the people, have generally descended from generation to generation, in three or four families at most."]

[27] "I prefer (says De Mably) to all the rest the Constitution of Massachusetts as prescribing the narrowest limits to the Democracy, and as preparing the republic for its inevitable transition to Aristocracy" [De Mably, *Remarks*, p. 204.]

[28] [See notes 48, 51.]

hand their Respect, and on the other their faithfull Service, than
dignity and splendor in the offices of government and high salaries to support them therein.

The cry of high salaries both in the members and officers of
Congress became general and even fashionable, and those that
would not fall in with the Idea [came to be] considered as unfit
for a public office and, if In, unworthy and to be turned out. The
effects of the neglect of the Rotation began soon to operate. The
distresses in many parts of the country created by a depredatory
war occasioned a more than ordinary change in the Members of
the Legislatures, while on the contrary the Members of Congress
were said to be necessary to be continued. Instead of serving no
more than three years which would have been the means of dis-
concerting them In their Destructive plans, they Remained some
even near nine years; By means whereof they had not only an
opportunity to cabal and concert but, when concerted, to get
others combined to assist and support it.[29]

The Journals of the Continental Congress Reveal the
Progress of the Conspiracy

The Perusal of the Journals will cast light upon this matter. On
the 6th February 1778 The Treaty was concluded with the King of
France; the News is Received at Congress the 2 May 1778;[30] 27
August a Committee is appointed "to consider the state of the
Money and of the Finances of the United States and report thereon

[29] [For the importance of rotation to the drafters of the Articles, see Merrill
Jensen, The Articles of Confederation: An Interpretation of the Social-Constitutional History of the American Revolution, 1774-1781 (Madison, 1940),
p. 242. Yates may have been thinking particularly of his political opponent
James Duane, who served in the Congress from 1774 to 1783 with a break of
only one year. Others with long terms of consecutive service in the Congress,
however, included "radicals" Samuel Adams (1774-1782) and Richard Henry
Lee (1774-1780). See Lynn Montross, The Reluctant Rebels: The Story of
the Continental Congress, 1774-1789 (New York, 1950), pp. 426-431.]

[30] [Journals of Congress, IV, 255.]

from time to time";[31] 19 September 1778 "This Committee having made report the same was read: Resolved that 60 copies of the said Report be printed for the use of the members, and that the printer be under an Oath not to devulge any part of the said Report, nor strike off more than 60 copies together with the proofs and finished sheets; That the Members of the House be enjoined not to Communicate the report or any part of it, without leave of the House."[32]

On the 16 December 1778 Congress Resolved to pay expenses of the presidents that have been, or [may be] elected presidents of Congress, [and] to pay the expenses incidental to this office; and all the former presidents were called upon to Exhibit their accounts before the Board of Treasury. It was also Resolved "that a convenient furnished dwelling House be hired and a Table Carriage and Servants provided at the public Expense for the President of Congress for the time being." A Steward [was] to be appointed to have the Superintendence of the Household of the President and of the Necessary expenditures.[33]

It is observable here that until 1779 the Members of Congress, joined with certain officers appointed from time to time for that purpose, had managed the Exchequer or treasury Business. The 30 July Congress passed an Ordinance for "Establishing a Board of Treasury and proper officers for managing the finances of the United States," the Board now to consist of five Commissioners whereof two to be Members of Congress.[34]

The 18 January 1780 it was ordered that the Journals for the

---

[31] [*Ibid.*, IV, 500. The key member of the committee was Yates's New York antagonist, Gouverneur Morris; see Morris to Robert Livingston, Aug. 17, 1778, in *Letters of Members of the Continental Congress*, ed Edmund C. Burnett (Washington, D.C.; 1921-1936), III, 376 and *note*.]

[32] [*Journals of Congress*, IV, 550.]

[33] [*Ibid.*, IV, 716.]

[34] [*Ibid.*, V, 300-306. The New York conservative James Duane was chairman of both the new and old Treasury Boards; see Edward P. Alexander, *A Revolutionary Conservative: James Duane of New York* (New York, 1938),

current year be published Monthly without the yeas and nays.[35] 18 March 1780 Congress Resolved that the Principal of all Loans should be discharged by paying the full value of the Bills when Loaned;[36] 26 June 1780 Ordered that the Journals of Congress of the year 1779 be Immediately reprinted in one volume omitting the yeas and nays;[37] 28 June 1780 Congress fixed the Period to Calculate the Interest from to be the first of September 1777, a Period Notoriously known [as a time by which] the Money had Depreciated Above half, or in other words, that it passed at the rate of above two to one.[38] This was supposed to gratify certain Individuals.

The 7 November 1780 a Committee was appointed "to prepare and lay before Congress a plan for arranging the finances [and] paying the debt, and economizing the Revenue of the United States."[39]

---

pp. 109 ff., 136, and more generally on Duane's central role in Continental finances before 1781. Essay 5, p. 119.]

[35] [*Journals of Congress*, VI, 26.]

[36] [*Ibid.*, VI, 92-94: "That the bills which shall be issued, be redeemable in specie, within six years after the present, and bear an interest at the rate of five per centum per annum, to be paid also in specie at the redemption of the bills." The author of the plan for currency devaluation of Mar. 18, 1780—the first significant victory of the nationalists in Congress—was again a New York conservative, in this case Philip Schuyler; see Schuyler to George Washington, Mar. 7, 11, 13, 1780, in *Letters of Continental Congress*, V, 62, 67, 71.]

[37] [*Journals of Congress*, VI, 193.]

[38] If the Reader will turn up the Journals [of] Congress of the 15 January 1784 he will find it out that the Interest on Loan office Certificates bearing Date between the 1 September 1777 and the last Day of February 1778 are not subjected to any Depreciation [Yates is referring to the following passages in the act of June 28, 1780, *ibid.*, VI, 195: "That the value of the bills when loaned, shall be ascertained for the purpose above mentioned, by computing thereon a progressive rule of depreciation, commencing with the first day of September, 1777," and "that the same interest and mode of payment on certificates taken out before the first day of March, 1778, shall be continued as at present, until the principal . . . be ready to be discharged."]

[39] [*Ibid.*, VI, 362.]

Robert Morris Is Appointed Financier

While this was in agitation and the country in the utmost distress, [there] was brought forward the impost system and that for appointing the Superintendent of Finance.

On the 3 February 1781 Congress "Resolved that it be recommended to the several states as indispensably Necessary, that they vest a power in Congress to levy for the use of the United States a duty of five per cent," etc.[40]

On the 7 February 1781 was brought forward this New System,[41] of the complexion of that of the Court of France, untill then unknown in America. What in England is called the exchequer or treasury, in holland Chamber of Accounts,[42] in france finances, had the name of the Treasury or treasury Board in America.

By this System they determined to appoint a *superintendent of finance* and defined the duties of his office, afterwards called the *Fiscal Administration*.[43] On the 20th Robert Morris Esq., then or lately one of the Committee of Secrecy, was appointed: a gentleman perhaps as fruitfull of Invention, and from his former experience and high Notions of funding the public debt as well calculated to act the Part of a Financier, as any in the Reign of Louis the 14th. But this was not the only Requisite. They gave the Financier Liberty to trade.[44] That could [be] of Little use to Congress:

[40] [*Ibid.*, VII, 25-26. Yates actually summarizes rather than quotes the resolution of Congress. A federal impost had been included in the devaluation plan of Mar. 1780, but the states ignored it; in Aug. 1780, Robert R. Livingston of New York revived the idea of a Federal impost and also moved the creation of a committee to report a plan for centralizing the executive departments (see *Letters of Continental Congress*, V, xxx,xxxiii).]

[41] [*Journals of Congress*, VII, 29-30.]

[42] 27 Universal History 346 [*An Universal History, from the Earliest Accounts to the Present Time* . . . (London, 1779-1784), XXVII, chap. 75, "Chamber of Accounts."]

[43] 2 Spirit of Laws 347:354 [Apparently a reference to Book XIII, "Of the relation which the levying of taxes and the greatness of the public revenues have to liberty."]

[44] [Before accepting the position of Financier, Robert Morris stipulated

he might thereby by Impowered to *scrape* and to commit *usury* with Impunity but Neither, Except to himself and Associates, were like to be productive in the Coffers of Congress. It therefore followed that there could be no great expectations of the New System [unless] the powers of Congress were augmented.

The Financier in Action

It appears from the various Schemes [we] have had in contemplation that the following was adopted, viz:

To make the financier the center of communication and to put all the officers that had any connections with the Treasury under his controul, and to try to Introduce and get the appointment of some Influential officers in Every state (and they also under the controul of the Financier); so that Congress, by means of the Financier and these officers, might keep up a correspondence, and by acting in concert they might be Enabled to influence the several Legislatures in favour of Congressional Measures, and so get the powers of Congress augmented.[45]

This was carried on with such art and secrecy between certain Members of Congress and the Financier that few in the states, and even the Honest part of the Members of Congress, were acquainted with the Intention. The Abbe Robin must have been let into the secret, when in his Letter of the 15 November 1781 after the cap-

---

that he must have what Yates calls "Liberty to trade"—that is, freedom to continue his private business enterprises while serving Congress—and the power to discharge any officer of Congress handling Federal moneys. See Clarence L. Ver Steeg, *Robert Morris, Revolutionary Financier: With An Analysis of His Earlier Career* (Philadelphia, 1954), pp. 59-61.]

[45] [See the statement of E. James Ferguson in *The Power of the Purse: A History of American Public Finance, 1776-1790* (Chapel Hill, 1961), p. 142, that Morris "employed the receivers as his personal agents to lobby with state legislatures and inspire favorable publicity for his measures." The letters of Alexander Hamilton, as Receiver of Taxes in the state of New York, support Yates and Ferguson on this point; see, e.g., Hamilton to Robert Morris, Aug. 13, 1782, as cited in note 8 of this essay. See also Ver Steeg, *Robert Morris*, p. 101.]

ture of Lord Cornwallis he says, "The power of Congress heretofore weak and wavering will be consolidated."[46]

On the 21 April 1781 all the officers in Connection with the Finances were ordered to be subordinated to him, and [the Resolution] of the 2nd of November 1781 gave him a Constructive power to appoint a Receiver of Taxes in the Room of the Loan Officers in Every State.[47] Another Reason that was given in favour of this office of Receiver of Taxes in every State was to instruct the Committees of Ways and Means in the Art and Mystery of financing. Altho this Committee generally possessed sound judgment and Common Sense, it was [held to be] insufficient in the Line of financing, which was a Business so intricate that it Required a person of uncommon Sense.

While this was in agitation, the Financier by his letters of the 27th of February and the 29th of July [1782], under a Mistaken Idea that the impost had already been vested in Congress, was urging in *America* the Necessity of funding the public Debt to provide for the Interest thereof, and an additional Land Tax of one dollar upon every hundred acres of Land, a Pole tax of one dollar upon [every male] above sixteen, and an excise of [one-eighth of] a Dollar per Gallon upon all distilled Spirituous Liquors; while in *Europe* he was temporising with our ambassador in France, to persuade him that the 3,000,000, understood to be granted as a donation, should be acknowledged as a debt and included in the obligation given to the Court of France as money borrowed, and assigned as a Reason that this Country ought not to lay under any obligation to any Foreign power for money given.[48]

[46] Abbé Robin 19:104 [Abbé (Claude C.) Robin, *New Travels Through North-America: In A Series of Letters* . . . (Philadelphia, 1783), p. 79.]

[47] [*Journals of Congress*, VII, 89-90, 219.]

[48] [Morris proposed the taxes described by Yates in his letter to the President of Congress of July 29, 1782. Yates's reference to Morris's correspondence with the American ambassador to France probably concerns the Financier's letter to Benjamin Franklin, Nov. 27, 1781, in which Morris urged that the United States rather than France should henceforth pay the interest on the

Had this Revenue and the mode of Collecting taken place, it would have put the people of America either in the same situation the People of Great Britain have been in since their Revolution, who, says Blackstone, "in the time of King William had generously struggled for the Abolition of the then prerogative and by an unaccountable want of foresight Established this System in their stead. The entire collection of so vast a Revenue being placed in the hands of the Crown, has given rise to such a Multitude of new Officers created by and Removeable at the Royal pleasure, that they have extended the influence of government to every corner of the nation";[49] or as in France, where many of the taxes and Revenues are let out for a time to the best bidder, or as it is their called, farmer, and these Harpies, the farmer general and the underlings, make no scruple of fleecing the people most unmercifully.

And altho the measure was not adopted, yet the prospect of success (it was at one time said that all the states except Rhode Island had come in) had led both Congress and the Financier to actions, and into such management, as if they were not to be accountable to god or Men for their Conduct.

The Financier and His Collaborators Dishonestly Promote
Their Nationalist Program by Pretending That It
Is Essential for Victory in the War

We recollect that Lord Cornwallis with his army were captured on the 19th October 1781, from which time says Dr. Ramsay

domestic public debt. Ferguson, *Power of the Purse*, p. 149, substantially agrees with Yates's interpretation of the latter; Ver Steeg also points out that Morris had falsified the amount of French aid in a letter to the state governors so as to make the domestic crisis seem more urgent (*Robert Morris*, pp. 103-104). The pertinent passages in these letters will be found in *The Revolutionary Diplomatic Correspondence of the United States*, ed. Francis Wharton (Washington, D.C.; 1889), V, 17, 627.]

[49] [William Blackstone, *Commentaries on the Laws of England in Four Books* (Philadelphia, 1771-1772), I, 334. The passage begins: "Our national debt and taxes . . . have also in their natural consequences thrown such a weight of power into the executive scale of government, as we cannot think was intended by our patriot ancestors." Yates was one of five members of his family who subscribed to this first American edition of the *Commentaries*.]

every thing tended to peace and an acknowledgment of our Independence;[50] that on the Fourth of March 1782 the House of Commons addressed the King and entered into a Resolution, "That
they would consider all those as enemies to his Majesty and the
Country, who should advise or by any means attempt the further
prosecution of the war on the continent of America for the purpose of reducing the revolted Colonies to obedience by force"; that
in Consequence thereof the campaign of 1782 passed by almost
without any hostilities; that on the 30th November 1782 the preliminary Articles were signed, by which these united states were
declared free and independent.

Compare these with the Letters of the Financier of the 27th
February and 29 July 1782, Recommending to fund the public
debt, and to grant the Congress the aforesaid Land Tax, Pole Tax,
and Excise;[51] with the Letter from Congress on the 11 December
1782 in respect to the duty of Imposts to the Governour of the
state of Rhode Island,[52] viz:

Sir

Congress are equally affected and alarmed by the information they
have received, that the Legislature of your state, at their last meeting,
have refused their concurrence in the *establishment* of a *Duty* on imports. *They consider this measure, as so Indispensable to the prosecu-*

[50] [David Ramsay, *The History of the American Revolution* (Philadelphia,
1789), II, 306: The "great change of the public mind in Great Britain, favorable to American independence, took place between November 1781, and
March 1782. . . . Seven years experience had proved to the nation that the
conquest of the American States was impracticable; they now received equal
conviction, that the recognition of their independence, was an indispensable
preliminary to the termination of a war, from the continuance of which, neither
profit nor honour was to be acquired."]

[51] [Morris's letter of Feb. 27, 1782, is referred to in *Journals of the Continental Congress, 1774-1789*, ed. Gaillard Hunt *et al.* (Washington, D.C.; 1904-
1937), XXII, 115n; his letter of July 29, 1782, is printed in *ibid.*, 429-446,
and in *Revolutionary Diplomatic Correspondence*, as cited in note 48.]

[52] Supposing what was then said to be ill founded, That a noted Writer
[Thomas Paine] was sent from Philadelphia to Rhode Island to advocate the
Necessity of adopting the Measure; and that the Money to pay the expenses,
whether any, and what sum, was taken out of the Treasury without the Consent of Nine States.

tion of the war, that a *sense of duty,* and Regard to the common *Safety,* compel them to renew their efforts, to engage a compliance with it; and in *this view* they have determined to send a deputation of three of their members to your state . . . [Yates's italics] [;] [53]

with the Letter to Congress from the Financier Dated Office of Finance 24 January 1783: [54]

Congress (he says) will recollect that I expressly stipulated to take no part in past transactions. My attention to the public Debts, therefore arose from the conviction that *funding* them on solid *Revenues,* was the last essential work of our Glorious Revolution. The accomplishment of this Necessary Work, is among the objects, *nearest my Heart,* and to Effect it I would continue to sacrifice time, prosperity, and domestic Bliss etc. If effective Measures are not taken by that period (the last day of May) to make permanent provision for the public debt, of every kind, Congress will be pleased to appoint some other man to be Superintendent of Finances. I should be unworthy of the confidence reposed in me by my follow citizens, if I did not explicitly declare that I will never be the minister of injustice . . . [Yates's italics] [;]

with the letter of the Committee of the Army dated Philadelphia 8 February 1783, from which it Evidently appears that there was a *Combination* between some of the *Members of Congress* and the Committee to *assist Each other,* the *one* to obtain *continental funds* for Congress, the *other half pay* or the *equivalent* for the Army; [55] [and] with the Letter from the Minister of France dated Philadelphia 15 March 1783. [56]

[53] [This letter is printed in *Journals of Congress,* VIII, 31-32.]

[54] [The text of Morris' letter is printed in *Revolutionary Diplomatic Correspondence,* VI, 228-229; it is referred to in *Journals of the Continental Congress,* XXIV, 92n., 151.]

[55] [Yates evidently has in mind the Army memorial written in Dec. 1782 and presented to Congress in Jan. 1783; it is printed in *Journals of the Continental Congress,* XXIV, 291-293. The Army-Congress plot of early 1783 is described by Ferguson, *Power of the Purse,* chap. 8; Ver Steeg, *Robert Morris,* chap. 9; and Merrill Jensen, *The New Nation: A History of the United States during the Confederation, 1781-1789* (New York, 1950), pp. 69-84.]

[56] [The letter of the Chevalier de la Luzerne to Robert Morris, Mar. 15,

They will appear to be out of Character, void of truth or good policy.[57] Even supposing what has been said, that it was a combination wholly intended to scare Rhode Island into a compliance, and supposing too that *they Realy believed* that if Rhode Island had complied with the System it would have been for the *good of the People* (which is supposing a great deal), still, were they not justified? [No.] They were not to do Evil that good Might come.

In the mean time the Financier got to be very Dictatorial and Impertanent. His Letter of the 24 January 1783 shows how Difficult it is to Manage Servants when their Masters have Employed them to pursue Indirect Measures.

Having Failed to Enact Their Program in Wartime, the Conspirators Plan the Annapolis and Philadelphia Conventions

If we advert to the crooked measures of the Leading Characters after the Treaty with France in 1778 both in and out of Congress

---

1783, was forwarded by Morris to Congress, and printed in *Journals of the Continental Congress*, XXIV, 288-290; it stated that "*without a speedy establishment of solid general revenue, and an exact performance of the engagements which Congress have made, you must renounce the expectations of loans in Europe*."]

[57] [Yates's argument in the preceding paragraphs—that the nationalists in Congress attempted to establish Federal revenues under cover of a war emergency which, after Yorktown, did not in fact exist—is supported by Ferguson, *Power of the Purse*, pp. 125, 147: "After Yorktown, a military force had to be maintained until the spring of 1783, but the emergency was over.... Morris' plea that the impost was necessary as a war measure was forceful, but it lost much of its urgency when he managed to obtain foreign loans without the tax. He deliberately understated and tried to conceal the amount of aid being received from abroad, but the fact was that, under his astute management, it was enough to support the limited campaigns after Yorktown. Although he still warned that the hope of the enemy was in the 'derangement of our finances,' his arguments were vitiated in the spring of 1782, when changes in the British ministry forecast peace." See also Ver Steeg, *Robert Morris*, pp. 166-168, and the letters of Morris there quoted; and Robert Morris to Alexander Hamilton, July 2, 1782, in *Papers of Hamilton*, III, 98, "what remains of the War being only a War of Finance solid arrangements of

(which about that time became the Center of Intrigue and cabal), [we see them] playing into each others hands *progressively* to enlarge the powers of Congress at the expense of the Liberties of the People; calling out that the confederation was like *a rope of sand*, without Energy or sufficient power to protect us, that we ought to proclaim a Dictator. At the same time public affairs were suffered to run into confusion, while the cry was all through this state, the worse the better: out [of] confusion a good government would arise.[58] The newspapers Every day were almost filled with the disadvantage we were under by the British act of trade; the Algiers capturing our vessels; and the Danger we were in from the Indians[59] on our Borders—untill Matters were brought about by that Confusion that they could add, that now Everybody could see that it was become Necessary (no Matter how) that something should be done, that it was evident Congress had not sufficient powers, that it was Necessary the federal government should for fifteen years be invested with full powers to regulate trade.

When this was done, It was said that altho it Evidently appeared from the Respective Acts that *all* the States aimed at a compliance with the Recommendations of Congress, yet the several acts

Finance must necessarily terminate favorably not only to our Hopes, but even to our Wishes."]

[58] [Conservative New Yorkers did on occasion express themselves much in the manner Yates describes. For example, James Duane wrote to Philip Schuyler, June 16, 1780: I "contemplate the approach of distress itself with serenity, and I had almost said with some Mixture of Contentment. It is an Evil which will be productive of essential good." Schuyler Papers, N.Y.P.L.]

[59] The Dread of an Indian war, from the Barbarous Manner it is carried on, has ever been alarming, and as such a great handle for sinister purposes to politicians, both under the former and the present government. Witness the maneuvering of the Governor of Pennsylvania between 1750 and 1760 and that of Congress set on foot 20 October 1786 [*Journals of Congress*, XI, 258-259] to increase the Army. I have no doubt that by considering the Natives as Human Beings and not as Wolves and Bears, and acting agreeable to the Laws of Nature and Good conscience and purchasing the Lands from them, more may be done with one Dollar than with 10,000 [dollars] by extinguishing the Indian Right by War.

differed in their Phraysialigy, commencement, and duration, so that
it could not be made an Article in the Confederation; that therefore it would be necessary for the several states to appoint persons
to meet, agree upon and report a Draught of a Bill to be Laid
before the respective Legislatures to be passed into a Law in the
very Words.

The meeting at Baltimore, altho an Insufficient Number, Reported not the Draught of a Law but the propriety of another
meeting at Philadelphia with powers to amend the Confederation.

The meeting at Philadelphia in 1787 for the sole and express
purpose of revising the Articles of Confederation, got the name of
a Convention (I believe before long that of a Conspiracy would
have been more Significant), [and] paid no more regard to their
orders and credentials than Caesar when he passed the Rubicon.
Under an Injunction of Secrecy they carried on their works of
Darkness untill the Constitution passed their usurping hands.

It did not pass through Congress without an attempt for an
approbation. When it was sent on to the respective states, [what]
Management and Deceptions were used by the advocates in representing in their publications the perfection of the instrument,
[what] meetings and processions of the different classes of the
inhabitants (as if they wandered after and worshipped the Beast)
to dupe, Infatuate and ensnare the unwary! [What] violence and
Intrigue [was] used in other states: The members of the Legislature of Pennsylvania were dragged by violence, those of Rhode
Island by menaces of the Higher powers, into the Measures; those
of New Hampshire, Massachusetts, New York, Virginia and North
Carolina were flattered and deceived; those of Massachusetts were
made to believe that by making it a standing Instruction to their
Members in Congress they would infallibly succeed.[60] The Con-

[60] [The ratification process has been most fully described by Jackson T.
Main, *The Antifederalists*, chaps. 9, 10; for his treatment of the incidents in
Pennsylvania and Massachusetts mentioned by Yates, see *ibid.*, pp. 188, 205-
206.]

vention of New York went a step further in agreeing to write a Letter which was signed by every member of the Convention, Directed to every Legislature in the federal Union, expressive of the Indispensable Necessity of Speedy Amendments. All the Members in the Convention unanimously agreed to and Signed this Letter: those that have Religiously Done their Endeavors to perform their promises have acted Honorably.

The Prospect for Amendments Is Dark

I must confess I never heard that the Members of either Massachusetts or New York were more strenuous for amendments than those of other States; and if we judge from the prints, it appears that the one they try to frighten from the attempt, the other [they try to frighten] into despair. To this they insinuate that it is Dangerous to examin Systems of Government; to the others: You stand in a precarious situation, like that of the Priest in his flock (the Priest having by his call undertaken to supply them with Rain when they called for it, and when they did he said they must be unanimous). And we are told that there [are] not a few in every state who in their tender mercies, Rather than to amend the faults in the Constitution, would overset the whole and have another chance for an aristocracy.

And [consider] the Solemn Mocking carried on by the Legislature at their first sessions after it was organized, as if they intended to vie with the Tyrants of Babylon, who, when their Prisoners the Jews were in the utmost Calamity and distress, required Mirth of them, [saying], Sing us one of the songs of Zion.[61] They recommended a Day of thanksgiving to the People of the United States for the favor bestowed on them by almighty God, and Especially for affording them an opportunity Peaceably to Establish a form of government *calculated to promote their happiness*—when they were conscious of the preceding facts!

[61] Psalm 133:3 [actually, Psalm 137].

Besides that [the Constitution] was filled with ambiguity and duplicity, and the far greater number of the Inhabitants were apprehensive that, unless amended, it would sooner or later turn out the greatest curse that ever befell the Rights of Mankind in America. At the very time, too, examples had just come fresh out of their hands, viz: under the colour of a co-ordinate power with the Respective State Legislatures they had passed a Law entitled, "An act to regulate the time and manner of administering certain oaths," whereby the Members of the State Legislatures and all the executive and judicial officers of the several states should within a certain time take an oath or affirmation to support the Constitution;[62] and the Bill before the Senate[63] to Enact by Law, "That from and after the first day of July next no goods wares or Merchandizes of the growth or Manufacture of whatsoever country shall be brought into the United States from the state of Rhode Island and Providence plantations by Land or by Water etc.: the Law to Continue in force until a Convention of the State of Rhode Island and Providence plantations shall assent to and Ratify the Constitution and give notice thereof to the President of the United States."[64]

[62] ["An Act to regulate the Time and Manner of administering certain Oaths," passed June 1, 1789, *The Public Statutes at Large of the United States of America* . . ., ed. Richard Peters, I (Boston, 1850), Session I, chap. I.]

[63] Barbers paper [*Albany Register*] 24 May 1789 ["An act to regulate the Collection of the Duties imposed by law on the tonnage of ships or vessels, and on goods, wares and merchandises imported into the United States," *Statutes at Large*, Session I, chap. V; Section 39 of this law states that goods from Rhode Island and North Carolina not of their own growth or manufacture should be subject to impost duty as if imported from a foreign country.

[64] See the Proceedings on the Boston Port Bill: ". . . until his Majesty should be satisfyed in these particulars and publicly declare in Council on a proper Certificate of the good Behaviour of the Town that he was so satisfyed" (I Ramsay 103:147) [Yates is quoting Ramsay's paraphrase of the British Minister's argument, *History of the American Revolution*, I, 103; at *ibid.*, I, 147, Ramsay tells how the following November, opponents of a coercive policy toward America reminded the ministry of its confidence the preceding spring that the Americans could be humbled and punished.]

To take a Retrospective View of the pains that from time to time have been taken to accumulate and perpetuate the public Debt,[65] by Assumptions [and] Loans even in time of professed Peace; the number of useless Officers and Pensions, and the extravagant Salaries, to augment the army;[66] the Misrepresentations and Impositions daily practiced to make the people believe it is for their own good: we find that those who have Led the People have Carried them Estray and have Loaded them with unnecessary Burthens, to obtain which they have turned a *Convention* into a *Conspiracy*, and under the Epithet *Federal* have destroyed the Confederation. It is yet apprehended that under the name of the Community they will erect a Nobility. "The Prophets prophesy falsely and the priests bear Rule by their means and my People will have it so, and what will ye do in the End thereof."[67]

Postscript on Shays' Rebellion

I shall add another Transaction more which will show as great an insincerity, and that we Americans need not turn our hands to any Europeans at Contrivance. I mean the Resolutions of Congress of the 20 October 1786, Representing, as if they were serious, That we were on the Eve of Hostilities, threatened by the Shawanese, Puteotamies, Chippawas, Tawas, and Twightwas (savage Nations, that live toward the Mississippi, Behind and to the southward of Virginia); [and] the Necessity of reinforcing the continental army with 1340 Non-Commissioned officers and privates.[68] This delu-

[65] Count De Mirabeau [*Considerations on the Order of Cincinnatus . . .* (Philadelphia, 1786).]

[66] I Newton 5: 155: 199: 300, 2 Do 2: 64, 3 Do 8: 146: 399: 306: 376: 436: II Journals 258:259 ["Newton" is apparently not a writer on finance, but Thomas Newton, author of *Dissertations on the Prophecies, which have Remarkably been Fulfilled, and at this Time are Fulfilling in the World*, three volumes (London, 1760); the reference to the Journals of Congress is to that resolution of Oct. 20, 1786, ostensibly concerning the menace of Indians but actually concerned with Shays' Rebellion, cited also in notes 59, 68.]

[67] Jeremiah 5 and 31 [Jeremiah 5:31.]

[68] [*Journals of Congress*, XI, 258-259.]

sion or if you please this Resolution carried with it a suspicious appearance. The ordering 1220 men of the Number to be raised in the four New England states—It was said near 2000 miles from the Country where they were said to be wanted—showed that it was a Contrivance; intended at the same time to get the Continental Establishment augmented, and to terrify the Insurgents in the state of Massachusetts, who were openly Reprobating the conduct of their Rulers and had attempted to obstruct the Courts of Justice. The defection was so strong, that at one time it was a matter of doubt, whether they were not the Majority of the Inhabitants in that State.

Be that as it may, It appears to me that the Insurgents, and so Congress (if it was Realy their intention to employ these troops to terrify them), were Both wrong, in beginning where they should have ended. The Insurgents should first have taken every Legal Measure, to obtain Redress: they should have Instructed their Members, they might have Petitioned and Remonstrated before they had attempted to obstruct the Courts of Justice. So Congress had no business with the Internal Commotions in that State, until it had been determined, who were the Majority, and whether the Rulers had not governed too much. For the people by the Constitution in that state "have an incontestable, unalienable and indefeasible right, to Institute government, and to Reform, alter, or totally Change the same, when their protection, safety, prosperity and happiness require it": a power absolutely Necessary in the hands of the people, and that was not, or ought not to be, in the power of Congress to alter or in any wise to instruct or impede. For the contrary principle, would put in the power of bad Rulers, countenanced by Congress (as Sir Edward Poynings by Henry the 7th), by a Law, if Ever obtained by strategem, irretrievably to violate the Rights of a whole country, and make the Majority tributary to the Minority.

Upon the whole, If upon comparing the usurpation of the Crown of Great Britain upon the parliamentary Rights, with the usurpations of the American Congress upon the sovereignty of the individual states (which was the design of this discussion), upon the contrast I have made it appear (which I trust I have) that American Rulers, if not worse than British, are every way as likely to abuse their powers, to act the wolf in sheeps cloathing; [then] I submit whether it is not High time that we should be upon our guard, while we leave not a stone unturned to obtain the Necessary amendments to the new System, to avert the curse (Next to that of Adam) which we will Entail upon our Descendants without Amendments.

10

Beard, Jefferson,
and the Tree of Liberty

The distinction between "personalty" and "realty," brought forward by Charles A. Beard as the key to the genesis and ratification of the United States Constitution, has not survived the critical onslaught of the last decade. The present essay seeks to explore the intellectual background of Beard's unfortunate classification. The essay's point of departure is the fact that the distinction between "personalty" and "realty" emerged in a period when, under the influence of Populism, Turner and those historians like Beard who followed him pictured American history as a continuing contest between the city capitalist and the exploited farmer.[1] But this vision of our history did not appear *de novo* in the 1890's. Populist historiography itself was a latterday variant of the Jeffersonian mythos which saw nature's nobleman, the yeoman farmer, fleeced and oppressed by the paper speculators of the cities. Thus the quest to grasp Beard runs back to Jefferson. The crux of Beard's exposition, his list of the security holdings of members of

[1] [See Essay 6.]

247

the Constitutional Convention, is a lineal descendant of Jefferson's 1793 "list of paper-men."[2]

What Beard did was to adopt the Jeffersonian ideology of the 1790's and apply it to the events of 1787-1788. Compare the following passages, in which Jefferson characterizes the party battles of the 1790's and Beard the earlier ratification struggle:

(Jefferson)	*(Beard)*
Trifling as are the numbers of the Anti-republican party, there are circumstances which give them an appearance of strength & numbers. They all live in cities, together, & can act in a body readily & at all times; they give chief employment to the newspapers, & therefore have most of them under their command. The Agricultural interest is dispersed over a great extent of country, have little means of intercommunication with each other. . . .[3]	Talent, wealth, and professional abilities were, generally speaking, on the side of the Constitutionalists. They resided for the most part in the towns or the more thickly populated areas, and they could marshall their forces quickly and effectively. The money to be spent in the campaign of education was on their side also. The opposition on the other hand suffered from the difficulties connected with getting a backwoods vote out.[4]

This was fatally to muddy the waters, for what happened in the 1790's was certainly less the continuation of the 1787 alignment than the division of the Constitutional coalition into its Northern and Southern components.

Nor was Jefferson's portrait adequate even for the 1790's. As Federalist critics never tired in observing, Jeffersonians made the paradoxical assertion that the slaveholding South was the heartland of republicanism, and the plantation owner the sentinel of representative government. Beard, while insisting that Jefferson did not seek to give more political power to the poor, never freed him-

[2] Jefferson's list is in the "Anas" for Mar. 23, 1793, *The Works of Thomas Jefferson*, ed. Paul Leicester Ford (New York, 1904-1905), I, 262-263.

[3] "Notes on Prof. Ebeling's Letter of July 30, 95," *ibid.*, VIII, 210.

[4] Charles A. Beard, *An Economic Interpretation of the Constitution of the United States* (New York, 1913), pp. 251-252. I have rearranged the order of Beard's sentences but not in a way that does violence to his argument.

self from the assumption that the Jeffersonians—slaveholders or no—were defending economic democracy. This assumption then became the source of another series of historiographical half-truths in the interpretation of Civil War and Reconstruction; half-truths giving rise to versions of the "Second American Revolution" which hardly noticed slavery and the Negro in their emphasis upon the conflict of Southern agrarianism and Northern industry.

My object, therefore, is to show that the failure of Beard's interpretation rests essentially upon an error in Jefferson's perception of his own time, and to locate the source of that reverberating error.

I.

Beard believed that the party struggle of the 1790's was simply an extrapolation of the conflict between capitalists and farmers over the Constitution. When compared to the earlier *Economic Interpretation*, the *Economic Origins* shows more awareness of the role of slavery and therefore less naïveté about agrarian democracy. Yet, for example, in characterizing the Jeffersonian spokesman Jackson of Georgia, Beard calls him an "Anti-Federalist leader," "the famous champion of agrarianism," and "the leader of the opposition to the funding bills";[5] but does not mention that this same Jackson declared in 1790 that slavery is commanded by the Bible and that

the people of the Southern states will resist one tyranny as soon as another. The other parts of the continent may bear them down by force of arms, but they will never suffer themselves to be divested of their property without a struggle. The gentleman says, if he was a Federal Judge, he does not know to what length he would go in emancipating these people; but I believe his judgment would be of short duration in Georgia, perhaps even the existence of such a Judge might be in danger.[6]

[5] For these and other references to Jackson, see Charles A. Beard, *Economic Origins of Jeffersonian Democracy* (New York, 1915), pp. 136-138, 147-149, 150-153, 191, 248-249.

[6] *The Debates and Proceedings in the Congress of the United States,* ed. Joseph Gales (Washington, D.C.; 1834), II, 1200.

Jackson's rhetoric indicates the inadequacy of any simple equation of Jeffersonianism and democracy, as in Main's statement that Antifederalism was "peculiarly congenial to those who were tending toward democracy, most of whom were soon to rally around Jefferson."[7]

Beard, while insisting that "Jeffersonian Democracy" did not seek suffrage extension or any other "devices for a more immediate and direct control of the voters over the instrumentalities of government," and "simply meant the possession of the federal government by the agrarian masses led by an aristocracy of slave-owning planters," nevertheless failed to emphasize sufficiently the extent to which Jeffersonian Democracy was essentially Southern. Manning Dauer has shown that in the late 1790's non-commercial farmers in the Middle and Northern states deserted the Federalist party.[8] But the original opposition to Hamilton, which played the same role in the genesis of Jeffersonian Democracy as had "personalty" in instigating the movement for the Constitution, was overwhelmingly sectional.

The key evidence for this contention is to be found in the votes of the Congresses which followed the Constitution's ratification, in 1789-1792. I think what they show is the intricate interaction of interest and ideology in the following three ways: 1) although the South—and subsequently Charles Beard—conceptualized the planter as a "farmer" and the regional interest of the South as a "landed interest," in fact the opposition which crystallized by 1792 did not include all farmers and was almost exclusively Southern; 2) although the upper and lower South had quite different discrete interests, the tendency was toward the subordination of immediate pocketbook interests and increasing concern with the broader struggle for sectional dominance; 3) although in general the influence of slavery was in differentiating the entire institutional fabric

---

[7] Jackson T. Main, *The Antifederalists: Critics of the Constitution, 1781-1788* (Chapel Hill, 1961), p. 281.

[8] Manning J. Dauer, *The Adams Federalists* (Baltimore, 1953), *passim*.

of the South from that of the remainder of the nation, still there was in this early period explicit anxiety about Federal interference with slavery which intensified resistance to expansion of Federal power in other areas.

Upper and lower South, Virginia and South Carolina, differed in 1789-1790 about whether to discriminate against British shipping, about whether the Federal government should assume state debts, and about slavery. When on July 1, 1789 the House of Representatives voted on Madison's motion to insist that British shipping pay higher duties than vessels of other foreign countries, 9 of 14 Congressmen from the tobacco states of Maryland and Virginia voted for the motion while 6 of 7 from the rice states, South Carolina and Georgia, were opposed.[9] When on March 23, 1790 the House voted—in rehearsal for the gag-rule struggle of the 1830's and 1840's—on whether to enter in its journal certain committee reports on two antislavery petitions, South Carolina and Georgia voted solidly in opposition while the Virginia delegation divided evenly.[10] Similarly, voting on assumption of state debts on July 24, 1790, three of four representatives from South Carolina were in favor of sustaining the Senate's addition of assumption to the funding bill passed by the House, while 11 of 15 Congressmen from the tobacco states opposed.[11]

Nevertheless, it was in the spring of 1790 that the various concrete differences between the interests of upper and lower South began to be overshadowed by broader sectional concerns. Georgia split from South Carolina on assumption, voting solidly against it. North Carolina, as its representatives trickled into Congress during March and April 1790, aligned itself with Virginia on the issues both of tariff discrimination and assumption. And while the alignment of Congressmen in voting on the Bank in 1791 was essentially similar to the pattern of voting on assumption in 1790, there

[9] *Debates and Proceedings*, I, 618-619.
[10] *Ibid.*, II, 1473.
[11] *Ibid.*, II, 1710-1711.

is the important difference that for the first time a majority of every Southern state delegation voted against Hamilton on a major measure.[12] Not only were 19 of the Bank's 20 opponents in the House Southerners; not only did Southern Congressmen vote 19 to 5 against the Bank; but 2 of the 3 South Carolina delegates who voted joined their fellow-Southerners to form for the first time a solid South. In the debate before the vote Jackson of Georgia, Stone of Maryland, Smith of South Carolina and Giles of Virginia all said that, consistent with Madison's observation in 1787, the votes of Congress were divided by the geographical line which separated North and South.[13]

The South as a whole had by 1792 adopted essentially the philosophy articulated by Antifederalists in 1787-1788. In the fall of 1789, William Grayson wrote to Patrick Henry that Southern gentlemen in Congress were beginning to attend to the reasoning of the "antis," who had said that the South would be a milch cow for the North.[14] In the debates on assumption that following February one Virginia Congressman said bitterly that had the Virginia ratifying Convention known that a direct tax would be laid so soon, and without necessity, it would have hesitated to approve the Constitution; while another cried: "This is the very thing which the opponents of the new Constitution thought they foresaw; this is that consolidation, as they called it, which they predicted."[15] In the fall of 1790 the Virginia legislature articulated Southern opposition in resolutions drafted by Henry, the old Antifederalist, virtually identical with the philosophy which Jefferson, the new opposition leader, would begin to expound a few months later.[16]

[12] *Debates and Proceedings*, II, 1960.

[13] *Ibid.*, II, 1919, 1928, 1930, 1937-1938.

[14] William Grayson to Patrick Henry, September 29, 1789, *Patrick Henry: Life, Correspondence And Speeches*, ed. W. W. Henry (New York, 1891), III, 405.

[15] *Debates and Proceedings*, II, 1348, 1345.

[16] *Statutes At Large . . . Of Virginia*, ed. W. W. Hening, XIII (Philadelphia,

The philosophy of Antifederalists, North and South, in 1787 had special charms for Southerners in 1790 because the issue of Federal interference with slavery had already appeared. Jackson of Georgia, previously quoted, expressed a common Southern response to the antislavery petitions of 1790 intermittently debated in the midst of the funding and assumption drama. Senator William Maclay, at the time of the excitement in the House over one of the petitions, wrote under date of March 22, 1790: "I know not what may come of it, but there seems to be a general discontent among the members, and many of them do not hesitate to declare that the Union must fall to pieces at the rate we go on. Indeed, many seem to wish it."[17] The same thing was true in the Senate. Two days later Maclay's entry recorded: "Izard and Butler both manifested a most insulting spirit this day, when there was not the least occasion for it nor the smallest affront offered. These men have a most settled antipathy to Pennsylvania, owing to the doctrines in that state on the subject of slavery."[18] Thus the Senators from South Carolina, the Southern state hitherto staunchly Hamiltonian, were sensitized to the dangers of loose construction; and in the House, similarly, South Carolina's staunchest Federalist Congressman, William Smith, made a long speech March 17 which began and ended on the theme of Federal interference and in the middle developed every argument for slavery as a positive good which Calhoun would bring forward half a century later.[19] Broadus Mitchell believes this conflict about slavery in the week of March 16 induced enough Southern Congressmen to stiffen in their attitude toward Federal power to account for the repudiation by the

1823), 237-239. See also Henry to James Monroe, Jan. 24, 1791: "As to the Secretary's Report with which you favored me, it seems to be a consistent part of a system which I ever dreaded. Subserviency of Southern to N-n Interests are written in Capitals on its very Front. . . ." (*Henry*, ed. Henry, II, 460).

[17] *The Journal of William Maclay, United States Senator from Pennsylvania, 1789-1791* (New York, 1927), p. 216.

[18] *Ibid.*, p. 217.

[19] *Debates and Proceedings*, II, 1453-1464.

House of its initial acceptance of assumption by four or five votes on March 13.[20] John Bach McMaster merely observes that "from this wrangle the House came back in no good temper to the funding and assumption bills."[21] In either case, the episode must have been in the minds of Southern Congressmen as they haggled about the constitutionality of the Bank for a week the following February.

What Southerners counted on in 1787, what they still hoped for in 1790, was that—to use Madison's words—in only a few years "the Western and S. Western population may enter more into the estimate" so that the South would have a majority in the House.[22] But the results of the 1790 Census were not encouraging. The Northern majority of seven created by the Constitutional Convention's apportionment in 1787 would become a majority of nine even if, as Southerners hoped, Congress apportioned one Congressman for every 30,000 persons. If, as Northerners consistently voted, apportionment were on the basis of one Congressman to every 33,000 persons, then the Southern situation would be still worse. One or two votes were not trifling matters in a Congress where a switch of two or three votes had determined the fate of assumption. In the long debates on apportionment between October 1791 and April 1792 the discussion, as at the Constitutional Convention, began with abstract political theory, moved on to the interests of small and large states, and ended on the conflict between North and South. Never had sectionalism been so forcefully articulated. Williamson of North Carolina said the South "had suffered so much under the harrow of speculation" that he hoped it would not

[20] Broadus Mitchell, *Alexander Hamilton: The National Adventure, 1788-1804* (New York, 1962), p. 73.

[21] John Bach McMaster, *A History of the People of the United States, from the Revolution to the Civil War*, I (New York, 1883), 579.

[22] The South's hope in 1787-1788 that it was "growing more rapidly than the North" and Jefferson's hope in 1792 "that census returns would . . . strengthen the South," are described in John R. Alden, *The First South* (Baton Rouge, La.; 1961), pp. 75, 131. [See also Essays 7, 8.]

be denied the proportion of representation to which it was entitled. Murray of Maryland noted that the long debate had been "entirely constructed on the tenets of Northern and Southern interests and influence." Sedgwick of Massachusetts said still more sweepingly that "there existed an opinion of an opposition of interests between the Northern and Southern states. The influence of this opinion had been felt in the discussion of every important question which had come under the consideration of the Legislature." Summing up, William Branch Giles argued that a larger Congress would be more sympathetic to "the landed interest" and that "he felt a conviction that the agricultural or equalizing interest was nearly the same throughout all parts of the United States." He was wrong: 31 of the 34 votes for a smaller House came from the North; 25 of their 30 opponents were Southerners.[23]

Thus while one unifying theme of these first Federalist years is Hamilton's promotion of his closely-coordinated measures to enhance public credit, a second unifying theme is the resurrection of that chronic sectional antagonism which had plagued both the Continental Congress and Constitutional Convention. If from the first standpoint we can view these years as the completion of the Union, from the second we must see them as prefiguring its dissolution. Joseph Charles says of congressional response to Hamilton's financial bills: "A sharp sectional division appeared in the voting upon the measures of that program, a division which foreshadowed the first phase in the growth of national parties."[24] John C. Miller's summary states explicitly:

The gravest weakness of the Federalists was that their power was based upon a coalition of northern businessmen and southern planters. In all probability, this uneasy alliance would have succumbed sooner or later to the strains and stresses generated by the divergent economic

[23] *Debates And Proceedings . . . Second Congress* (Washington, D. C.; 1849), 244, 269, 272, 546, 548 and (final vote in the House) 548-549.
[24] Joseph Charles, *The Origins of the American Party System* (Williamsburg, Va.; 1956), p. 23.

interests and social and political attitudes of Northerners and Southerners. As might be expected, victory—in this case, the adoption of the
Constitution—hastened the dissolution of the coalition, but the event
was not ensured until 1790, when Hamilton launched his fiscal and
economic programs.[25]

II.

Jefferson's perception of what was happening in
America in the 1790's went through two clearly-defined phases. In
neither phase did he squarely confront the Southern sectional
character of his support.

From 1791 until his election to the Presidency Jefferson believed
that Hamilton and his associates were attempting to create an
American monarchy. Historians have found this view of American
realities somewhat puzzling, if not somewhat paranoid. After making all due allowance for the energy, deviousness, and admiration
of things English of Secretary Hamilton, there clings to the Jeffersonian rhetoric of the '90's something excessive for which Douglass
Adair uses the word "obsession."[26]

What might be called Jefferson's proto-Populism after 1791 is
all the more odd when contrasted with his temperate pragmatism
in 1790, the first year back from France. In his correspondence of
that year there was no dichotomy of "purity" and corrupt "interest." Jefferson wrote to Lafayette in April 1790: "I think, with
others, that nations are to be governed according to their own interest; but I am convinced that it is their interest, in the long run,
to be grateful, faithful to their engagements even in the worst of
circumstances, and honorable and generous always." As in foreign
affairs, so in domestic. "Energy in our government" was, as yet,

[25] John C. Miller, *The Federalist Era, 1789-1801* (New York, 1960), pp.
100-101.

[26] Douglass Adair, "The Intellectual Origins of Jeffersonian Democracy"
(Doctoral dissertation, Yale University, 1943), 2: ". . . the Jeffersonians' obsession that the result most greatly to be feared from the Federalist fiscal
policy was not the obvious—to us—plutocracy, but an American monarchy."

welcome. Writing to the former Antifederalist, George Mason, about assumption and the location of the national capital, Jefferson said in June: "In general I think it necessary to give as well as take in a government like ours." Although funding would require direct taxation by the general government, "this, tho' an evil, is a less one than any of the others" which might result from the assumption crisis in Congress.[27]

After as before his famous understanding with Hamilton, Jefferson was mentally prepared for compromise. He wrote to Francis Eppes on Independence Day: "I see the necessity of sacrificing our opinions some times to the opinions of others for the sake of harmony"; and told the same correspondent three weeks later: "It [assumption] is a measure of necessity." The mood, in another letter of late July, was still essentially that of successful North-South bargaining as in 1787:

I saw the first proposition for this assumption with as much aversion as any man, but the development of circumstances have convinced me that if it is obdurately rejected, something much worse will happen. Considering it therefore as one of the cases in which mutual sacrifice & accomodation is necessary, I shall see it pass with acquiescence.[28]

Writing again to Mason in February 1791, Jefferson had adopted a new vocabulary. Give and take, the lesser evil, "necessity" and "mutual accomodation" had given way to the perils of "sect" and

[27] Thomas Jefferson to the Marquis de Lafayette, Apr. 2, 1790; to Thomas Mann Randolph, May 30, 1790; to George Mason, June 13, 1790; to George Gilmer, June 27, 1790 (*Works*, VI, 40, 64, 75, 84). On June 20, the approximate date at which Jefferson invited Hamilton and Madison to dinner to effect a sectional compromise, Jefferson wrote to James Monroe: "in the present instance I see the necessity of yielding for this time to the cries of the creditors in certain parts of the union, for the sake of union, and to save us from the greatest of all calamities, the total extinction of our credit in Europe" (*ibid.*, VI, 80).

[28] Thomas Jefferson to Francis Eppes, July 4, 1790 and July 25, 1790; to John Harvie, July 25, 1790 (*ibid.*, VI, 85, 107, 109). Writing to Edward Rutledge on Independence Day, Jefferson said that he hoped that, with assumption and the location of the capital settled, "nothing else may be able to call up local principles [i.e., sectional conflict]" (*ibid.*, VI, 88).

"heresy," to a contest of "stock-jobbers" with the "untainted" mass. Fifteen months later, in his letter urging Washington to serve a second term, Jefferson added "profit . . . taken out of the pockets of the people," "barren" capital, a "corrupt squadron" of bribed Congressmen, and the explicit charge that the American monarchists, foiled at the 1787 Convention, "are still eager after their object, and are predisposing every thing for it's ultimate attainment." Jefferson had come to regard his opponents as "Conspirators against human liberty."[29]

Why this change? Hamilton had brought in bills for an excise and a national bank. In themselves, however, these laws do not explain so startling an alteration in ideological Gestalt. Something symbolic about the measures beyond their financial consequences or their widespread unpopularity in the South, apparently triggered an opposition ideology latent in Jefferson's mind. As when the pieces of a kaleideiscope are shaken and, although themselves unaltered, settle into parts of an entirely new pattern, so Jefferson reverted to a pre-Revolutionary mindset. His tone was no longer common-sensical, for he must have felt that he no longer shared the consensus of those who governed. Once more the world seemed divided into Whigs and Tories, conspirators and counter-conspirators.

The detection of conspiracy in high places was a major preoccupation of eighteenth-century politics.[30] Jefferson himself, using language borrowed from the Glorious Revolution, had discerned behind the "long train of abuses" committed by the government of George III a fixed "design" of enslavement. "Excise" and "bank" were words charged with conspiratorial meaning for Jefferson because of their associations with English history. When US Bank

[29] Thomas Jefferson to George Mason, Feb. 4, 1791; to George Washington, May 23, 1792; to James Madison, May 12, 1793 (*Works*, VI, 186, 490-491; VII, 324).

[30] See Bernard Bailyn, "The Transforming Radicalism of the American Revolution," General Introduction to *Pamphlets of the American Revolution, 1750-1776*, I (Cambridge, Mass.; 1965), especially 86-89.

stock fell in 1792, he commented: "No man of reflection who had ever attended to the south sea bubble, in England, or that of Law in France, and who applied the lessons of the past to the present time, could fail to foresee the issue tho' he might not calculate the moment at which it would happen."[31] Political results, more serious than financial ones, could be predicted on the basis of the same analogy. Rome furnished the archetypal plot of republican corruption; viewed with Rome in mind, English history of the previous hundred years seemed one long tale of wicked kings and ministers using profits and offices provided by an inflated public debt to corrupt the representatives of the people. English "independent Whigs" or "commonwealthmen," such as those dogged investigators of South Sea bubbles and Papist plots, Thomas Gordon and John Trenchard, furnished Jefferson a model for his portrait of the Hamiltonian cabal. As Charles II (according to Trenchard) acquired "a vast Revenue for Life" which enabled him "to raise an Army, and bribe the Parliament,"[32] so (according to Jefferson) would Hamilton employ his swollen public debt.

Yet Jefferson's change of front toward Hamilton in 1791 was not a mere reversion to the ideology of English Whigs. Jeffersonian democracy linked political alienation to agrarianism: its central image was the independent farmer abused by an unholy combination of capitalist and bureaucrat. In the writings of Trenchard and Gordon one finds instead, the unJeffersonian assertion that trade

is a grateful and beneficent Mistress; she will turn Desarts into fruitful Fields, Villages into great Cities, Cottages into Palaces, Beggars into Princes, convert Cowards into Heroes, Blockheads into Philosophers.

Trenchard and Gordon call for the election to Parliament of persons who are "interested in Trade and Commerce"; "give me the

[31] Thomas Jefferson to Francis Eppes, April 14, 1792 (*Works*, VI, 478-479).
[32] John Trenchard, "A Short History of Standing Armies in England," *A Collection of Tracts. By The Late John Trenchard, Esq.; And Thomas Gordon, Esq.* (London, 1751), I, 59. See, more generally, H. Trevor Colbourn, *The Lamp of Experience: Whig History and the Intellectual Origins of the American Revolution* (Chapel Hill, 1965).

man," they write, "that encourages Trade."[33] *Cato's Letters* were not addressed to an essentially rural constituency. And that is why the origins of the tradition which passed through Jefferson and culminated in Populism, Turner, and Beard turn out to be Tory as much as Whig.

III.

The political influence of Henry St. John, Lord Viscount Bolingbroke, has been obscured by the epithet "Tory." Some notorious Whigs seem to have borrowed heavily from him. John Adams said in 1813 that he had read Bolingbroke more than five times, the first time more than fifty years before. Did Parliament cry that the influence of the Crown had increased, was increasing and ought to be diminished? Bolingbroke had written that "the power of the crown to corrupt" has "increased" and "must continue to increase" unless a "stop be put" to it.[34] Did Jefferson

[33] *Cato's Letters: Or, Essays On Liberty, Civil And Religious, And Other Important Subjects*, (third edition; London, 1733), II, 267; *Tracts*, II, 8, 276. See also: "Merchants [are] a sort of Men always in the Interests of Liberty, from which alone they can receive Protection and Encouragement" (*Letters*, II, 272).

[34] "As the means then of influencing by prerogative, and of governing by force, were considered to be increased formerly, upon every increase of power to the crown, so are the means of influencing by money, and of governing by corruption, to be considered as increased now, upon that increase of power, which hath accrued to the crown by the new constitution of the revenue since the revolution. Nay farther. Not only the means of corrupting are increased, on the part of the crown, but the facility of employing these means with success is increased, on the part of the people, on the part of the electors, and of the elected. Nay, farther still. These means and this facility are not only increased, but the power of the crown to corrupt, as I have hinted already, and the proneness of the people to be corrupted, must continue to increase on the same principles, unless a stop be put to the growing wealth and power of one, and the growing depravity of the other" ("A Dissertation Upon Parties," *The Works Of The Late Right Honourable Henry St. John, Lord Viscount Bolingbroke* [London, 1809], III, 290). In his "Machiavelli, Harrington, and English Political Ideologies in the Eighteenth Century," *William and Mary Quarterly*, third series, XXII (1965), 549-583, J.G.A. Pocock presents a view of Bolingbroke similar to that of this essay.

write that the tree of liberty must be watered with the blood of tyrants? Bolingbroke had invented the metaphor:

Though the branches were lopped, and the tree lost it's beauty for a time, yet the root remained untouched, was set in a good soil, and had taken strong hold in it: so that care, and culture, and time were indeed required, and our ancestors were forced to water it, if I may use such an expression, with their blood. . . .[35]

The works of Bolingbroke were among the first books Jefferson owned. He praised them chiefly for their style and for their intellectual courage in discussing religion; but in 1821 made the remarkable declaration:

You ask my opinion of Lord Bolingbroke and Thomas Paine. They are alike in making bitter enemies of the priests and pharisees of their day. Both were honest men; both advocates for human liberty. Paine wrote for a country which permitted him to push his reasoning to whatever length it would go. Lord Bolingbroke in one restrained by a constitution, and by public opinion. He was called indeed a tory; but his writings prove him a stronger advocate for liberty than any of his countrymen, the whigs of the present day.[36]

[35] "A Dissertation upon Parties," *Works*, III, 254-255. The tree of liberty, incidentally, came from the Teutonic forests: "Both their [the French] ancestors and ours came out of Germany, and had probably much the same manners, the same customs, and the same forms of government. But as they proceeded differently in the conquests they made, so did they in the establishments that followed" (*ibid.*, III, 251).

[36] Thomas Jefferson to Francis Eppes, Jan. 19, 1821 (*Works*, XII, 194). There are more than fifty pages of extracts from Bolingbroke's philosophical writings in Jefferson's student notebooks, and it is the general opinion of his biographers that Bolingbroke more than any other writer stimulated Jefferson to question received religious opinions. See *The Literary Bible of Thomas Jefferson: His Commonplace Book of Philosophers and Poets*, ed. Gilbert Chinard (Baltimore, 1928); Dumas Malone, *Jefferson the Virginian* (Boston, 1948), pp. 106-109; and Marie Kimball, *Jefferson: The Road to Glory, 1743 to 1776* (New York, 1943), who dates Jefferson's Bolingbroke extracts 1764-1767 and comments: "With the exception of Montesquieu, whose works he did not acquire until December 1769, no writer had greater influence on the formation of Jefferson's ideas" (p. 113). In the first of the several lists of books which Jefferson recommended to friends throughout his life, the works of Bolingbroke are suggested for both religious and political study (Thomas

Caroline Robbins excludes Bolingbroke from the succession of genuine Whigs. During the reign of George II, she says, "The journal most powerfully and prominently against the government was *The Craftsman*, run by Nicholas Amhurst, the disgruntled Oxford Whig, and adorned by the effusions of Bolingbroke." The writings of William Talbot, a Real Whig, "might almost come from Bolingbroke's *Dissertation On Parties* where the Revolution was termed 'a new Magna Charta.'" And again: "Bolingbroke was a freethinker and a Tory, albeit one who could put Scripture to his own uses and cite the canonical Whig writers in defense of his own devious ways."[37] Perhaps it would be simpler to conclude that Bolingbroke and the Whig remnant were saying the same thing. But no; for, according to Miss Robbins:

All Whigs until the French Revolution maintained that in theory at least tyrants could be resisted, and by so doing, justified the events of 1689. This was their chief advantage over Tories like Bolingbroke and Hume who accepted the Revolution without a logical defense for it.[38]

Jefferson to Robert Skipwith, Aug. 3, 1771, *The Papers of Thomas Jefferson*, ed. Julian P. Boyd [Princeton, 1950–], I, 76-81).

[37] Caroline Robbins, *The Eighteenth-Century Commonwealthman* (Cambridge, Mass.; 1959), pp. 274, 284, 295.

[38] *Ibid.*, p. 8. I believe that Miss Robbins not only exaggerates the conservatism of Bolingbroke, but also the radicalism of the "commonwealthmen." On p. 125 of her book Miss Robbins quotes several sentences from *Cato's Letters* and sums up their content with the phrase: "The time had not come for a more equal commonwealth." But the conclusion which "Cato" himself draws is: "the Phantome of a Commonwealth must vanish, and never appear again but in disordered Brains" (*Cato's Letters*, III, 162). In what sense were Trenchard and Gordon commonwealthmen? Gordon said of his collaborator: "he was sincerely for preserving the Established Church, and would have heartily opposed any Attempt to alter it. He was against all Levelling in Church and State, and fearful of trying Experiments upon the Constitution. He thought that it was already upon a very good Balance; and no Man was more falsely accused of an Intention to pull down. The Establishment was his Standard; and he was only for pulling down those who would soar above it, and trample upon it" (*ibid.*, I, liii-liv). Bolingbroke turned the concept of the "balance" to at least as radical an end as did the commonwealthmen. He writes of Rome: "How inconsistent, indeed, was that plan of government,

This is just not true. Bolingbroke made himself quite clear:

The legislative is a supreme, and may be called, in one sense, an absolute, but in none an arbitrary power. "It is limited to the publick good
of the society. It is a power, that hath no other end but preservation,
and therefore can never have a right to destroy, enslave, or designedly
to impoverish the subjects; for the obligations of the law of nature
cease not in society, etc." [Here Bolingbroke cites: "Locke's Essay on
civil Government, c. 11, of the extent of the legislative power."]—If
you therefore put so extravagant a case, as to suppose the two houses of
parliament concurring to make at once a formal cession of their own
rights and privileges, and of those of the whole nation to the crown,
and ask who hath the right, and the means, to resist the supreme legislative power? I answer, the whole nation hath the right; and a people
who deserve to enjoy liberty, will find the means.[39]

Is there any ambiguity here? If so, Bolingbroke seeks at once to
dispel it:

From hence it follows, that the nation which hath a right to preserve
this constitution, hath a right to resist an attempt, that leaves no other
means of preserving it but those of resistance. From hence it follows,
that if the constitution was actually dissolved, as it would be by such
an attempt of the three estates, the people would return to their original, their natural right, the right of restoring the same constitution, or
of making a new one.[40]

Bolingbroke's political originality, and his essential contribution
to Jeffersonian democracy, lay in his identification of resistance to
centralized corruption with the landed interest. He said in his last,
unfinished political pamphlet (in 1749): "The landed men are the
true owners of our political vessel: the moneyed men, as such, are

---

which required so much hard service of the people; and which, leaving them
so much power in the distribution of power, left them so little property in the
distribution of property? Such an inequality of property, and of the means
of acquiring it, cannot subsist in an equal commonwealth; and I much apprehend, that any near approaches to a monopoly of property, would not be
long endured even in a monarchy" (*Works*, III, 220).

[39] "A Dissertation Upon Parties," *ibid.*, III, 271-272.
[40] *Ibid.*, III, 272.

no more than passengers in it."[41] The metaphor neatly expressed the vision of a commercialized society governed by agrarians. A similar ambiguity inhered in Bolingbroke's use of the word "country," as in his advocacy of "the representation of the country by the independent gentlemen of the country."[42] What this meant was that the people should be represented by their landlords.

In Locke, according to Adair, the classical concept of "the struggle between the few and the many" was "translated into the conflict of the few as the rulers against the many as the ruled." Bolingbroke carried the translation one step further:

The idea of the balance of social classes so strong in Aristotle, still perceptible in Polybius, almost entirely disappeared in the writings of Bolingbroke, the most famous eighteenth-century English expounder of the system, whose view of the contemporary economic conflict was cast, not in terms of the rich against the poor, but of the landed versus the moneyed interest.

Adair concludes that "Bolingbroke's use of 'the separation of powers' theory to fight Walpole's use of the funding, debts, etc. to corrupt and manage Parliament set the pattern for the Jeffersonian opposition to Hamilton."[43]

According to Bolingbroke's reading of party history, a unified "country party" had existed in opposition to Charles II but broke into Whig and Tory parties at the time of the exclusion crisis. The country party had been founded on principle, indeed a "party, thus constituted, is improperly called party; it is the nation, speaking and acting in the discourse and conduct of particular men." The Whig and Tory parties, on the other hand, were based on "the prejudices and interests of particular sets of men."[44] (One finds in

[41] "Some Reflections On The Present State Of The Nation," *ibid.*, IV, 388. On Bolingbroke's conception of the "moneyed interest," see Jeffrey Hart, *Viscount Bolingbroke: Tory Humanist* (London and Toronto, 1965), X, 29, 30, 46, 65.
[42] "Remarks On The History Of England," *Works*, II, 370.
[43] Adair, "Intellectual Origins," pp. 172, 202n.
[44] "A Dissertation Upon Parties," *Works*, III, 82-83.

this concept of two kinds of parties, I believe, the germ of that intolerance of opposition which Leonard Levy has noted in Jefferson.) The sole intention of his *Dissertation On Parties*, Bolingbroke said, was to break down the "ridiculous" and "nominal" division of Whig and Tory parties, to reorganize English politics on the basis of opposition between court and country, to reduce "our present parties to this single division, our present disputes to this single contest."[45]

Jefferson took from this tradition the identification of patriotic purity with the farmer which became a cliché of one strand of American radical thought. When Jefferson wrote to Mazzei that "the whole landed interest is republican,"[46] he meant something more than that the weight of numbers and wealth in the countryside was anti-Hamiltonian. He meant also that the nation should turn to rural men for political leadership. Like Bolingbroke a half century earlier, Jefferson declared in 1797:

All can be done peaceably, by the people confiding their choice of Representatives & Senators to persons attached to republican government & the principles of 1776, not office-hunters, but farmers, whose interests are entirely agricultural. Such men are the true representatives of the great American interest, and are alone to be relied on for expressing the proper American sentiments.[47]

If city people adhered to the republican cause, they might be viewed as somehow agrarian, too. When the common people of Philadelphia flocked to the wharves to cheer a French frigate with British prizes, Jefferson described them as "the *yeomanry* of the City (not the fashionable people nor paper men)."[48] One hundred and twenty years later Beard, seeking to explain urban support for

[45] *Ibid.*, III, 305.
[46] Thomas Jefferson to Philip Mazzei, Apr. 24, 1796 (*Works*, VIII, 239).
[47] Thomas Jefferson to Arthur Campbell, Sept. 1, 1797 (*ibid*, VIII, 337-338).
[48] Thomas Jefferson to James Monroe, May 5, 1793 and to Thomas Mann Randolph, May 6, 1793 (*ibid.*, VII, 309, 312).

Jefferson in 1800, suggested that it came from the truck gardeners, laborers and farmers of the outlying districts—as it were, the city agrarians.[49]

Bolingbroke's vision of a patriot king served Americans well during those years when their analysis of the English conspiracy placed the blame on Parliament. Thus Stourzh writes of Franklin:

The American interest obliged him to fight against Parliament—an aristocratic body in those days—while remaining loyal to the king; in recognizing the king's sovereignty while denying Parliament's rights over the colonies, Franklin by necessity was driven into a position which, historically speaking, seemed to contradict his Whig principles. The complaining Americans spoke, as Lord North rightly said, the "language of Toryism."[50]

When the time came to indict the "royal brute" as well, only a slight turn of the kaleidoscope was required. Burke had shown how to do it in 1770. One recognized that: "The distempers of monarchy were the great subjects of apprehension and redress, in the last century; in this, the distempers of parliament." One did not deny that the present danger was corruption rather than prerogative, or as Jefferson later put it, "that fraud will at length effect what force could not." What one did was simply to blame corruption on the king instead of (this had been Bolingbroke's theme) on his ministers. So Burke thundered: "The power of the crown, almost dead and rotten as Prerogative, has grown up anew, with much more strength, and far less odium, under the name of Influence." Conspirators were still at work, but they had "totally abandoned the shattered and old-fashioned fortress of prerogative, and made a lodgment in the strong hold of parliament itself." The

[49] Beard, *Economic Origins*, p. 246, "Note to Chapter VIII," pp. 387, 466. I am indebted for this insight to Alfred Young.

[50] Gerald Stourzh, *Benjamin Franklin and American Foreign Policy* (Chicago, 1954), p. 28. When one recalls that Madison (according to Douglass Adair) and Hamilton (according to Clinton Rossiter) were intellectually indebted to the Tory David Hume above all others, one begins to wonder whether *any* of the ideologues of the American Revolution drew on an essentially Whig tradition.

people's cause, therefore, only seemed to be a contest between themselves and Parliament. "The true contest is between the electors of the kingdom and the crown; the crown acting by an instrumental house of commons."[51]

In such fashion, a Whig ideology which Tories had transformed into political agrarianism was made Whig once more by recasting the chief conspirator as the king. The farmer continued as the protagonist of political purity. And the script came to be called, Jeffersonian Democracy.

III.

Even as early as the 1780's there were two alternative sources for an American radical tradition. The first was the agrarian version of Whiggism inherited from Bolingbroke, and reinforced by Montesquieu (another favorite author of Jefferson's student days). All three libertarian landlords stressed common themes: the protection of provincial autonomies, distrust of the commercial city, a cyclical theory of history based on the proposition that prosperity corrupts.

The second available vision was the artisan radicalism of Paine. As the friendship of Paine and Jefferson attests, agrarian and artisan radicalism agreed in many things. They shared a sociology "which divided society between the 'Useful' or 'Productive Classes' on the one hand, and courtiers, sinecurists, fund-holders, speculators and parasitic middlemen on the other."[52] Yet in the long run the two streams of thought diverged. The radicalism associated with city workingmen made affirmations—that strong central government accessible to the people was more democratic than decentralized rule by gentlemen; that common men, whether or not formally educated, had the capacity to govern; that slavery must stop—

[51] "Thoughts On The Cause Of The Present Discontents," *The Works of the Right Honorable Edmund Burke* (Dublin, 1792), I, 420, 466, 478, 490; Thomas Jefferson to Aaron Burr, June 17, 1797 (*Works*, VIII, 312).

[52] E. P. Thompson, *The Making of the English Working Class* (London, 1963), p. 99.

which agrarian radicalism proved unable to assimilate. By the middle of the nineteenth century in Europe, the historical perspective of a Bolingbroke or a Burke, a Montesquieu or a de Tocqueville, was virtually dead. In America, sustained by the availability of Western land, Jeffersonian agrarianism lived on and became the recurrent ideology of dissent.

Beard, seen in this context, was a latterday Jeffersonian. The central thrust of his historiography was to impose on all periods of American history the static dichotomy of capitalist and farmer characteristic of the agrarian tradition. What was wrong was not so much Beard's emphasis on economics as the Jeffersonian economics he espoused. "Personalty" and "realty" were a part of that system, as was the emphasis on conspiracy and corrupt self-interest. So too was an ultimate fatalism.

For all his well-known optimism about human nature, Jefferson absorbed and passed on to his Populist and Progressive successors a fundamentally pessimistic view of history.[53] The Golden Age, when Saxon ancestors had lived "under customs and unwritten laws based upon the natural rights of man,"[54] was in the past. Revolutionary America approximated those conditions, but only for the moment.[55] The growth of commerce would corrupt manners in America as it had in Rome, and once manners were corrupted, the best of statesmen could not save the republic.

Jefferson's hostility to capitalism, as to slavery, ended in pessimism about controlling it. In this he differed not at all from Hamilton, who in 1788 told the New York ratifying convention:

> While property continues to be pretty equally divided, and a considerable share of information pervades the community; the tendency

[53] [Compare the discussion of Madison and slavery in Essay 7, part V.]

[54] *The Commonplace Book of Thomas Jefferson: A Repertory of His Ideas on Government*, ed. Gilbert Chinard (Baltimore, 1926), pp. 55-56.

[55] See Jefferson's significant letter to William Branch Giles, Dec. 17, 1794: "The attempt which has been made to restrain the liberty of our citizens . . . has come upon us a full century earlier than I expected" (*Works*, VIII, 155).

of the people's suffrages, will be to elevate merit even from obscurity. As riches increase and accumulate in few hands; as luxury prevails in society; virtue will be in a greater degree considered as only a graceful appendage of wealth, and the tendency of things will be to depart from the republican standard. This is the real disposition of human nature: It is what, neither the honorable member nor myself can correct. It is a common misfortune, that awaits our state constitution, as well as all others.[56]

In 1819, in his famous correspondence with that other Federalist, John Adams, Jefferson raised the question whether Brutus, had he conquered, could have restored republicanism to corrupted Rome. Adams responded:

Will you tell me how to prevent riches from becoming the effects of temperance and industry? Will you tell me how to prevent riches from producing luxury? Will you tell me how to prevent luxury from producing effeminacy intoxication extravagance Vice and folly? When you will answer me these questions, I hope I may venture to answer yours.[57]

Jefferson did not answer.

"Absolute stability is not to be expected in any thing human," Bolingbroke had written. "The best instituted governments, like the best constituted animal bodies, carry in them the seeds of their destruction." For agrarian radicalism, decay did not hold the promise of renewal and transcendence. "All that can be done, therefore, [is] to prolong the duration of a good government."[58] The tree of liberty could be pruned and grafted, and this was the duty of men of public spirit. History taught, however, that in the long run the rot was irreparable. In the last analysis, one stood by and watched the great tree fall.

[56] Speech of June 21, 1788, *The Papers of Alexander Hamilton*, ed. Harold C. Syrett (New York, 1961—), V, 42.

[57] Jefferson to Adams, Dec. 10, 1819, and Adams to Jefferson, Dec. 21, 1819 (*The Adams-Jefferson Letters*, ed. Lester J. Cappon [Chapel Hill, 1959], II, 549-550, 551).

[58] "The Idea Of A Patriot King," *Works*, IV, 272-273.

Index

Abernethy, Thomas P., 140

Abolition (emancipation), 95; Constitution on, 153–154; political parties ignore, 146; prospects for, in Revolution, 179–183; protection against, 202, 213

Abolitionists, 135, 180–181; Beard's view of, 136; criticize Constitution, 147, 153–158, 178–179, 183; Mill's definition of, 154; Turner's view of, 143

Adair, Douglass, 19, 256, 264, 266n.

Adams, John, 6, 126–127, 178, 269; Bolingbroke's influence on, 260; in peace commission, 166; Yates and, 223, 225, 229

Adams, John Quincy, 180–181

Adams, Samuel, 126, 225, 230n.

Agrarian-capitalist coalition, 255–256

Agrarian-capitalist compromises, 11, 26n.; over Constitution, 14, 17, 150; with mechanics, 128

Agrarian-capitalist conflicts, 3–4, 10–18, 20, 248–250; American history as, 247; Beard's interpretation of, 10–11, 12, 14–18, 136, 145–146, 148–151, 247–250, 266; over Constitution, 248–249; Jefferson's view of, 11–12, 247, 259–260, 263–269

Agrarianism, 191; radical, 267–269; slavery as, 20, 136, 145–151, 250

Agrarians: aristocrats' conflicts with, see Tenant-landlord conflicts; freehold, see Freehold farmers; slave-owning, see Slaveholders

Alabama, 140n., 175

Albany (N.Y.), 70, 71, 118; creditors' convention in, 120; prisoners dispersed to, 74; state legislature at, 41, 42; Yates in, 219, 220n.

Albany Committee of Safety, 72

Albany County (N.Y.), 219; see also Livingston Manor

Alden, John, 18

271

Class conflicts (*cont.*)
8–9, 31, 33, 63–77; of urban mechanics, 79–108, 122–126, 128–132; white community views, 21; Yates and, 219–221, 223; *see also* Agrarian-capitalist conflicts; Tenant-landlord conflicts
Clinton, George, 36, 40–41, 50, 65, 109*n.*, 218; as challenge to conservatives, 115; on manor tenants, 76; as military leader, 73; Schuyler's opinion of, 114; tax program of, 116; Yates' services for, 220
Clinton, Sir Henry, 71, 104*n.*
Coles, Edward, 188–189, 205, 207
Columbia (Albany) County (N.Y.), 219; *see also* Livingston Manor
Columbia University, 150
Common people (laboring class), 82; nineteenth-century, clash with capitalists, 135; Turner's view of, 141; *see also* Mechanics; Tenant-landlord conflicts
Compromise of 1787, 153–213; abolitionist critique of, 147, 153–158; chief figure in, 182; counterrevolution begun with, 178; fundamentals of, 213; Northwest Ordinance contrasted to, 185–188; sectionalism and, 161–175, 177, 185*n.*, 188, 190–191, 194–198, 199–205, 207, 212–213
Confederation, attempts to strengthen, 120, 227, 240
Confederation, Articles of, 159, 241; Dickinson draft of, 163–164
Confiscation of lands, 32, 34, 42–43, 45–55, 67, 99–100; conservative position on, 117–118; democratization through, 54; as radicalism, 98, 115–116; significance of, 59–60; Yates' opposition to, 220
Congress, U.S.: amends Constitution, 221–222; anticipated Southern ma-

Congress, U.S. (*cont.*)
jority in, 173–175, 203, 254; basis of representation in, 156, 160–164, 173, 185, 188, 200, 202–204, 206, 254–255; Jefferson's fears about, 257–258; powers of, 116, 121, 168–169, 171–173, 196*n.*; sectional conflicts resumed in, 251–255; states admitted by, 206, 209; *see also* Continental Congress; House of Representatives; Senate
Connecticut, 6, 200*n.*
Conservatism, 80, 110–111, 117–123, 125, 240*n.*; economic conversion of, 118–119; liberal character of, 110; nationalist sentiments of, 118, 120–122, 128; in Philadelphia, 129*n.*
Constable, William, 129
Constitution, U.S., 8–11, 14–21, 196*n.*, 209*n.*, 252, 256; abolitionist critique of, 147, 153–158, 178–179, 183, 211*n.*, 212*n.*; amendments to, 221–222, 242–244; Bill of Rights of, 179*n.*, 221–222; common people's support of, 130–132; drafting of, *see* Compromise of 1787; Constitutional Convention; failure of Beard's interpretation of, 249; fugitive slave clause of, 154, 159, 189, 205, 213; leaders of opposition to, 32; motive for formation of, 14; New York governing class supports, 111–112; New York ratification of, 25–26, 33, 58*n.*, 108, 112, 122–123, 126, 130, 220, 222*n.*, 241; Northwest Ordinance influences, 205–207, 212; personalty-realty view and, 247; produced by class conflict, 4*n.*, 148–149; as settlement of Revolution, 113; three-fifths clause of, 153–154, 156–157, 160–161, 178, 182, 185, 192, 200, 202, 206, 213; Yates' history of movement for,

House of Representatives, U.S. *(cont.)*
sectionalism in, 251–255; Southern
strength in, 153, 175, 209, 254
Howe, Gen. William, 75
Hudson River, 42, 71, 73
Hudson Valley, *see* Dutchess County;
Livingston Manor
Hughes, Hugh, 129
Hume, David, 223, 228, 262, 266*n*.
Hunt, Daniel, 54*n*.
Hunter, Robert, 65

Illinois, 175, 190, 195
Impost, national, 118–119, 129, 223,
229, 232, 235, 237–238, 239*n*.
Indian Queen tavern (Philadelphia),
211, 212*n*.
Indiana, 175, 190, 195
Indians, American, 163–164, 187*n*.,
240; ambivalence toward, 180–181;
in Shays' Rebellion, 244; Turner's
view of, 144
Inspection, Committee of, 92–94
Iredell, James, 159
Ivers, Thomas, 97, 99, 129
Izard, Ralph, 253

Jackson, Andrew, 149, 181; Turner's
view of, 139–141, 144
Jackson, James, 249–250, 252–253
Japan, 15
Jay, John, 68, 115, 117, 123, 125; as
conservative, 110–111; inhibits merchants, 126; in Mississippi controversy, 172, 194, 196–198; as nationalist, 42; in peace commission, 166–
167; Schuyler's gubernatorial campaign and, 65, 75
Jay, Mrs. John, 109*n*.
Jefferson, Thomas, 196, 252; abolitionist view of, 178; Bolingbroke's influence on, 261, 263–267; as class
spokesman, 4*n*.; interprets 1790's,
11–12, 248–249, 256–260; Madison's

Jefferson, Thomas *(cont.)*
letters to, 168–169, 172, 173, 179, 202;
Northwest Territory divisions of,
190; in peace commission, 166–167;
pessimism of, 268–269; proposes ban
on slavery, 180, 186, 193; as section-
alist, 164–165, 254*n*., 256; slavery
rationalized by, 20; Southern democracy of, 250; Virginian trade
and, 175–176
Jefferson-Hamilton conflict, 3–4, 256–
259, 264
Jensen, Merrill, 56, 218
Johnson, William Samuel, 187
"Junius" (pseudonym), 223, 226
Justice, 72, 183; Constitutional, 154–
155; execution of rebel tenants, 73–
74; for common people, 27–28
"Juvenis" (pseudonym), 100

Kean, John, 186
Kentucky, 140*n*., 175, 177, 191
Kenyon, Cecilia, "Where Paine Went
Wrong," 6–7
"Ketch, Jack," 73
King, Rufus, 161, 162, 200*n*., 211*n*.; on
admission of states, 203–204; Missis-
sippi controversy and, 197–198,
206*n*.; Northwest Ordinance and,
186*n*., 187, 188*n*., 190, 191, 209, 210;
on potential Southern power, 173–
174; on sectionalism, 201
"Kings Book," 69–70
Kingston (N.Y.), 42, 71, 74
Kipp, Henry, 100

Labaree, Benjamin, 82
Laboring class, *see* Common people
Lafayette, Marquis de, 159, 256
Lamb, John, 54*n*., 91, 101*n*., 104; as
Antifederalist, 109*n*.
Land confiscation, *see* Confiscation of
lands